Religion, regulation, consumption

MANCHEStER
1824

Manchester University Press

Religion, regulation, consumption

Globalising kosher and halal markets

JOHN LEVER AND JOHAN FISCHER

Manchester University Press

The right of John Lever and Johan Fischer to be identified as the authors of this work has been asserted by them in accordance with the Copyright, Designs and Patents Act 1988.

Published by Manchester University Press
Altrincham Street, Manchester M1 7JA
www.manchesteruniversitypress.co.uk

British Library Cataloguing-in-Publication Data
A catalogue record for this book is available from the British Library

ISBN 978 1 5261 0364 2 hardback
ISBN 978 1 5261 5598 6 paperback

First published 2018

The publisher has no responsibility for the persistence or accuracy of URLs for any external or third-party internet websites referred to in this book, and does not guarantee that any content on such websites is, or will remain, accurate or appropriate.

Typeset by Out of House Publishing

Contents

Figures

(All images authors' own)

Glossary

dhabh	Islamic ritual slaughter
glatt	a Yiddish word meaning 'smooth' (but also used to refer to a stricter standard of kosher)
hadith	traditions concerning the life and works of the Prophet Muhammad
halacha	kosher law
haram	unlawful or forbidden
hechsher	a rabbinical product certification (a stamp or logo)
kashrut	Jewish religious dietary laws
makruh	detestable
mashbooh	doubtful
shechita	Jewish ritual slaughter
shochet	qualified Jewish slaughterer: pl. *shochetim*
shomer	Jewish legal guardian: pl. *shomerim*
sunnah	the life, actions and teachings of the Prophet Muhammad
ulama	literally, those who know the law
ummah	the community of Muslims

Abbreviations and acronyms

BSE	Bovine Spongiform Encephalopathy
CRC	Chicago Rabbinical Council
DIT	Det Islamiske Trossamfund (Islamic Faith Community)
GMO	Genetically Modified Organisms
HFA	Halal Food Authority
HFCE	Halal Food Council of Europe
HMC	Halal Monitoring Committee
ICCOS	Islamic Cultural Center of Scandinavia
IFANCA	Islamic Food and Nutrition Council of America
ISO	International Standards Organization
JAKIM	Islamic Development Department of Malaysia
KOF-K	Kosher Certification and Supervision
LBS	London Board for Shechita
MBD	Manchester Beth Din
MFR	Muslim Joint Council (Muslimernes Fællesråd)
MH	Machzikei Hadass (Manchester)
MK	Manchester Kashrus
MSB	Manchester Shechita Board
MUI	Majelis Ulama Indonesia (Indonesian Ulema Council)
MUIS	Islamic Religious Council of Singapore
OU	Orthodox Union
RSPCA	Royal Society for the Prevention of Cruelty to Animals

Introduction: global kosher and halal markets

Over the last two decades or so the global markets for kosher and halal food, particularly meat, have grown rapidly. Kosher is a Hebrew term meaning 'fit' or 'proper' and halal is an Arabic word that literally means 'permissible' or 'lawful'. This book explores the emergence and expansion of global kosher and halal markets with a particular focus on the UK and Denmark. This is the first book of its kind drawing on contemporary empirical material to explore kosher and halal comparatively at different levels of the social scale, such as individual consumption, the marketplace, religious organisations and the state. During this period, kosher and halal markets have become global in scope, and states, manufacturers, restaurants, shops, certifiers and consumers around the world are faced with ever stricter and more complex kosher and halal requirements – most clearly exemplified by Jewish and Muslim groups' call for kosher and halal certification by third-party certification bodies. Hundreds of kosher and halal certifiers have emerged around the world and thousands of manufacturers, restaurants, shops and products have been certified. While kosher and halal requirements are comparable there are also many differences, and the book discusses how these similarities and differences affect consumption, production and regulation. The book is based on extended periods of research carried out among manufacturers, shops, Jewish/Muslim organizations, certifiers and consumers in the UK and Denmark, where kosher and halal are of particular significance. Empirically, the book compares the major markets for kosher/halal in the UK with those in Denmark, where kosher/halal are important to smaller groups of religious consumers. While religious slaughter without stunning is permitted in the UK, this is not the case in Denmark. Moreover, we explore linkages between the two countries with respect to exports of meat as well as non-meat products; for example, during fieldwork in Manchester we found Danish kosher butter on sale. In addition to the contemporary empirical material, we also draw on and update materials the authors have collected over many years.

Since the end of World War II, the kosher market has consolidated in many places within the Jewish diaspora, as new generations of migrants have sought to maintain traditional practices in new locations (Lytton 2013). While the

1

Figure 1 Danish kosher butter in Manchester

Jewish population is declining as a proportion of the global population, it is increasing worldwide, and it currently stands at around 14 million (JPPI 2015; Kooy 2015). The global demand for kosher products has been growing steadily, and many non-religious consumers now view kosher as a healthy food option: in the US over 60 per cent of kosher food consumption is linked to non-religious values associated with health and food quality. Globally there are estimated to be around 25 million kosher consumers and in 2008 sales of kosher foods in the US totalled US$12.5 billion (Mintel 2009). Kosher is one of the oldest food certification systems in the world (Campbell *et al.* 2011) and despite widespread acceptance of common practices there are many kosher certification and standard-setting bodies. The Orthodox Union (OU) is perhaps the best-known global kosher certification body, but there are many other national, regional and local rabbinical authorities and Jewish courts of law offering *kashrut* (Jewish religious dietary laws) services.

The market for halal food has also grown rapidly over recent decades. The value of the halal food market alone has been estimated at around US$632 billion annually (see Bergeaud-Blackler *et al.* 2015), and with the Muslim population projected to increase globally from 1.6 billion to 2.2 billion by 2030 the potential benefits to be accrued are vast. The market is expected to grow by more than 100 per cent in a number of European and North American countries and the demand for certified halal meat products is predicted to expand exponentially (Miller 2009). Over the last three decades, Muslim majority states in Southeast Asia, most notably Indonesia, Malaysia, Brunei and Singapore, developed the first halal standards and certification regimes, primarily for internal and latterly for external markets (Fischer 2011, 2015a).

The continuing expansion of the halal market over the last decade has created many opportunities for non-Muslim counties to export halal meat into Muslim countries (Lever and Miele 2012; Miele 2016) and this has led to a proliferation of certifying bodies to assure Muslim consumers. At the same time, governments in a number of other Muslim countries have started to offer certification and accreditation services, including the United Arab Emirates (UAE) and Saudi Arabia: significantly, many of these large, state-run bodies do not recognise each other. This continues to create tension, and certification and accreditation for the export of raw materials into Muslim countries is now often overseen by large private-sector accreditation bodies, including, most notably, the Islamic Food and Nutrition Council of America (IFANCA) and its sister company, the Halal Food Council of Europe (HFCE).

While kosher and halal requirements are comparable, there are also many differences and the book discusses how these similarities and differences affect consumption, production and regulation. The research question addressed in this book is: *What are the consequences of globalising kosher and halal markets?* We argue that the similarities and differences between kosher and halal consumption, production and regulation in different national contexts are not well understood. We argue further that to better understand global kosher and halal markets they need to be explored at different levels of the social scale. For example, as we shall see, many if not most of our informants are unaware of the extent to which enzyme production (Chapter 3) has undergone kosher/halal regulation over the last two decades. Paradoxically, kosher/halal-certified companies and kosher/halal certification bodies will argue that kosher/halal regulations are put in place to meet consumer-driven demands, but as we will show there is tension between these levels of the social scale in terms of understanding and practice.

What are modern kosher and halal production, trade and regulation?

Kashrut and kosher law (*halacha*) include a number of prohibitions such as a ban on pork, the mixing of milk and meat and a prescribed method of slaughter:

> Any animal that has true hoofs, with clefts through the hoofs, and that chews the cud – such you may eat ... And the swine – although it has true hoofs, with the hoofs cleft through, it does not chew the cud: it is impure for you. (Lev. 11:3, 11:7)

Thou shalt not seethe a kid in its mother's milk. (Exod. 34:26; Deut. 14:21)

You shall not kill of thy heard and thy flock which the Lord hath given you, except as I have commanded you. (Deut. 12:21)

Meat only qualifies as kosher if the animal of origin is slaughtered using appropriate *shechita* methods as interpreted through rabbinic commentaries and customary practices. Three key principles must be followed at all times (Lytton 2013). A qualified Jewish slaughterer – or *shochet* (pl. *shochetim*) – with the necessary skills and understanding of the laws and requirements of *shechita* must conduct the act of slaughter. *Shechita* must also be carried out with a razor-sharp blade on a special knife – a *chalaf* – in order to minimise the risk of damage to the body of the animal being slaughtered. And the knife must be well maintained to avoid bad practice. In addition to food, kosher is also widely used to designate the 'rabbinic properness' – that food is fit, proper and ready to consume, for example – or personalised understanding of a wide range of objects, products, activities, ideas and institutions (Ivry 2010: 662). Some of the points below are from the book *Kosher Food Production* (Blech 2008), which many companies use as a handbook for kosher production. Kosher law is ultimately the application of a system of religious precepts and beliefs that govern the types of foods that people of the Jewish faith eat. This system is based on a number of verses found in the Bible, rabbinic biblical exegesis, ordinances as presented in the Talmud (the written record of the oral law as redacted in the fifth century) and the writings and decisions of rabbinic authorities (Blech 2008: xxiii). Central concepts in kosher laws are related to acceptable plants and species of animals. Other important concerns are rennin, gelatine, lactose, sodium caseinate (a protein produced from casein in skimmed milk), vitamins, eggs, grape products, fruits, vegetables and Passover (Pesach, a major Jewish festival that commemorates the exodus from Egypt) items (Regenstein and Regenstein 1979).

A large and growing body of literature explores kosher from diverse perspectives. Some studies are basic introductions to kosher for food scientists and processors (Regenstein and Regenstein 1979; Blech 2008). Other studies demonstrate how these laws can be implemented in the food industry (Regenstein and Regenstein 1988). Some articles on kosher also discuss halal laws (Regenstein and Chaudry 2003a, 2003b) and their implications for biotechnology and genetic engineering. Another type of study deals with how diverse groups of Jews in the global diaspora negotiate kosher principles and practices. For example, dietary practices provide a common symbolic system through which the increasingly heterogeneous notions of Jewish identity in Denmark can be expressed, and one way to reinforce one's Jewish identity is by keeping kosher (Buckser 1999). Similarly, for Jews in suburban Canada keeping kosher signified the creation of a Jewish lifestyle, building religious observances and practices (Diamond 2000, 2002). Among Jews in Brazil kosher observance and practices help maintain identity vis-à-vis other ethnic groups, but kosher is also a contested question that marks the diversity present in the Jewish community (Klein 2012). These studies show that many Jewish groups are fastidious about their everyday kosher consumption and this point has reinforced regulation of global kosher production and regulation.

Another group of studies shows the increased significance of kosher regulation from the 1990s onwards, arguing that non-Jewish food industry management may understand how kosher laws specifically affect their own product without understanding the religious significance that they hold for kosher consumers and rabbis. In effect, as kosher proliferated and was lifted it out its traditional religious base, calls for increased market regulation (Regenstein and Regenstein 1991) and rabbinic–industry cooperation (Regenstein and Regenstein 1990) increased to address concerns about misuse and fraud (Regenstein and Regenstein 1999). The growing market for certified kosher foods offers opportunities for the expansion of markets for existing products and scope for the development of new products for particular market niches, while modern scientific methods such as genetic engineering play an increasingly important role in certification (Regenstein and Regenstein 1991). A study by Lytton (2013) shows that the US kosher market is an example of successful private-sector regulation in an era of growing public concern over the government's ability to ensure food safety. From the 1990s onwards the 'Big Five' kosher certification agencies – the Orthodox Union (OU), OK Kosher Certification (OK), Kosher Certification and Supervision (KOF-K), Star-K (Kosher Certification) and the Chicago Rabbinical Council (CRC) – have largely dominated the global kosher market.

Similarly, a study of the implications of switching from non-kosher to kosher wine production in Israel shows that crossing the kosher categorical boundary exposes these producers to experience-based penalties that are reflected in lower product quality ratings (Roberts *et al.* 2010). Another study (Campbell *et al.* 2011) demonstrates that although neoliberalism has opened up new spaces for audit activity, older political and social dynamics operating around food audits have a much longer history.

Important issues in the literature on kosher and halal concern how regulation in the form of certification, legislation and inspections was tightened as a response to increased consumer awareness among Muslim and Jewish groups on a global scale. The proliferation of religious production meant that it was no longer exclusively Muslims or Jews who were in charge of production and this strengthened the need for regulation by trustworthy certifying bodies. Even if there is a large and diverse body of literature on kosher and halal in existence, there is no study of modern and global kosher and halal in the context of how manufacturers, shops and consumers comply with rising religious requirements. In this book there is a distinct element of political economy present in the way in which kosher and halal in complex ways link the different levels of the social scale such as individual consumption, the marketplace, religious organisations and the state.

Halal literally means 'lawful' or 'permitted'. Industrial players, merchants and some Muslim scholars involved in halal trade and standardisation have based their halal food rulings on statements from selected verses from the Qur'an such as:

> Allah makes good things lawful to them and bad things unlawful. (7: 157)
>
> You who believe, eat the good things We have provided for you and be grateful to God, if it is Him that you worship. (2: 172)
>
> He has only forbidden you what dies of itself and blood and flesh of swine and that over which any other name than that of Allah has been invoked, but whoever is driven to necessity, not desiring nor exceeding the limit, then surely Allah is Forgiving, Merciful. (2: 173)

According to these passages, halal is that which is beneficial and not detrimental to Muslims. A number of conditions and prohibitions must be observed. Muslims are expressly forbidden to consume carrion, spurting blood, pork and foods that have been consecrated to any being other than God himself: these substances are called haram ('unlawful' or 'forbidden'). The lawfulness of meat depends on how it is obtained. During ritual slaughter, *dhabh*, animals should be killed in God's name by making a fatal incision across the throat, with the blood being drained as fully as possible. Among Muslim groups and individuals, the question of the stunning of animals prior to slaughter is highly contested. While some Muslims only consider meat from non-stunned animals to be halal, for many others it is lawful to consume meat prepared by all People of the Book (Jews and Christians as well as Muslims) and they thus accept that stunning is part of modern and ethical food production.

Sea creatures and locusts are considered halal. Because the sea is seen to be pure in essence, all marine animals, even if they have died spontaneously, are halal. Despite the fact that they are not mentioned in the Qur'an, land creatures such as predators, dogs and, in the eyes of some jurists, donkeys are haram. What is more, crocodiles, weasels, pelicans, otters, foxes, elephants, ravens and insects have been condemned by the *ulama* (Islamic scholars). Often some of these animals are seen as *makruh* or detestable and thus not halal (Denny 2006: 278). Differences also exist between different schools of Islamic jurisprudence (for example, between Hanafi, Maliki, Hanbali and Shafi'i jurists) around halal understanding and practice. Another significant Islamic prohibition relates to wine and any other alcoholic drink or substance, all of which are haram, whatever the quantity or substance (Denny 2006: 279) – though alcohol has become a highly controversial question in divergent halal zones. With the advent of Islam, ancient negative attitudes toward pigs and pork were reinforced. Inspired by Jewish law, the Prophet Muhammad banned the flesh of pigs as the only animal to be prohibited, and in the Qur'an, the ban is repeated several times (Simoons 1994: 32). In effect, Muslims were distinguished from their Christian adversaries. Some Muslim groups came to abhor pigs and pork to such an extent that everything touched by them was regarded as contaminated and worthless. Under Western colonialism, pig abhorrence declined in many parts of the world, only to increase again with the end of European colonial rule after World War II, and especially with Islamic revivalism (Simoons 1994).

The understanding and practice of halal requirements vary among countries and companies producing and importing halal food. This is the point made in the book *Halal Food Production* (Riaz and Chaudry 2004). This book by two US scholars is a popularised guide to producing and marketing halal (foods) for professionals in an expanding global food market. To our knowledge, this is the only book of its kind and it is widely used by companies (see, for example, in Chapter 3, below, the section on the enzyme manufacturer Novozymes) worldwide that try to understand and comply with the current transformation of halal and it is a unique piece of empirical material. Modern halal cannot be understood simply as part of a stable taxonomy. In addition to halal and haram, doubtful things should be avoided, that is, there is a grey area between the clearly lawful and the unlawful (Riaz and Chaudry 2004: 6–7). The doubtful or questionable is expressed in the word *mashbooh* (Riaz and Chaudry 2004), which can be evoked by divergences in religious scholars' opinions or the suspicion of undetermined or prohibited ingredients in a commodity. Hence, far more abstract, individual and fuzzy aspects of context and handling are involved in determining the halalness of a product. The problem in certifying food and other products with regard to these substances is that they are extremely difficult to discover. The interpretation of these *mashbooh* areas is left open to Islamic specialists and state institutions such as the Islamic Development Department of Malaysia (JAKIM), Majelis Ulama Indonesia (Indonesian Ulema Council (MUI)) and the Islamic Religious Council of Singapore (MUIS). In the rapidly expanding global market for halal products, Southeast Asia holds a special position, that is, in Malaysia and Singapore state bodies certify halal products, spaces (shops, factories and restaurants) as well as work processes. In shops around the world, consumers can find state halal-certified products from these countries that carry distinctive halal logos. Globally, companies are affected by the proliferation of halal that to a large extent is evoked by Southeast Asian nations such as Malaysia, Singapore, Indonesia, Brunei and Thailand (Fischer 2015a).

At the end of the day, the underlying principle behind the prohibitions remains 'divine order' (Riaz and Chaudry 2004: 12). Knowledge of the above requirements is, of course, essential to innovative companies that try to establish themselves in an expanding global halal market. The increased demand for halal products by conscientious and educated Muslim consumers has urged developed countries to export halal products. In this way, developed countries have entered a market that was previously dominated by Muslim countries. Moreover, the proliferation of Western franchised food has changed the international food market and subjected it to new standards of halal certification.

.In countries such as Malaysia, Singapore and Indonesia even paper/plastic labels and printing on food are seen as problematic. Glue used for labels as well as edible printing and dyes used directly on food may contain non-permissible ingredients. Some halal certifying bodies in importing countries feel that such seepage or cross-contamination may violate the halal status of food. Muslim dietary rules assumed new significance in the twentieth century, as some Muslims began striving to demonstrate how such rules conform to modern reason and the findings of scientific research. Another common theme in the revival and renewal of these dietary rules seems to be the search for alternatives to what are seen to be Western values, ideologies and lifestyles and this is reflected in globalised halal.

Religion, regulation and globalising religious markets

In 2000, as kosher and halal were globalising and standardising, a seminal article discussed capitalism at the new millennium as 'millennial capitalism': capitalism in its 'messianic, salvific, even magical manifestations' (Comaroff and Comaroff 2000: 293). In many ways the present study fits together with central points concerning religion and markets discussed in that article. Occult economies are economies with a material aspect based on the effort to conjure wealth, or to account for its accumulation by appealing to 'techniques that defy explanation in the conventional terms of practical reason' and ethical aspects transmitted in moral discourses generated by production of value through 'magical means' (Comaroff and Comaroff 2000: 310). We argue that both kosher and halal markets can be conceptualised as forms of millennial capitalism that incorporates kosher/halal certification bodies, companies and consumers – what we refer to as different levels of the social scale.

Most scholarship on moral economies or religious markets focuses on the compatibility of markets and religious practices. For instance, Weber (2001) understood the origins of modern capitalism to be religious ethics. More recent work explores religious moralities as formative of 'market cultures' (Hefner 1996) or 'spiritual economies' (Rudnyckyj 2010). Rudnyckyj and Osella (2017) demonstrate the increased stress on calls for reforms of financial markets and for the consideration of moral values in economic practice, that is, how market practices engender new forms of religiosity that again shape economic actions.

Much of this research overlooks the fact that over the last couple of decades or so moral economies have been subjected to new forms of regulation and standardisation. Only recently have these markets become global in scope, and states, manufacturers, restaurants, shops, certifiers and consumers around the world are faced with ever stricter and more complex requirements within a framework of moral economies. Global kosher and halal markets are examples of modern religious or moral economies that are embedded in social action, for example production, trade, consumption and regulation in organisations and networks (Granovetter 1985). Thus, in this book we try to move beyond more classical and textual studies of the way in which Jews and Muslims conceptualise 'us' and 'them' through food (Freidenreich 2014) by studying kosher and halal in an era of globalisation. We also move beyond the compatibility of religion and economy to explore modern religious forms of regulation in the UK and Denmark as 'secular' case countries.

Understandings and practices of kosher/halal in these two countries are framed by ways in which 'the secular' offers signs of quite different trajectories and meanings. In other words, our focus is on the ways in which Jewish and Muslim consumers negotiate kosher and halal in the interfaces between political discourses, religious organisations and the marketplace. We show that unpacking the various assumptions that constitute 'secularism' as a political doctrine is necessary in order to explore 'the secular' as comprising concepts, practices and sensibilities that conceptually are prior to secularism (Asad 2003: 16). The secular is ubiquitous in modern life and not easily grasped, so it may most fruitfully be 'pursued through its shadows' (Asad 2003: 16). Thus, we provide empirical specificity to meanings and practices associated with 'the secular' and secular government as part of divergent state practices in the UK and Denmark. In the majority of debates about secularism, 'there is an unfortunate tendency to understand the secular state in rather undifferentiated terms: modern, homogenising and driven by objectifying scientific modes of governance' (Hansen 2000: 255). Unpacking secularism involves a focus on how Jews and Muslims live 'the secular' as well as divergent modes of secular government in everyday life.

Einstein's (2008) work on the 'supply-side theory of religion' is useful in this context in that it stresses the increasing interdependence between religious and commercial culture. Einstein argues that unlike most consumer goods, where demand can be manipulated, the supply of religious goods can only be increased because a market already exists. In opposition to proponents of the secularisation thesis, who argue that the decline in traditional forms of religious participation signals a waning of religious belief, Einstein suggests that different religious packages now offer individual consumers alternative and competing benefits. In a study of the expansion of European halal markets, Lever and Miele (2012) argue that halal certification bodies play a key role driving market differentiation in this sense, providing consumers with competing visions of 'authentic' halal.

Lee (1993) argues similarly that rules and understandings for the attainment of salvation 'have become important commodities in an expanding religious market that transcends international boundaries' (Lee 1993: 36). Politicians, bureaucrats and entrepreneurs use the popular mass media to manipulate popular wants. Planners of a religious economy try to package 'convincing soteriologies and devise practical means of delivery for their target populations in order to achieve popularity, maintain or advance a religious vision, legitimate a political hegemony, or simply gain wealth' (Lee 1993: 48). Thus, we explore modern kosher and halal as examples of globalised religious markets subjected to tensions at different levels of the social scale.

Kosher and halal standards

In this section we explore why and how standards are essential concepts when studying the global emergence, consolidation and expansion of kosher and halal markets. In other words, standards play important roles in the ways in which kosher and halal markets function. Ferguson and Gupta's (2002) concept of transnational governmentality grasps how new practices of government and new forms of 'grassroots' politics are being set up on a global scale. Examples are new strategies of discipline and regulation, exemplified by kosher and halal regulation and standards, but also transnational alliances forged by activists and grassroots organisations and the proliferation of voluntary organisations supported by complex networks of international and transnational funding and personnel. The outsourcing of the functions of the state to NGOs and other ostensibly non-state agencies is a key feature, not only of the operation of national states, but of an emerging system of transnational governmentality (Ferguson and Gupta 2002: 990). These political entities are integral parts of a transnational apparatus of governmentality. This apparatus does not replace the older system of nation-states, but overlays and coexists with it. It is necessary to treat state and non-state governmentality within a common frame and as an ethnographic problem (2002: 994). An example of this is not only the US kosher market as a successful private-sector regulation in an era of growing public concern over the government's ability to ensure food safety (Lytton 2013), but also more generally increasing regulation of kosher and halal globally. Globalised grassroots groups and NGOs are good examples of how scales have collapsed into each other. Ferguson and Gupta (2002: 995) call for an ethnography of encompassment, an approach that would take as its central problem the understanding of processes through which governmentality by state and non-state actors is both legitimated and undermined across domains. This book tries to honour this call by exploring kosher and halal at different levels of the social scale.

Processes of standardisation are apparent in kosher and halal certification, but standardisation is also market-driven. We take kosher and halal standards and standardisation to mean several things. First, they can refer to the design and qualities of products as well as proper conduct of states, organisations and individuals, for example with regard to production, preparation, handling and storage of products. Standards and standardisation can be seen to be instruments of control and forms of regulation attempting to generate elements of global order (Brunsson and Jacobsson 2000: 1). At the same time, the meanings of standards may evoke ideas of similarity and uniformity – the standardised is that which supposedly is similar and follows rules (Brunsson and Jacobsson 2000: 14). Busch (2000) argues that standards are part of the moral economy of the modern world that set norms for behaviour and create uniformity and this point is important for the emergence and expansion of kosher and halal standards. Standards standardise things or products: workers with regard to uniformity and discipline; markets in relation to fixed/uniform prices as well as the packaging of products; the way in which capitalists behave and use capital; standards themselves, that is, standardised methods that produce consistent results; the makers of standards such as scientists and technicians; consumers as a product of capitalist development and socially regulated consumption; as well as the environment. It is through standards that the moral economy is produced and reproduced (Busch 2000: 274). Moreover, standards are the recipes by which we create realities and they invoke the linguistic categories we use to organise the world (Busch 2013: 2) – material as well as ideal (Busch 2013: 3). Moral and religious behaviours are subject to standards of tolerance as they work as limits of tolerable behaviour in divergent settings (Busch 2013: 25) – for example kosher standards verses 'civic' standards in the US (Busch 2013: 259).

Kosher and halal are no longer expressions of esoteric forms of production, trade or consumption, but part of huge and expanding globalised markets where standards play important roles. In sum, based on our contemporary empirical data this book explores standards and their stories (Star and Lampland 2009) at and across different levels of the social scale, that is, how people interact with standardised forms, technologies and conventions built into infrastructure (Star and Lampland 2009: 3). We are inspired by the ideas that standards are nested inside one another; distributed unevenly; relative to divergent communities; are linked to and integrated across organisations, nations and technical systems; and signify ethics and values (Star and Lampland 2009: 5)

Kosher and halal audit culture in business organisations

Organisations such as kosher and halal certifiers, manufacturers, restaurants and shops possess shared characteristics such as explicit rules, divisions of labour and aims that involve acting on or changing everyday life, and a have governing ethos (making money or a management principle, for example)

11

(Gellner and Hirsch 2001). Important themes in our study of how organisations think about and practice kosher and halal production, trade and regulation are conflicts, diversity and power relations as well as 'the bigger picture', that is, competition between organisations and their relationship to the state and society at large. Kosher and halal regulation is premised on ways in which certifiers generate authority among individuals such as company representatives and participants in halal training.

There exists a particular trade relation in the market for kosher and halal. Consumers buy commodities that ideally comply with certain religious standards, and the trader not only profits but also claims a measure of authority. Marking commodities with kosher/halal logos helps to personalise this form of exchange or transaction: ideally the producer, trader and consumer all share the symbolic content of the halal logo. Marking products with kosher and halal logos emphasises the religious, personal and social component in proper consumption. This is a form of 'logo logic' that works by attaching political and moral messages to lifestyle brands and communicating these branded messages (Bennett and Lagos 2007: 194). In general, systems of certification have grown considerably, but the diversity of these systems often confuses consumers (Bennett and Lagos 2007: 204) – more and more products carry an increasing number of logos. An important theme that runs through this book is the emergence and expansion of an audit culture around kosher and halal practice. Certifiers regulate kosher/halal by performing 'on-site' audits and inspections in manufacturers, for example. There is a large body of literature on the rise of an 'audit society' but there is need for further scholarship on the ways in which audits and inspections are understood and practised in locally specific contexts. The pervasiveness of an audit culture within and around kosher and halal practices is not well understood, and this book fills this gap.

Audit and inspection systems are a feature of modern societies. They exist to generate comfort and reassurance in a wide range of policy contexts (Power 1999: xvii). To a large extent auditing is about cultural and economic authority granted to auditors (Power 1999: xvii), based of course on the assumption that those auditors are competent and their practices effective. A central aspect of audit culture that is also highly relevant to the market for kosher and halal is the pushing of control and self-control further into organisations to satisfy the need to connect internal organisational arrangements to public ideals (Power 1999: 10). Staff policies and setting up positions for kosher and halal coordinators to handle these issues properly, as well as establishing sections in companies that specialise in halal compliance, are examples of the increasingly prominent role of internal control systems that can be audited.

Food scares and scandals relating to Bovine Spongiform Encephalopathy (BSE), for example, and salmonella have also increased the role of public and third-party certification bodies as a way of controlling internal organisational arrangements and food systems in the global marketplace. Organisations and their procedures have become more auditable and in practical terms this involves formalised procedures of application and negotiation with a certifier. Even if kosher and halal markets have proliferated within the last two decades, how these changes have affected manufacturers and shops is not well understood. This book fills this gap by exploring how kosher and halal requirements are understood and practised in the everyday lives of business organisations in line with changing market dynamics and the lifting of kosher and halal food out of their traditional religious base.

Kosher and halal food markets

Of course, interest in the relationship between religion and food is extensive. Claude Lévi-Strauss (1968: 87) argued that exploring food could generate 'a significant knowledge of the unconscious attitudes of the society or societies under consideration'. The underlying logic in this type of analysis is that religion, on the one hand, and dietary understandings and practices, on the other hand, are inseparable forces shaping human cosmology. In seminal studies of food and religion/cosmology by Lévi-Strauss (1968), Émile Durkheim (1995) and Mary Douglas (1972, 1975, 2002), binaries such as edible/inedible, sacred/profane, and raw/cooked are vital. Barthes writes that to eat is a behaviour that develops beyond its own ends and thus it is a sign vital to individual, group, and national identities (1975: 72). Simultaneously, basic food taxonomies 'incorporate the individual into the group' and 'situate the whole group in relation to the universe' (Barthes 1975: 172). We review a few of these seminal studies of food in the anthropology of religion to draw attention to the fact that few of these anthropologists could have anticipated the emergence of global markets for kosher and halal food.

In an increasing number of markets, product quality is contingent on cultural and political controversy amongst individual and collective actors attempting to influence product recognition in line with moral, aesthetic and other status-based criteria (Knight 1992). Market competition emerges between groups benefiting from such practice and markets are therefore characterised by quality uncertainty and contestation involving producers and consumers (see Beckert and Musselin 2013).

In order to explore how markets function, Callon and colleagues (2002: 199) examine how qualities are 'attributed, stabilized, objectified and arranged'. They argue that 'markets' evolve and, like species, become 'differentiated and diversified'. However, 'this evolution is grounded in no pre-established logic. Nor is it simply the consequence of a natural tendency to adapt. Economic markets are caught in a reflexive activity: the actors concerned explicitly question their organization and, based on an analysis of their functioning, try to conceive and establish new rules for the game' (2002: 194). These insights are particularly relevant for our purposes. We are interested in how food products become kosher and halal through successive processes of *qualification* and *requalification* linked to production, certification and retailing. This is a far from straightforward process and one not usually given much attention. Two key terms are relevant – the good and the product. The notion of an 'economic good' is associated with the characteristics that give it a degree of stability and explain 'why it is in demand and why, being wanted as such, it is traded'. A 'product', alternatively, is an 'economic good seen from the point of view of its production, circulation and consumption' (Callon *et al.* 2002: 197). While a product is therefore a process, a good is a state, a moment in a never-ending process. This conceptualisation is useful in that it allows us to explore how different certification bodies define kosher and halal though processes of inspection and labelling, and how authority and trust emerge in the supply chains through which certified products travel to the consumer. As we observe in subsequent chapters, the attribution of distinguishing qualities for kosher and halal meat starts at the abattoir and only ends when a product is placed on the counter of a trusted retailer, where it gains its full *quality*.

The global markets for kosher and halal food have grown dramatically in recent decades. While the kosher market has continued to grow steadily (Lytton 2013), the halal market has expanded rapidly to generate positive economic predictions (Bergeaud-Blackler *et al.* 2015) and complex social attitudes (Bradley *et al.* 2015). With global meat production expected to double to 460 million tonnes by 2050 (FAO 2006), largely on the back of increasing meat consumption in the developing world, the halal market is creating significant opportunities for export to Muslim-majority countries (Miele 2016). In 2012 it was reported that India exported 1.5 million tonnes of halal-approved water buffalo meat to countries in the Middle East, North Africa and South Asia in line with rising demand from price-conscious consumers. This increased to 2.082 million tonnes in 2015 to generate US$4.8 billion in export trade that made India the largest global exporter of beef (Weeks 2012). Kosher meat is also traded globally, and over recent decades Israel in particular has imported vast quantities of kosher meat from countries such as Argentina and Uruguay in South America (Grandin 2004).

The increasing visibility of kosher and halal meat products in non-Muslim countries in recent decades has also been accompanied by controversy about the religious slaughter of animals. There has been intense political debate over stunning in a number of European countries, including the UK and Denmark (Lever and Miele 2012; Mukherjee 2014; Miele and Rucinska 2015). In the UK, following the longstanding position of kosher-certifying bodies that do not accept pre-slaughter stunning, there has been growing pressure from some halal certifying bodies to promote 'non-stunned' halal meat as being of a more 'authentic' and traditional quality (Lever and Miele 2012). While it is clear that some Muslims see halal as a way of reinforcing their identity in the face of wider global pressures (Marranci 2009), the discourses engendered have been the source of much tension and misunderstanding. Some European countries – Norway, Iceland and Switzerland – banned religious slaughter without stunning in the 1930s or earlier, but European Union legislation now grants a derogation from stunning that respects religious freedom in line with Article 10 of the Charter of Fundamental Rights of the European Union. In countries with large Muslim populations where the derogation is legal and applied – for example, in the UK, Netherlands, Germany, Italy and France – there are now halal markets for meat from *both* stunned and non-stunned animals (Lever and Miele 2012). Apart from Germany, where there are controls on the number of animals that can be slaughtered without stunning in line with consumer demand, a number of European countries also use the derogation from stunning to supply export markets (Miele 2016).

While all meat in the much smaller kosher market comes from non-stunned animals, evidence suggests that around 80 per cent of all halal meat in the UK comes from pre-stunned animals (FSA 2012) – though it should be noted that this figure has recently started to decrease, particularly for sheep and goats (FSA 2015). However, the high volume of meat produced and marketed as halal in the UK has led to widespread concerns about its availability in supermarkets, fast-food restaurants and public institutions. The issues involved are complex and evidence also suggests that negative social attitudes towards halal slaughter, (and to a lesser extent kosher slaughter) are wrapped up with wider public concerns about integration and immigration disseminated and enhanced through the mass media (Bradley *et al.* 2015). There are similar tensions in other countries. In Denmark, although it had not been practised for over a decade, non-stunned religious slaughter was banned in 2014, which religious minorities interpreted as anti-Semitic and Islamophobic (Fischer 2014). Danish meat production companies are now struggling to meet halal guidelines for export to some Muslim majority countries (O'Dwyer 2015) and some Danish cities have ordered pork to be made mandatory in schools and on menus in public institutions. Similar arguments have been made about Islamophobia and anti-Semitism restricting market growth and development in the UK (Shabbir 2015), and since the Brexit vote in 2016 there has been talk of new production restrictions on non-stunned kosher and halal meat.

It is clear that the functioning of these markets for certified religious food products sits uneasily between religion, regulation and consumption. But this book not only explores developments in relation to food, it also takes this comparison further by exploring globalised kosher/halal certification in biotech production (Chapter 3). Within the last couple of decades, these expanding religious markets for kosher and halal production have moved beyond meat to include enzyme production, for example, for a wide range of food and drink products. Thus, in modern and globalising industry, it is not only for food, but also for biotechnology products that requirements to avoid substances that may be contaminated with porcine residues (kosher/halal) or alcohol (halal) are being met.

Religious consumers in the age of globalised mass production

Many of our Jewish and Muslim informants are urban middle-class individuals acutely aware of the dilemma of practising class through legitimate and proper forms of (food) consumption while performing religious identities, yet it is also clear that many other middle-class consumers react against this kind of 'food piety'. More specifically, their knowledge of manners or styles as symbolic manifestations constitutes one of the key markers of class and is an ideal weapon in strategies of distinction (Bourdieu 1984: 66). However, Bourdieu's theories of distinction and practice alone are not able to capture the immense complexity involved in modern religious consumption. Michele Lamont (1992) has critiqued Bourdieu's theory of distinction through an exploration of the symbolic boundaries individuals draw when they categorise people and the high-status signals that underpin our evaluative distinctions. She argues that Bourdieu's theories of cultural capital and habitus exaggerate cultural and socioeconomic boundaries and consequent hierarchies of power while ignoring moral (religious, for example) status signals and national repertoires (history, mass media, state–market nexus, educational system, demographic mobility, stratification systems, as well as ethnic diversity, among other things). Lamont also argues that Bourdieu's method of studying status signals in questionnaires misses important qualitative aspects such as practices involved in the construction of symbolic boundaries between different middle-class groups. Based on research among the upper middle class in France and the United States, she draws attention to the complexity involved in mapping several and often overlapping symbolic boundaries (Lamont 1992). Lamont studies what it means to be a 'worthy person' by analysing types of symbolic boundaries between *self* and other (Lamont 1992: 4). The most important type of boundary for this study is moral. Religious 'fundamentalists' tend to draw these moral boundaries defending not only a religious position but also traditional values such as family life, neighbourhood, community and a religious lifestyle based on moral choices against materialism, individualism, elitist meritocracy, secular humanism and cosmopolitanism (Lamont 1992: 56). These insights supplement Bourdieu's theories and draw attention to the broader aspect of food, religion and identity.

The work of Elias (2012) also provides useful sociological insights into the relational nature of symbolic boundaries in a way that moves beyond Bourdieu's more rigid position. Although he does not focus on religion,

Elias draws attention to the competitive element of power within intergroup relations, and the ways in which food rituals, for example, help to maintain intergroup distinction through symbolic practices. Mennell (1985) draws on Elias to explore how eating habits reflect changing social relations between individuals and groups over time, and how cultural tastes are transformed in line with changes in political power and socioeconomic organisation. To fully understand food preference and avoidance effectively, Mennell argues that we thus need to examine how such changes influence food practices over an extended period of time – more specifically, we explore how consumers experience and practise everyday religious consumption on levels of the social scale: locally, nationally and globally. For example, as we shall see, many if not most of our informants are unaware of the extent to which enzyme production (Chapter 3) has undergone kosher/halal regulation over the last two decades. Paradoxically, companies and global certification bodies will argue that kosher/halal regulations are put in place to meet consumer-driven demands.

Warde's (2016) recent work specifically focuses on understanding food consumption in contemporary Western societies. He observes that agribusiness, sustained economic growth, multinational companies and ever greater international trade has not only transformed the economic foundations of Western diets, but also created possibilities of eating in much more varied ways. In short, food systems experience the effects of globalisation (Warde 2016: 1–2), which, as we demonstrate throughout this book, is essential in understanding contemporary kosher and halal practices. Drawing on practice-theoretical approaches, Warde (2016: 2) sees eating as a type of cultural consumption inseparable from aesthetics and everyday life. Most importantly, perhaps, we are inspired by the term 'compound practice' that captures the complexity of eating in the intersections between different levels of the social scale. Compound practices are shaped by the sharing of practices (Warde 2016: 5) among family members, for example, and are subject to 'pressures' from other areas (Warde 2016: 165) – for example, 'health' and 'spirituality'. Moreover, food practices condition and are themselves conditioned by the learning of new tastes, handbooks and manuals on eating, cultural intermediaries as well as controversies in popular judgements and justification (Warde 2016: 5). As we shall see throughout this book, in contemporary secular Europe significant religious observance (Warde 2016: 93) coexists with a proliferation of well-advertised specialised diets, that is, it is a feature of the modern world that many options associated with religious conviction, health concerns, political commitment and aesthetic consideration coexist and overlap (Warde 2016: 145). In this sense kosher and halal consumption encompass issues such as 'nutrition' and 'spirituality' (Coveney 2000). For modern consumers, 'nutrition' functions as both a scientific and a spiritual/ethical discipline. It serves this dual function by providing a range of scientific knowledge about food and the body as 'spiritual' disciplines: spiritual here not only means theological, but also refers to the means by which individuals are required to construct themselves with a 'correct' concern for the 'proper' way of behaving in relation to eating (Coveney 2000: xvi).

Our study of kosher and halal consumption thus examines social occasions, food selection, processes of bodily incorporation (Warde 2016: 150) and the ways in which these elements are orchestrated in everyday food consumption. Food practices are subject to direction, coordination and regulation by different (secular/religious) stakeholders and texts that are dedicated to describing and prescribing proper eating practices. Media in liberal state regimes validate pluralism by courting dispute to strengthen bias towards hegemonic preferences and unpalatable alternatives (Warde 2016: 152–3). But this does not mean that religious consumers in contemporary Western societies always know what to eat. As the Eliasian the notion of informalisation (Wouters 2008) suggests, as questions of what to eat, where to eat and how to comport the body become more open to judgement, the need for more elaborate forms of justification increases and consumers must practise more self-discipline when deciding what is and is not acceptable. Contemporary and historical social environments, institutions and organisations thus condition compound eating practices, as we show throughout this comparative study of kosher and halal consumption in the UK and Denmark.

In sum, we are inspired by studies that explore how the diversity of religion draws attention to debates about what religion is or ought to be (Bowen 1993) and the divergent responses produced by these controversies; that is, the field of debate and discussion in which participants construct discursive linkages to texts, phrases, ideas and rituals held to be part of the universal traditions of Judaism and Islam. As we shall see, kosher and halal consumption is closely linked to ritual and 'ritualisation' and to the ways in which certain social actions strategically distinguish themselves in relation to other actions (Bell 1992: 74). Ritualisation constitutes a way of acting that distinguishes and privileges practice against the quotidian – most often as sacred and profane. Thus, ritual and ritualisation become significant through their interplay and contrast with other strategic and value-laden distinctions (Bell 1992: 90). We therefore explore everyday kosher and halal consumption in the context of a ritual economy, that is, ways in which economic processes are driven by and integrated with religious ritual (Fischer 2008a). We take kosher and halal to be such fields of debates or lenses between Judaism and Islam, and also internally amongst divergent groups of Jews and Muslims.

A note on methodology

The methodology of this study is based on participant observation, on interviews undertaken in 2015–16 and also on our earlier work with state bureaucracies, religious organisations/schools and at kosher/halal network events, companies/shops/restaurants and with consumers. We also draw on a range of primary sources such as advertisements, newspapers and websites as well as reviewing existing scholarly literature on kosher and halal. Organisations were selected to obtain a good representative spread, that is, to cover types of organisations with different histories, sizes, cultures, structures, hierarchies and values to observe and analyse; and the same was the case with informants. Empirically the study is based on extended periods of qualitative research carried out in the UK and Denmark.

Our research strategy and methodologies allowed us to explore how kosher and halal are understood at different levels of the social scale in the UK and Denmark: more specifically, it translated theoretical and conceptual approaches to kosher/halal production, trade, regulation and consumption into questions asked during semi-structured interviews with actors at different levels of the social scale. This allowed us to compare the UK and Denmark as well as actors at different levels of the social scale. Moreover, this data was compared to others types of qualitative data such as observations during our extended periods of fieldwork.

We explore why and how the historical, political and institutional settings in the case countries give shape to kosher and halal markets, their regulation as well as particular forms of consumer practices. Thus, this book is comparative in nature as it compares not only kosher and halal, but also how these religious markets are understood and practised in divergent contexts. Epistemologically we use comparison as a powerful conceptual mechanism that fixes attention on kosher and halal similarities and differences. This can also be said to be a reflexive comparison (Herzfeld 2001) building on fieldwork in the case countries. Freidenreich (2014) explores how ancient and medieval Jewish, Christian and Muslim scholars conceptualised 'us' and 'them' through rules about the preparation of food by adherents of other religions and the act of eating with such outsiders. He analyses the significance of food to religious formation and the ways in which food restrictions generate ideas about the 'other'. Freidenreich (2014: 8) concludes that Jews, Christians and Muslims have imagined their respective communities in qualitatively different 'styles'. These communities employ divergent methods when classifying humanity, leading to differences in self-identification. Our book updates Freidenreich's study by looking at contemporary understandings and practices of kosher and halal in an era of globalised mass production, trade, regulation and consumption while keeping in mind historical and textual perspectives. We are inspired by Freidenreich's (2014: 10) method of 'comparative jurisprudence', that is, comparing understandings and practices of kosher and halal along four axes: firstly, comparing kosher in the UK and Denmark; secondly, comparing halal in the UK and Denmark; thirdly, comparing kosher and halal in the UK; and finally comparing kosher and halal in Denmark. More specifically, we have focused on the major markets for kosher and halal around London, Manchester and Copenhagen, with our methodology capturing and comparing the major UK markets for kosher/halal with Denmark, where kosher/halal are important to smaller groups of religious consumers. Thus, we compare the UK and Denmark when exploring historical and contemporary contexts of Judaism/kosher and Islam/halal (Chapter 1), meat production and trade (Chapter 2), biotech (Chapter 3), kosher consumers (Chapter 4), halal consumers (Chapter 5) and in the book's Conclusion.

We endeavoured to follow 'the people' (bureaucrats, representatives from kosher/halal certifying bodies, scientists, activists, company representatives and consumers); 'the thing' (the circulation of kosher/halal commodities as manifestly material objects of study) (Marcus 1995: 106) as well as 'the metaphor' (kosher/halal embedded in particular realms of classification, discourse, and modes of thought) (Marcus 1995: 108). Thus, we follow people, kosher/halal things and metaphors between Judaism/Islam, consumption, production and regulation. We introduce relevant chapters by reviewing research conducted over the last 15 years or so in order to put the contemporary material into perspective. Altogether, for this entire project we carried out around 50 interviews (certifiers, companies and consumers) and practiced participant observation. This included interviews with eight Jewish and ten Muslim consumers in each country. The reason for this is that demographically Muslim groups are more diverse and kosher is arguably more complex compared to halal, resulting in more extensive narratives of informants. In sum, the above methodologies and the research strategy allowed us to answer our central research question.

Organisation of the book

The book is in five chapters. Chapter 1, 'Kosher and halal in the UK and Denmark', serves as an introduction to Judaism/kosher and Islam/halal in the UK and Denmark. The main function of these discussions is to give the reader a broader context for exploring kosher and halal in greater empirical detail in subsequent chapters, so in this chapter we also discuss how this present study fit our previous studies on kosher and halal to flesh out similarities and differences. Chapter 2, 'Manufacturing and selling meat', explores and compares kosher and halal meat production and retailing in the two case countries, while Chapter 3, 'Beyond meat' looks at biotech and dairy production in manufacturing companies. In Chapter 4, 'Kosher consumers', we explore how Jewish consumers in the UK and Denmark understand and practise kosher consumption in their everyday lives. A specific focus in this chapter is how consumers make sense of the issues raised in previous chapters, that is, buying/eating meat and non-meat products. With regard to halal, Chapter 5,

'Halal consumers', addresses the same issues as Chapter 4. Both chapters are organised so that in each we start out by discussing consumers who are very observant about kosher/halal and then gradually we move towards more non-observant or relaxed consumers at the other end of the spectrum. The book's Conclusion ties the findings together and explores some broader issues and themes.

1

Kosher and halal in the UK and Denmark

This chapter serves as an introduction to Judaism/kosher and Islam/halal in the UK and Denmark. The main function of these discussions is to give the reader a broader historical and societal context for exploring kosher and halal in greater empirical detail in subsequent chapters; we also discuss broader similarities and differences between kosher and halal in the UK and Denmark. We firstly explore Judaism/kosher and Islam/halal in the UK before moving on to Denmark. Thus, we examine important background aspects of Judaism/kosher and Islam/halal in their national contexts and this knowledge is invaluable in subsequent chapters. Generally, compared to the UK context sources on Judaism/kosher and Islam/halal in Denmark are more limited and the section on Denmark in this chapter is to a larger extent based on our fieldwork than the UK section.

Kosher and halal in the United Kingdom

In the UK secular government predominates at a cultural level in the context of institutionally complex ties between church and state. The ruling monarch is the head of state and Governor of the Church of England, and 26 unelected bishops sit in the House of Lords. In theory, secularism does not seek to curtail religious freedoms, but to ensure freedom of thought and conscience for believers and non-believers alike. The secular and plural nature of UK society has generated competing identities for centuries and the state has a long history of accommodating religious minorities, including Protestant non-conformists, Roman Catholics and Jews (Fetzer and Soper 2005; Anasri 2009). In the 1970s, educational policy was multicultural in state-supported schools and religious education covered Judaism, Islam and Sikhism as well as Christianity. However, the arrival of Muslims in greater numbers in the second half of the twentieth century once again tested the intimate ties between church and state. Throughout the 1980s and 1990s, a range of issues related to Muslim schools created wide-ranging controversy and education officials consistently refused applications for state aid, and it was not until 1998 that the government approved two independent Islamic schools. Over time Islamic practices have thus been recognised, but the constitution does not establish religious rights as fundamental and these are left to the political arena (Fetzer and Soper 2005). As we observe in subsequent chapters, current exemptions that allow Jews and Muslims to slaughter animals without prior stunning as an expression of religious freedoms continue to create considerable tension in the political sphere.

Judaism and kosher in the United Kingdom

In 1656 a small colony of Sephardi Jews was found living in London and this group formed the UK's first embryonic Jewish community (Roth 1978). Today, outside Israel and the US, London has one of the largest Jewish populations, at around 200,000 (Kooy 2015), and a number of well-established *kashrut* boards and rabbinical authorities are located in the city. While Anglo-Jewry has been in decline in terms of size and religiosity for more than a century as more Jews have integrated, there has also been a concurrent rise in ultra-Orthodoxy in communities across the UK (Wise 2006). This is strongly evident in London and in Manchester, which has the largest Jewish community outside London and the fastest growing in Europe, with a population of approximately 40,000. Much like London, Manchester has a number of leading *kashrut* boards and rabbinical authorities operating at the local, national and international level.

The origins of Manchester's Jewish population can be traced back to the middle of the eighteenth century, when a small group of Ashkenazi traders of German origin arrived in the city. By the 1780s, a small group had settled permanently and they would soon establish Manchester's first synagogue and kosher eatery (Williams 1976). The first legal dispute over *shechita* slaughter in the UK was heard in London in 1788 (Wise 2006) and in 1804 local Sephardi and Ashkenazi congregations established the London Board for Shechita (www.shechita.org) (LBS). When the first synagogue opened in Manchester in 1825 the congregational *shochet* slaughtered animals and supervised the sale of kosher meat at licensed butchers with the authority of the 'chief rabbi' and a London based Beth Din (Williams 2006).

As the economic and professional standing of Manchester's original Jewish settlers began to improve they started to move out of the disease-ridden city centre (Engels 2009) towards the rural suburbs of Broughton and Cheetham Hill, establishing themselves as leaders of the community. As Jewish immigrants continued to arrive in the city from Eastern Europe and Russia throughout the eighteenth century, the dominance of this emerging middle class became unacceptable to large sections of the community, and divisions subsequently emerged between those who wanted to retain Jewish traditions and those who wanted to modernise in line with the wider reform movement (Williams 1976). In 1858 these established–outsider relations (Elias 2008) were formalised within the community, as the Orthodox Great Synagogue and the British Reform Synagogue emerged within half a mile of each other in Cheetham Hill. A small Sephardi community of Spanish and Portuguese merchants also became established in the city during this period, yet by the end of the century these families had also started to move out to the more affluent southern suburbs, where they were soon joined by Arabic-speaking Sephardim from Syria, Iraq and Morocco. A number of synagogues thus also emerged in south Manchester, including the *Sha'are Sedek* in West Didsbury in the 1920s.

The London Board for Shechita – endorsed by the chief rabbi – was first given authority to grant licences to immigrant Jewish slaughterers (*shochetim*) in 1868 and over the coming century this was to facilitate an ongoing debate over *shechita* that continues to this day (Alderman 1995; Lever and Miele 2012). When the Manchester Shechita Board (MSB) was formed in 1892 to coordinate independent *shechita* across the city it quickly found itself defending religious slaughter from wealthy merchants and patrons of the local RSPCA (Wise 2006). MSB initially made a number of concessions to their gentile neighbours to protect the image of the Jewish community, including the adoption of post-mortem stunning (stunning animals post-slaughter) and in 1896 MSB considered using some form anaesthetic to desensitise animals prior to *shechita*. This was strongly opposed on the grounds that it would be difficult ascertain the exact cause of death, thus rendering the carcasses of animals *treifa* (unfit) under Jewish law. By the turn of the century, MSB was stuck between the two camps and they subsequently formed the Manchester Beth Din (www.mbd.org.uk) (MBD) to provide full-time rabbinical advice and religious supervision for its slaughterers and licensed retail outlets (Wise 2006).

As the Jewish community continued to spread out into the northern and southern suburbs, the degree to which Jewish customs were adhered to varied amongst different groups (Williams 1976; Wise 2006). Those who strayed too far felt the wrath of the more strictly observant and Orthodox members of the community, most notably from businessmen and textile dealers who had arrived in the city from Eastern Europe in the early nineteenth century. In 1925 this group signalled their opposition to the erosion of traditional Jewish practices by forming the Machzikei Hadass (MH) society. From this point onwards MH became the centre of strict Orthodoxy in the city through community activism and repeated demands for higher *kashrut* standards, yet it was not until 1965 that the Chief Rabbi agreed to license an independent MH *shochet* to conduct *shechita*. In Manchester today, both MBD and MH offer *shechita* services.

In recent decades MBD has become a well-established *kashrut* organisation at the local, national and international level. The organisation supervises companies in Europe, the United States, China, India and Japan, amongst other places, and the Manchester Kashrus (MK) stamp and *hechsher* is visible on hundreds of food products at major global companies such as Kellogg's, Heinz and Kraft. Kellogg's Trafford Park factory, not far from Manchester United's famous Old Trafford stadium, is the biggest cereal factory in the world and produces 1 million boxes of cereal a day – around 400 million boxes a year (Kalmus 2012). All of the cereal produced at the factory is now kosher-certified, including over 30 of the 100 Kellogg's products currently manufactured in the UK. Kellogg's first started thinking about kosher certification in the late 1970s. At this time they spent a couple of hours every month producing cereal for Israel, which meant that they had to close down production completely at great expense to comply with kosher requirements and a decision was eventually made for the factory to go completely kosher.

Rabbi Osher Yaakov Westheim – a former senior *dayan* at MBD for around 20 years – explained that this change in production was not without its problems. As some suppliers could not supply the gelatine-free vitamin mixes (derived from non-kosher animal ingredients) required for kosher production they often became uncooperative and secretive. To complicate matters, when MBD auditors were trying to work out where various ingredients listed on Kellogg's products originated – vegetable oil in fried banana chips from the Philippines, for example – the company sometimes couldn't provide the information they required. In other instances Kellogg's had added ingredients to products as experiments, which often carried on for a number of years when it was totally non-effective: on occasions MBD thus made Kellogg's aware that they would save considerable amounts of money by eliminating such ingredients from production. Rabbi Westheim claimed that the Kellogg's operation was thus a significant turning point in MBD's reputation and that from this point onwards they 'grew into a major setup', earning 'a reputation of being high-standard kosher'.

During a recent spot check and visit to Kellogg's Manchester factory, another former MBD *dayan*, Rabbi Yehuda Osher Steiner, inspected a series of large machines in the enormous five-floor factory where ingredients are sorted; before he entered the factory, MBD has already checked the ingredients used in production from hundreds of sources and dozens of factories. While many of the cereals inspected by Rabbi Steiner are vegetarian, he points out that this this does not ensure that they are fully kosher. In relation to Fruit 'n Fibre, for example, he states that: 'You've got the raisins and sultanas, which kosher laws have to ensure have no problem of insect infestation, and that coatings on raisins are vegetable oil and not the animal derivatives used by some companies'. After the inspection of these machines is complete, Rabbi Steiner moves on to oversee the 'kosherisation' of equipment to prevent contamination by way of non-kosher infusion. In a huge hall on the fifth floor of the factory there are over 20 rotating cylindrical pressure cookers cooking millions of corn grits using steam, which, the rabbi explains, has the potential to create many problems for kosher production. On the third floor, where Corn Flakes are toasted, flavoured and tossed on conveyor belts on their way to giant mixers upstairs, engineers are again consulted to understand the heating process (Kalmus 2012; see also Blech 2008). Taken in its entirety, this is a comprehensive process and to a get an overall picture of production at Kellogg's Rabbi Steiner must speak with engineers in many parts of the factory.

The processes involved in kosher production are also increasing in complexity. Food production is changing rapidly and informants suggested that as well as opportunities this presents many challenges from a kosher perspective. While 50 years ago an individual food product might contain between five and ten ingredients, today it might contain over a hundred. Not surprisingly, as we observe in subsequent chapters, MBD offers certification for innovative UK biotech companies manufacturing enzyme blends for food and non-food products globally.

As property prices in London have continued to rise in recent decades, the Manchester community has grown considerably, becoming more strictly Orthodox in the process (Wise 2006). Between the population census of 2001 and that of 2011, the predominantly and strictly Orthodox *haredi* ward of Sedgley in Greater Manchester grew by almost 42 per cent (Graham 2013). When the leading historian of *haredi* Judaism in Manchester, Yaakov Wise, moved back to the city from London in 1991 he explained that there were very few local kosher restaurants and takeaways. Today, a quarter of a century later, the north Manchester community has a wide range of eateries, bakers, delicatessens and other businesses certified by MBD (see www.mbd.org.uk/site/licensees). More recently, as the community has become more strictly Orthodox, the *mehadrin hechsher* (which designates more meticulous observance of *kashrut* laws and *shechita* practice) of the Machzikei Hadass Kashrut Board has become increasingly visible, with a number of our informants explaining that strictly Orthodox Jews will not buy MBD-certified products or go anywhere near a supermarket to buy kosher food: Yaakov Wise confirmed this trend, pointing out that he only eats *glatt* kosher from strictly Orthodox sources. While the expansion and development of the kosher market in Manchester mirrors the growth of a more Orthodox and demanding community, Yaakov also notes that young people have more disposable income than they once did and hence like dining out more than the older generation. Growth is also part of the trend towards middle-class suburbanisation, even within the strictly Orthodox community (Wise 2006).

Halpern's Kosher Food Store and Delicatessen – one of the leading kosher businesses in the UK – is an MBD licensee. Located in Broughton near the Salford–Manchester boundary, the business has origins that stretch back three generations, and since opening as Higgins in 1924 the name of the business has changed three times; in 1951 Shimon Halpern purchased the shop and it retains this name. From 1983 to 1993 the shop flourished under

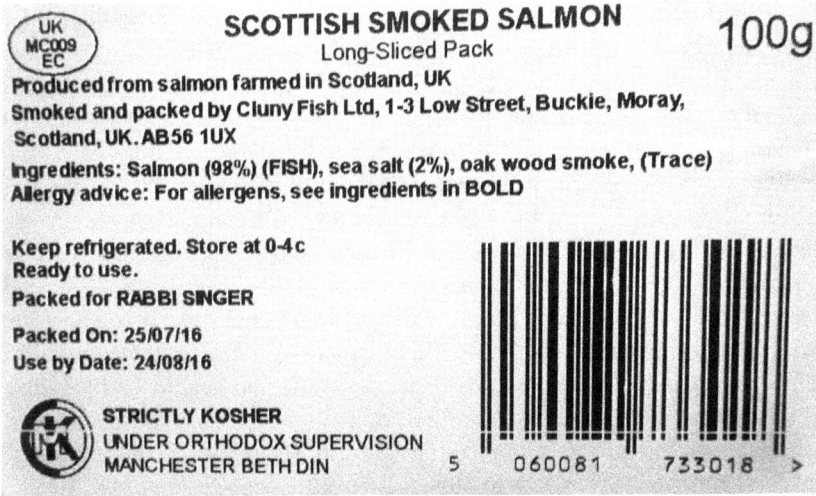

Figure 2 Kosher-certified Scottish smoked salmon certification

Figure 3 MH Meats on Leicester Road in Salford

the ownership of David Weisz and this has continued since David Salzman and his wife bought the business. Salzman explains that Halpern's mainly sells fresh and frozen meat and poultry, and also cold cuts (processed meats), predominantly under local kosher certification from MBD and MH. However, he also points out that Halpern's has to provide as wide a range of kosher certification as possible, as this has been paramount to their success over the last 90 years. Recognising that the strictly Orthodox community has grown significantly in the last couple of decades, he argues that this continues to create increasing market growth for kosher brands and kosher certification. As well as small kosher shops, David points out that mainstream supermarkets in the area have also increased their selection of kosher food products. In line with trends among the wider population, David suggests that healthy eating is also becoming a more prominent factor for kosher consumers and for the business. Halpern's own-label Deli'n'Dine fresh food products are free from colourings and preservatives and are very popular within the Jewish community, offering a range of traditional and Middle Eastern cuisine to address the demands of both the Sephardi and Ashkenazi Jewish communities.

Kosher food is now widely available in public institutions around Manchester and Salford. A number of informants explained that some mainstream Jewish schools in the UK provide kosher food from recognised certification bodies: some schools serve pre-packed kosher meals from the company Hermolis (www.hermolis.com), which provides kosher meals for British Airways. Many Jewish schools in north Manchester also provide their own kosher catering. This wasn't always the case. One informant from south Manchester noted that when he was a schoolboy in the 1950s he travelled for lunch every day to a kosher canteen in Salford that fed Jewish children from regular primary and secondary schools across north Manchester. While some informants argued that provision could be better in public institutions, others pointed out that if strictly observant families are overly concerned about such issues they can and do send their children to Jewish state and private schools. Hospitals have similar arrangements, providing food from Hermolis, though it was argued by one informant that this is not the healthiest food for a hospital. Hospitals offer other services. The Manchester Royal Infirmary has a *shabbat* room provided by the community, and Salford Royal has Jewish rooms where kosher 'snack foods' are provided for patients. One informant pointed out that while the provision of kosher food in schools and hospitals in Manchester is generally very good, it is not at the same level as halal simply because the Jewish population and kosher market are much smaller.

Despite the development of the kosher market over recent decades in London, Manchester and beyond, kosher meat production continues to be controversial. As soon as it was established in 2003, Shechita UK (www.shechitauk.org) – an independent body established to unite representatives from the Board of Deputies of British Jews, the National Council of Shechita

Boards and all UK *kashrut* authorities – was called upon to respond to a Farm Animal Welfare Council (FAWC 2003) report calling for a ban on slaughter without stunning. Vigorous opposition and sensitive relations with Muslim communities forced the UK government to retract their endorsement of the recommendation, yet as the halal market has expanded rapidly over the last 15 years, there have been repeated calls for a ban on slaughter without stunning.

Islam and halal in the United Kingdom

During the eighteenth century the East India Company recruited young men from the Indian subcontinent to work as cheap labour in the merchant navy, and Yemini and Somali seamen, as well as Ottoman Turks, were some of the first Muslims to settle in the UK. The number of lascars, as these sailors became known, increased greatly after the opening of the Suez Canal in 1869 and from this point onwards many began to settle and form distinct Muslim communities of their own in ports such as London, Cardiff, Liverpool and Manchester (Ansari 2009). While Islam in the UK is often equated with recent colonial migrations from Pakistan, India and Bangladesh, Ansari (2009) points out that by the end of the nineteenth century there was already an established Moroccan community with its own places of worship and halal butchers.

Today Muslims constitute almost 5 per cent of the total UK population and between 2001 and 2011 the population increased from 1.55 million to 2.71 million: 47 per cent are UK-born and 73 per cent identify themselves as British (MCC 2015). Although there has been a movement outwards into new areas in recent years, 76 per cent of UK Muslims still live in the inner-city neighbourhoods of London, Birmingham, Manchester and Yorkshire and Humber. Demographically these communities are changing fast. Between 2001 and 2011 the Muslim population increased in London by 66.8 per cent to reach 1,012,823, while in Manchester it reached 79,496, an increase of 121.9 per cent (43,690) (MCC 2015): there are fewer Muslims (4 per cent) over the age of 65 than there are in the rest of the population (16 per cent) and many communities have a younger and increasingly educated population (MCC 2015). Today Moss Side, Longsight and Rusholme in the south of the city and Cheetham Hill to the north are the major centres for Manchester's diverse Muslim population. Cheetham Hill in particular, as noted above, has long been a centre for Jewish migrants arriving in the city, but today it is largely Muslims who reside in the area: between 2001 and 2011 the Cheetham ward had the highest increase in Muslim residents (5,000) across the city overall (MCC 2015). The nine other local authorities of Greater Manchester, places such as Rochdale and Oldham, for example, also have high Muslim populations, and the 2011 census reported that 356,450 Muslims reside in northwest England overall.

By the late eighteenth century, Manchester's position as an emerging 'cotto-nopolis' and flourishing commercial centre was attracting Arabs and Muslims from the Middle East and beyond. Cotton was initially exported to Morocco around this time and by the mid-nineteenth century a number of Fasi merchants from Fez had settled in the city (Ansari 2009). While most of these merchants were Muslims, some were also Sephardi Jews who purchased kosher meat from the *Sha'are Sedek* synagogue in West Didsbury, and before they could source meat from their own communities in Rusholme and Fallowfield, Muslim merchants also bought meat from the synagogue (Halliday 1992; Seddon 2012). One of our informants pointed out that as late as the 1960s some Muslims were still buying sheep and chickens at local farms and ritually slaughtering them on the spot or at home later, a practice that could be a source of tension with their English neighbours.

The earliest traders from the Indian subcontinent started arriving in Manchester from Jullunder and the Punjab in the 1920s and 1930s. The early entrepreneurs were significant: not only did they open some of the first Asian cafés in the city, they also constituted the first movements on the mass migration chains involving migrants from Pakistan, India and Bangladesh that expanded during the 1950s, and which laid the foundations for contemporary Muslim communities in places such as London, Birmingham and Manchester (Werbner 1990; Ansari 2009). By the early 1950s many of these early migrants had become established market traders and some of our informants noted their movement into other business niches. These businessmen also played a central role in the foundation of the Pakistan Society and in the control of Manchester Central Mosque (also known as Victoria Park Mosque), which started out as two houses owned by Syrian textile merchants and the local Indian community in the early 1900s.

During the 1950s and 1960s, immigration to the UK from Pakistan increased considerably and by 2011 there were 1.1 million Pakistanis living in the UK (ONS 2015). The Commonwealth connection made migration easier, and prior to the Commonwealth Immigrants Act of 1962, citizens of British Commonwealth countries could migrate to the UK unopposed. During this period Pakistani migrants helped to resolve labour shortages in the steel and textile industries, while doctors were recruited to work in the National Health Service (Ansari 2009). Until this point, Muslims from diverse cultural and religious backgrounds interacted with each other openly. But as the numbers of migrants continued to increase many began to anticipate stricter immigration controls and Muslims began to cluster along more distinct ethnic lines. Many saw themselves as settlers rather than temporary migrants and they thus started to look to tribal, kinship, ethnic and sectarian affiliations to secure their status and position (Ansari 2009). In the coming period, mosques and religious schools took on greater significance and Muslims were reminded of their traditional values and practices more regularly. Muslim organisation increased significantly and specific cultural norms and religious practices were more widely adhered to: 'What emerged at the end of the 1970s was a patchwork of communities, each impressing its particular national, ethic, linguistic doctrinal character on the organisations it had created' (Ansari 2009: 343).

During the late 1960s, what has since become known as the 'Curry Mile' in Rusholme to the south of the city centre, started to change into what it is today – the thriving hub of the South Asian community in Manchester. At the time, Wilmslow Road was full of banks, jewellers, hairdressers, pubs and other traditional English businesses. One of our informants reminisced about his uncle opening a Bangladeshi café in the area at this time, only to close it down quickly because he wasn't making any money. From this point onwards, however, the Pakistani community began to settle in the area in greater numbers, and by the late 1970s the area of Wilmslow Road leading out of the city, beyond Manchester University, had been completely transformed. Increasing numbers of cafés and restaurants emerged and these quickly became meeting places for the vast number of factory workers who had arrived from the subcontinent (Goswami 2009). Another informant talked about his factory-owning father sending him down to cafés in the area every day for halal lunches of samosas, curries and breads for his workforce. As the Asian restaurant and food trade in the city expanded both economically and culturally, Werbner (1999: 562) discusses how 'hundreds of grocery stores selling halal meat became the base for the emergence of food wholesalers and manufacturers, making anything from frozen samosa and Asian savouries to chutneys'. Notably, it was during this period that some of these businesses started selling products to mainstream supermarkets for the first time.

Mirroring developments in the Jewish community over a century earlier, by the 1980s Muslims were beginning to feel more secure in the UK and they thus began to agitate for greater clarification of their rights as British citizens (Ansari 2009). This was most evident in campaigns for better provision for Muslim education, for example, which grew in intensity during the 1980s and 1990s. Two events in Bradford in particular propelled halal meat to the forefront of public debate during this period. Between late 1982 and early 1984, Bradford Metropolitan Council's decision to provide halal meat to Muslim children in schools across the city generated widespread debate locally and at the national level, significantly enhancing, in the process, greater consciousness and self-awareness amongst UK Muslims (Charlton and Kaye 1985; Kaye 1993). The issues involved were given greater prominence in 1984 after the headmaster of a local school in Bradford, Ray Honeyford, wrote an article on education and race for the right-wing *Salisbury Review* (www.salisburyreview.com). Critical of multiculturalism and its effects on British education, Honeyford's attack on the council's education policy had far-reaching consequences. While a multi-ethnic alliance formed to have Honeyford removed from his post, the affair also generated renewed opposition to religious slaughter by animal welfare groups and right-wing political parties (Charlton and Kaye 1985; Kaye 1993; Lewis 1993; Ansari 2009). Concerns were expressed about the dilution of British culture and when the Farm Animal Welfare Council petitioned for the abolition of religious slaughter in 1985, Muslims mounted a more concerted response at the national level for the first time.

It was at this point that a national body of halal butchers was put forward as a way of protecting Muslim identity, and with encouragement from the Muslim Parliament, the Halal Food Authority (www.halalfoodauthority.com) (HFA) eventually emerged in 1994. Masood Khawaja – a former president of HFA – explained that the initial remit of HFA was to oversee a network of approved slaughterhouses and shops that could provide the Muslim community with independently halal-certified red meat and poultry. HFA was the first UK halal certification body to grant licences to businesses in line with inspections and audits that assessed compliance with Islamic principles alongside UK and EU regulation. One of HFA's early innovations was a proposal for a reliable system to tag carcasses before they left the slaughterhouse, yet Masood Khawaja pointed out that it soon became apparent that carrying out halal slaughter in segregated slaughterhouses was problematic and that it was difficult to separate halal from non-halal meat in practice. He also noted that one of the major problems HFA has faced over the years has been explaining to various supply chain actors what halal actually means to Muslims. Initially this led to a more strict separation of halal and non-halal meat within slaughterhouses and meat plants, though as we observe in Chapter 3 this distinction has become increasingly blurred as the market has expanded.

Initially HFA certified non-stunned meat as halal. But as they established themselves as the major halal certification body in the UK they began to accept stunning, as this aligned them more clearly with mainstream scientific practice and animal welfare considerations to increase their authority (Lever and Miele 2012). For almost a decade HFA operated unchallenged. In 2003, however, the more orthodox Halal Monitoring Committee (www.halalhmc.org) (HMC) emerged. Much like the emergence of strictly Orthodox *kashrut* and *shechita* bodies within the Jewish community in the early twentieth century, HMC emerged as a result of rapid social change and attempts to bolster to Muslim identity at the global level (Marranci 2009). Based in Leicester, the organisation operates across the UK and exemplifies the emergence of organisations dedicated to maintaining the trust of Muslim consumers and addressing concerns about what they see as 'falsely labelled' halal meat. Until this time, most Muslims in the UK considered the meat sold in supermarkets and food service outlets to be produced and slaughtered by 'People of the Book' and therefore to be suitable for Muslim consumption (Lever and Miele 2012). From the outset, however, HMC mounted a challenge to the hegemony of HFA by opposing their position on pre-stunning and mechanical slaughter, and by questioning the halal qualities ascribed to meat through their production processes. As stated on HMC's website some years ago:

> Stunning the animal before slaughter leaves a huge doubt into the halalness of the animal as many could be killed by the stunning especially in the case of poultry. Furthermore, it prevents the drainage of entire blood resulting in it being retained in the animal and retained blood causes germs and bacteria, it deprives animals from the benefits of *tasmiyah* due to it being unconscious, it is inhumane to animals and causes unnecessary pain and suffering, it is in reality done not for animal rights purposes, but in order for the industry to kill more animals quicker so as to increase profits. (Abu Ibrahim, quoted in HMC 2012)

It is this controversy about the effectiveness of stunning that has driven competition to define what is and is not 'authentic halal' over the last 15 years (Lever and Miele 2012), with the outsiders from HMC challenging the boundaries of HFA's authority and their established practices (Elias and Scotson 2008).

A number of HMC-licensed grocers and butchers we spoke with in Manchester explained that there is a very real need to have HMC certification to attract customers and succeed in the current market climate. Abid Khan, Assistant Imam, and director of education at the Cheadle Mosque just outside Manchester, argued that in recent years HMC has become the default position for Muslims who want guarantees about the authenticity of the halal meat they consume. Those adopting this strictly orthodox position do so, he argues, because they are concerned about what they are putting into their body in the name of God.

Abid also pointed out, however, that the way HMC operates makes some Muslims uneasy, not least because it undermines rather than reinforces trust between Muslims. He provided an example of this situation from his own experience:

> I was out with a friend a while ago and we went into a local bakery in Trafford. And he is a very orthodox, kind of traditional Muslim and he's very strict on this issue of halal meat. So we went in there and I got a chicken pasty and he asked is it halal, they said yes it's halal. So I got a chicken pasty and he said is it HMC. And the lady behind the counter said no it's not HMC, but I can guarantee it's halal, but he said he didn't want it. But then the lady behind the counter got a bit upset … She said 'look, I'm telling you it's halal, you know you should be taking my word for it, it's halal, but you're not going to have it just because it's not HMC'.

Our informant did recognise, however, that there are many more Muslims, whom he does not regard as any less religious or pious, that do not go to such lengths. And he argued further that unless there is serious reason to doubt a Muslim businessmen selling halal meat and food, most Muslims should and do trust them.

This situation was also evident in the Italian restaurant Don Giovanni (www. dongiovanni.uk.com) in central Manchester. Although the restaurant is not halal-certified, the general manager (who comes from Egypt) showed us a certificate from an HMC-certified supplier in Greater Manchester that he shows to customers when they ask if the meat at the restaurant is halal. Interestingly, our informant indicates that customers never ask whether the meat is from stunned or non-stunned animals, and that once they have seen a certificate they never ask to see it again on subsequent visits; he also indicates that he personally does not pay much attention to the competition between certification bodies and that he simply trusts the supplier he has chosen to provide halal meat, much as the customers trust him when he tells them that the restaurant's meat is halal. Another informant, an imam in north Manchester, stated that he was personally against stunning, particularly for poultry, but argued further that slaughter conducted by Muslims, Jews or Christians ('People of the Book') is permissible and only 'unacceptable' if it is conducted by a non-religious person. He also recognised that stunning is acceptable to many Muslims and by what he described as a 'dissident' and 'minority' group of scholars.

As these discussions illustrate, the UK halal market has developed considerably in recent years to reflect changing social relations between individuals and groups and transformations in cultural taste and socioeconomic organisation (Mennell 1985). Yet unlike the broad range of issues that kosher certification bodies are concerned with, halal certification bodies in the UK generally focus on meat and food. While the HFA has attempted to cover many parts of the market in recent decades in partnership with some of the major global accreditation bodies in Malaysia and Indonesia, for example, and with multinational companies such as Kellogg's and Tesco, as we observe in Chapter 3 they are largely known for their work with meat producers and slaughter facilities in the UK. While HMC does not recognise the legitimacy of many international bodies, it has also built relationships with multinational companies, yet it is still largely known for its work with restaurants, grocers and butchers at the local level. Other bodies have a similar narrow focus. The Muslim Food Board (www.tmfb. net), for example, is known for its work in food processing as well as cosmetics and pharmaceuticals, while HFCE, registered in Belgium but operating across the UK and many other countries, focuses on the export of raw materials, which means that they are more engaged in enzyme certification than either HFA or HMC. Nevertheless, much like the kosher market, the international halal market continues to expand in new directions and this is creating new pressures as well as opportunities. Saqib Mohammed, chief executive at HFA, argued that to position itself in the market going forward, the organisation will have to give due consideration to new opportunities in pharmaceuticals and cosmetics, oils and fats, for example, as well as enzyme production and food processing, whilst maintaining good working relationships with long-term international partners in the meat industry. Paradoxically, as the market continues to expand and

34

Figure 4 Kellogg's cereal with HFA (halal) and MBD (kosher) certification

differentiate at the global level, controversy over halal meat and halal slaughter practice is becoming more controversial at the national level in the UK, though not currently to the same extent as it is in Denmark.

Kosher and halal in Denmark

The Evangelical-Lutheran Church of Denmark is the dominant church/religion in the country, but even so Denmark is characterised by religious diversity. Arguably the room for accommodating religious diversity in Denmark is premised on a particular configuration of secularity dominated by the state-supported Evangelical-Lutheran Church. Most importantly, however, is the widely held and strongly embedded popular perception that the public sphere is strictly secular (Nielsen 2014). Denmark stands out as being highly secular and highly non-secular at the same time, that is, state and church are tightly intertwined (Nielsen 2014: 251). Ethnic Danes are less likely to favour an active accommodation of religious diversity because they consider themselves to be highly secular – they consider religion to be a private matter that should not be explicitly or publicly accommodated beyond the legal right to practise one's religion (Nielsen 2014: 263). In effect this means that issues relating to Islam in particular, such as burial or halal, especially post-9/11, became hotly debated topics. As we shall see, while halal has a strong public presence in

Figure 5 HMC Halal Meat on Ayres Road, Old Trafford

urban public spaces such as the Nørrebro neighbourhood in Copenhagen, this is not the case with kosher. Our focus in this chapter is on Copenhagen, which is not only home to the majority of Jews and Muslims in Denmark, but also to kosher and halal markets and organisations involved in their regulation.

A ban on kosher and halal slaughter without prior stunning of animals came into effect in Denmark in 2014. This decision followed previous debates in Denmark about religious slaughter and stirred deep controversy among Jewish and Muslim groups both within the country and beyond. In announcing the ban, the Danish Minister for Food, Agriculture and Fisheries, Dan Jørgensen, referred to a Danish animal protection law that allows the minister to make a decision like this without first taking it to the Danish national parliament. Jørgensen once served as president of the Animal Welfare Intergroup, which advocates animal welfare and conservation issues (Fischer 2014). It is in this context that the empirical data provided below should be seen. In general we can say that in the public sphere and in the media in Denmark halal is more prominent than kosher, but also more problematic and linked time and again to what are considered the excessive rights of Muslims vis-à-vis the ethnic Danish majority, especially in institutions such as schools.

Judaism and kosher in Denmark

Jewish migration to Denmark started around the early eighteenth century and today there are about 7,000 Jews in Denmark (Ahlin *et al.* 2012: 410). The mainstream Jewish organisation in Denmark is Det Jødiske Samfund (the Jewish Community), which maintains a synagogue in central Copenhagen. The Jewish Community has about 2,400 members and a chief rabbi (Borup and Fibiger 2015: 57) and it is the central organisation involved in kosher in Denmark: below we discuss this organisation's involvement in kosher by exploring the work of the current and previous chief rabbis. Machzikei Hadass is a very small Orthodox group with a small synagogue in central Copenhagen. In contradistinction to Manchester, where it is an increasingly recognised kosher body, the group has virtually disappeared in Denmark because of emigration, intermarriage and secularisation. However, Orthodox Judaism is in no way extinct in Denmark and since 1996 Chabad, an Orthodox Jewish Hasidic movement, has occupied a house next to Machzikei Hadass.

The majority of sources on Judaism in Denmark are Danish and they focus on the earlier history of Danish Jews and their migration to Denmark (Blum 1973; Bamberger 1983; Jørgensen 1984; Blüdnikov 1986). Yet very little is written about kosher in Denmark and there are virtually no academic sources on the significant transformation of the kosher market within the last couple of decades or so. The standard work on modern Judaism and kosher in Denmark is Andrew Buckser's *After the Rescue: Jewish Identity and Community in Denmark* (2003; see also Buckser 1999, 2005). We consider this work at some length as well as developments since its fieldwork was carried out in the 1990s. Generally, compared to the UK context sources on Judaism/kosher and Islam/halal in Denmark are more limited and the sections on Denmark in this chapter are to a larger extent based more on our fieldwork than the UK section. Buckser explores how Jewish society developed in a Danish secular context of general acceptance towards Jews and what this means for modern Jewish identity. Paradoxically, the Jewish community of Denmark is characterised by both institutional integrity as well as fragmentation among its members, that is, disagreement about boundaries of the community; ritual practice; operation of Jewish institutions; or kosher practice (Buckser 2003: 4). The establishment of the state of Israel provided new international reference points for Jewish identity and this influence competes with that of the Jewish Community in the lives of Danish Jews. More broadly, the religious authority of rabbis in Copenhagen is now challenged by global influences (Buckser 2003: 53) and it is in this context that kosher understanding and practice should be seen.

Buckser (2003: 21–51) identifies six periods in the history of Danish Jewry. Early settlement (1673–1784) was characterised by Jewish merchants who became Danish Jews. In the reform era (1784–1814) a series of legal and religious reforms transformed Danish Jews into regular citizens. The decree of

37

1814 formally made Jews Danish citizens with civil rights and significantly increased positive attitudes towards Jews. The period of integration and assimilation (1814–1901) was marked by Eastern European immigration and improved livelihoods as well as the loss of tradition. The period of immigration, opposition and schism (1900–40) in turn embodied tensions between conservative and liberal factions and the continued inflow of Eastern European migrants. Occupation, exile and return (1940–45) was a critical period in the history of the Danish Jews. Under the Nazi occupation of Denmark the protection, rescue and return of Jews changed their role in Danish society and culture. The Danish government refused to take measures against Jews and in 1943 Danish resistance to the occupation turned increasingly violent and the relationship between Danish and German authorities deteriorated. That year the government resigned and plans for a roundup and deportation of Danish Jews started, but the Jews were warned and found refuge in Danish homes and institutions before most were ferried to neutral Sweden in fishing boats. Over 95 per cent of the Danish Jews survived and this cemented their relationship with Danish society; after the rescue (1945–2000) the last period is dominated by a polarisation between liberal and conservative wings of the congregation as Jews have entered mainstream society.

As we noted above, the three main groups are the Jewish Community (www.mosaiske.dk) (Mosaisk Trossamfund changed its name to Det Jødiske Samfund), Machzike Hadas (very small and mainly consisting of a few families) and from 1996 Chabad missionaries established a Hasidic chapter of the global organisation (www.chabadenmark.com). Arguably, three polarities exist: liberalism/conservatism; religiosity/cultural Judaism; and an ideal of Danish integration/ideal of Jewish distinctiveness (Buckser 2003: 51). Our empirical exploration of kosher focuses on the two most important organisations involved in kosher in contemporary Denmark, the Jewish Community and Chabad.

Because the Jewish community is rather small in Denmark, a handful of people have played important roles in Jewish organisations. In the Jewish Community, Bent Lexner was the chief rabbi from 1996 to 2014. Kosher products at Copenhagen Kosher carried Bent's seal of approval. He studied to become a rabbi as well as a *schechter* (literally, 'to slaughter'). In addition to his kosher supervision duties, in his capacity as chief rabbi Bent also helped design kosher kitchens and he performed kosher authorisations in private homes – he was the main authority on kosher living in Denmark. For 20 years Bent worked as a *schechter* in Denmark. As a chief rabbi Bent was solely responsible for 'national' kosher certification in Denmark under the auspices of the Jewish Community in Denmark. Bent was involved in making a kosher list for Jews in Denmark: a guide to kosher living as everyday consumption. The present

Rabbi Jair Melchior (see below) developed this list further and it can be found on the website of the Jewish Community in Denmark (www.mosaiske.dk/guide-to-keeping-kosher-in-denmark). Comparing Denmark to the UK, Bent concedes that generally the attitude in Denmark is more flexible due to the fact that there are only few products under supervision.

Comparatively, Bent concedes that Chabad is stricter about kosher in that they only eat what is produced under supervision. Another difference is that Chabad and its rabbi works as a kosher supervisor for the kosher certifier Circle K. This is different from the chief rabbi's own work in which he personally lends his name to kosher products and their certification. So in order to supervise and certify kosher in Denmark the chief rabbi has people who supervise for him. In kosher, contamination, transport and traceability have been important issues that require supervision and more generally kosher has been big business for a long time. Bent explains that his involvement is not about 'big business'. Instead, for example, he advised companies, on how to acquire OU certification, and checked papers on trucks from abroad to ensure traceability. The Big Five, the biggest kosher certifiers globally, have gradually increased their influence against local or national forms of certification in Denmark. Some exporting companies in Denmark are fine with national certification, whereas others turn to Circle K and other Big Five certifiers that they believe can give them an edge in the global market. Bent recalls that for a long time Israel only accepted national forms of certification by a chief rabbi, but that has changed and today the Big Five are more widely accepted.

The globalisation and commercialisation of the kosher market has also brought about calls to supervise and certify non-food products, but Bent maintains that the only type of non-food product that warrants certification is medication, which is mainly because of concerns over gelatine. When the Israeli airline El Al wanted to have its soda water kosher-certified because of concerns regarding the bottle, in Bent's eyes this was an example of kosher becoming excessive. Another example was when he was asked to look into Teflon baking paper that may potentially be unhealthy, but does not warrant supervision or certification.

Jair Melchior is in his thirties and he became the chief rabbi in 2014, taking over from Bent Lexner. Regarding kosher, his responsibilities include, firstly, informing and updating the congregation on what they can and cannot eat – especially in a globalised world when many different opinions, rabbinical and otherwise, circulate. More specifically, Jair's role is to create a national Danish opinion or ruling on the kosherness of products consumed by Jews in Denmark amidst other opinions from 'big' rabbis and other discourses found on the Internet. Being a relatively small country with a limited number of Jews actually necessitates thorough and systematic rabbinical supervision because kosher products are hard to come by: this means that many Jewish consumers will buy their products in ordinary shops or over the Internet and this warrants rabbinical supervision and opinions. The situation in Denmark is thus quite different from that in the UK or US, for example, where availability is better.

Secondly, Jair's work focuses on supervision and certification of Danish products exported to major markets such as Israel, the US or the UK. In this respect he carries out inspections and checks the kosherness of ingredients and the validity of certificates. In the filing cabinet in Jair's office there are many files on companies he is responsible for supervising. Normally, he sends members of the congregation to do supervision tasks in these companies – especially when a new company wants to be certified, a company starts manufacturing a new product or there are changes in ingredient lists. Generally, certified companies receive one yearly visit from Danish rabbinic representatives.

When discussing changes in supervision processes since Jair took over from Bent Lexner, he explains that such processes are increasingly being formalised: today, a contract is drawn up whereas previously supervision was mainly based on oral agreements and this creates 'increased transparency' locally as well as internationally. Jair also supervises Copenhagen Kosher, and because most products are imported and thus carry recognised kosher logos this relationship is uncomplicated. More effort goes into supervising the in-shop manufacturing of sausages with raw materials such as spices that are not certified, for example. It is complicated and expensive to find kosher-certified spices so this type of ingredient calls for a rabbinical opinion. Jair also supervises the vegetarian kitchen at Carolineskolen, the Jewish school in Denmark (see below), and focuses on products in the kitchen he is not familiar with. At the same time, the kitchen staff at Carolineskolen does supervision work for the Danish Rabbinate. Simultaneously three vegetarian restaurants have started to focus on kosher.

Jair uses several sources of knowledge when checking products and ingredients: the Internet as well as rabbinical contacts with London Beth Din, the Rabbinate of Israel and in Germany. As a global player, OU supervises and certifies over 500,000 products and Jair recognises that many companies prefer this kind of global and costly supervision – comparing the cost of supervision/ certification by the Danish Rabbinate and OU, seemingly the latter is around four to five times as expensive. Moreover, there's also a 'political' aspect to the relationship between supervision by the Danish Rabbinate and global forms represented by the Big Five: ideally, Jair would prefer more Danish companies to be certified by the Danish Rabbinate as this would cut costs and establish a local relationship between companies in Denmark and the Jewish community. Typically, companies with kosher certification in Denmark export to the US, the UK or Israel. In the US certification by the Big Five is of particular importance. In a Danish context the difference between the Danish Rabbinate and Chabad supervision is that Chabad does supervision for Circle K and not independently. Another difference is that the Danish Rabbinate does not have a specific logo on products/certificates or in Copenhagen Kosher.

When ritual slaughter without stunning was prohibited in Denmark in 2014 the Danish Rabbinate together with the Jewish Community opposed this decision. In general there is cooperation between the Rabbinate and Muslim organisations, and if a company is kosher-certified, halal certification is 'automatic' or relatively easily accessible. Comparing kosher and halal, Jair explains that stricter kosher rules and requirements mean that halal is not acceptable to observant Jews. Nor does the Danish Rabbinate allow kosher to be bought on the Internet and they argue that according to *halachic* Jewish law Jews should support local shops. Consequently, Copenhagen Kosher is the only local source of kosher meat in Denmark.

Chabad is a Hasidic revival movement from Brooklyn with a focus on scholarship in the scriptures as well as an emotional experience of the divine. The organisation sponsors an international network of religious centres to promote religious observance among Jews. Chabad has played a distinctive role among Danish Jews since the organisation arrived in Denmark in 1996. Rabbi Yitzi and Rochel Loewenthal, who funded this local chapter of the organisation, are an American couple that represent Chabad in Copenhagen. Chabad arranges Torah study sessions as well as Kabbalah and kosher cooking classes and Yitzi expounds the importance of a particular consciousness of one's connection with the divine (Buckser 2003: 61; 2005). In the eyes of Yitzi and Chabad, kosher is a religious obligation for religious Jews, even in a 'secular' Danish context where religious observance is declining. Yitzi explains that today in Denmark people make their own standards and that they are not so strict. Thus, not only does kosher have 'a rougher time' in secular Denmark, the only kosher shop, Copenhagen Kosher, has limited opening hours and the products are more expensive; keeping kosher thus requires more effort physically, mentally and financially vis-à-vis the UK or US, for example. Previously even 'cultural Jews' tended to keep kosher, Yitzi argues, while today the vast majority of Jews in Denmark buy what they need in regular shops.

When we discuss the relevance of kosher enzymes Yitzi makes the case that this question depends on the specific type of product enzymes are used for: for cheese, meat and wine it's clearly relevant because these types of products require constant rabbinical supervision, whereas this is not the case with regard to foods such as salt/sugar, pastas/rice and most drinks, as well as non-food products such as detergent that are not covered by Jewish law. Moreover, certification tends to drive up the cost of production and thus price. Yitzi is involved in the certification of several foodstuffs manufactured in Denmark that are exported to international markets, mainly Israel and the US. In connection with this work he specifically supervises the production of food ingredients for Circle K. While science is important for testing products for pork DNA, for instance, he argues that laboratory testing is often insufficient compared to the context in which the kosherness of a product is ascribed. Thus, kosherness hinges on a combination of factors: proper integration of religious laws with modern food science, technologies at the cutting edge of food science as well as applying and adapting ancient rules to a modern situation. Such questions as 'what's a freeze drier and how does it work?' and 'when does equipment need kosherising?' are essential in order to understand the ways in which products are manufactured and the information companies provide themselves.

At Carolineskolen food follows these kosher rules: food prepared at the school is kosher and under the supervision of the chief rabbi, including food for excursions, meetings and celebrations. Lunchboxes brought along by pupils should be vegetarian, but cheese, dairy products and fish are allowed. The school's website also lists ingredients that generally are not kosher (www.carolineskolen.dk). A single employee is responsible for the lunch arrangement at Carolineskolen. She is Jewish and religiously observant and has worked at the school for about three years. Previously, she also worked at Copenhagen Kosher and another kosher shop that is now closed. The school's lunch arrangement is vegetarian, but fish is also on the menu. Sausages are served once or twice a year at special events such as graduation. No meat is allowed into the school and it was not necessary to design a kosher kitchen. Less than half the pupils at the school actually keep kosher and out of about 20 teachers only three are Jewish. While a vegetarian kosher menu is more affordable, it's not easier to prepare or manage and putting the menu together is a demanding job: labels in supermarkets are carefully examined to make sure that no unwanted ingredients or E numbers are in the semi-manufactured produce she buys. Another big challenge for the school is to comply with the changing kosher environment in Denmark. In general, the employee explains that she knows enough about kosher to supervise the kosher menu herself without consulting the rabbi in office, even if the rabbi formally supervises the school's kitchen. When we look at labels on products in the school's kitchen several kosher logos are evident. Firstly, there's one by Canada's kosher certifier MK, stating that the product is 'kosher pareve' (neither meat nor milk). Secondly, there are Haribo wine gums. Haribo products are not kosher as such, but a kosher line of Haribo is sold through the Austrian company Paskesz, and it's this specific product we're looking at.

Even if the market for kosher products have shrunk over the years as the number of Jews has declined, the above discussion shows that Denmark is fully integrated into the global market for kosher that has developed from the 1990s onwards. Thus, kosher regulation in Denmark is more about exports to global markets than local consumption. We can say that kosher qualification in Denmark is to a large extent premised on this global market in which the Jewish Community and Chabad compete with Circle K of the Big Five.

Islam and halal in Denmark

There are an estimated 207,000 Muslims in Denmark (Statistics Denmark 2016). Muslims in Denmark come from many countries and the largest groups according to size are: Turks, Iraqis, Lebanese, Pakistanis, Somalis and Afghans; there is also a small number of Danish converts (Jensen and Østergaard 2007: 30). There are 56 Islamic congregations and Muslims make up the second largest religious community in Denmark, comprising an estimated 4 per cent of the total population (Jacobsen 2012). Compared to Judaism, there are many sources in English on Islam in Denmark, an abundance in Danish, but little scholarly work on halal. Halal food is widely available in Denmark and the country is a major exporter to the Muslim world. Both right-wing and left-wing political parties have tried to prohibit ritual slaughter since the mid-1990s (Jacobsen 2009: 106). Studies on halal among Muslims in Denmark mostly focus on halal in institutional settings such as schools. However, comparable to what we saw above regarding the globalisation and regulation of the kosher market over the last two decades or so, these processes have taken place since around 2000. Indeed while the market for kosher in Denmark is shrinking, the opposite is the case with the halal market – most of the chicken sold in Danish shops is halal-slaughtered and there are many halal butcher's shops in Copenhagen alone. However, even studies that explore Muslim immigrants in particular neighbourhoods such as Nørrebro in Copenhagen (Schmidt 2011a) with regard to space, relationships, neighbourhood and identity politics do not, or only in passing, examine halal (Schmidt 2011b).

Schmidt (2009) identifies four periods in the history of Islam in Denmark. 'History of Islam in Denmark prior to 1960' focuses on encounters between Danes and Muslims in connection with the European crusades and exploration in the Middle East, while 'Decades of settlement: Muslims in Denmark 1960–90' focuses on increasing Muslim immigration and tightening immigration rules from 1970 onwards. New waves of refugees, together with family/marriage reunification, affected the welfare state and its political landscape. 'New trends, new generations: 1990–2001' thus focuses on a transformative period in which a substantial number of Bosnian refugees came to live in Denmark in the wake of the civil war in the Balkans and increased awareness of the presence of Muslims in Denmark. In the media Muslims were often portrayed as taking advantage of Danish welfare state legislation and being unwilling to 'integrate'. The period defined as 'Islam and Muslims post-September 11, 2001' is thus characterised by 9/11, Denmark's participation in the occupation of Iraq and the 2005–6 cartoon controversy. In general, the country displays an often confrontational attitude towards migrants, and Muslims in particular.

A case study of Muslim practices in Danish primary schools shows how and why halal food practices are governed. The study demonstrates that the governance of Muslim practices is developed in the absence of national regulation and against the prevailing ideals in the Danish public. It is concluded that halal food in schools is not of major concern to teachers and generally there is a lack of consideration of formal policies concerning Muslim practices in schools (Jensen 2016b: 431). However, in general schools can relatively unproblematically accommodate halal in the everyday lives of Muslim pupils (Jensen 2014). Karrebæk (2014) explores how primary school children in Copenhagen use food to organise social space, drawing on different cultural and social models. Building on ethnographic material from primary school classrooms, the study focuses on the national food registers for 'health' and 'halal'. The food in the canteen was halal, and when food was served at social festivals halal would always be a choice. But in spite of this, halal was never explicitly discussed, resulting in unexplained discrepancies between the 'halal model' and the 'health model' (Karrebæk 2014: 22). There was no institutional discourse and instruction on halal and haram and thus halal understanding and practice exist primarily in peer-group conversations (Karrebæk 2014: 26). Ignoring the religious halal model combined with a strong focus on the health register made some of the Muslim children feel excluded (Karrebæk 2014: 31).

As we shall see in Chapter 2, approximately 99 per cent of chickens in Denmark are slaughtered at abattoirs approved for halal slaughter by the Islamic Cultural Center of Scandinavia (www.islamiccc.com/index.php/en/) (ICCOS) and/or Muslim World League's office in Copenhagen. ICCOS was founded in 1976 and is housed in a villa in the northwestern suburbs of Copenhagen. It is privately run and houses a mosque, has a Qur'an school and also arranges courses for local Danish Muslims, who for the most part are of Arab and Pakistani origin. ICCOS is the largest halal certifier of meat as well as non-meat products in Denmark. Denmark is a major exporter of both food and non-food products and thus halal is an important question for the state and companies. Danish embassies in Malaysia and other Muslim markets in which halal is important try to help Danish companies with their export and local manufacturing of products that must live up to halal requirements. Delegations from countries where halal is important come to Denmark to inspect abattoirs and other types of production. The ICCOS imam came to Denmark in 2001 and is the organisation's 'halal supervisor'. He is also involved in halal with companies in Germany, Sweden, Poland and the UK. The imam receives delegations from countries where halal is important and his function is also important, as meat and poultry following Danish law is stunned before slaughter. In the eyes of many Muslims and Islamic organisations that prefer non-stunned meat this is a controversial question and it seems to reinforce the need for proper Islamic handling of such products. A local halal certifying body such as ICCOS is responsible for ensuring that slaughtering follows proper Islamic procedures and record-keeping, including the appointment of the Muslim slaughterer.

In Denmark it is mandatory that a state veterinarian and a Muslim abattoir employee control the ritual slaughter process. ICCOS must approve the Muslim abattoir employee. He pronounces the phrase *Allahu Akbar* (God is Great) at the start of the slaughter process and after each break. Denmark also exports a wide range of non-meat food products such as cake, chocolate, chips and even enzyme products, as we have seen. So in order for Danish companies to export to Muslim countries these products must come with a certificate stating that no prohibited ingredients are involved in the production process. The imam recalls an episode where a Danish company called him and asked for halal certification. He asked why the company would want certification for its non-meat products and that this was surely not necessary. The company representative said that this was because a foreign halal certification body wanted halal certification for this particular product.

The imam asks companies to send him samples he can submit for laboratory testing for alcohol and pork gelatine. The interest in halal and its regulation is to a large extent generated from Southeast Asian countries such as Malaysia, Singapore and Indonesia. ICCOS educates butchers employed at abattoirs across Denmark about the meaning of halal and how to practise halal requirements. ICCOS also looks into the question of the halalness of raw materials that are sent to laboratories for testing. However, the imam stresses that companies are 'honest' and send all the requested information needed to verify production, and that much of this information is readily available on company websites that the imam can refer to when dealing with foreign halal certification bodies. At times, ICCOS receives visits from foreign certification bodies and the organisation is thus not only carrying out inspections, but is also subject to inspections itself. The imam thinks of the relation between ICCOS and certification as characterised by a 'responsibility' to exchange 'Islamic information'. Even if halal requirements set by certifiers are strict and tend to increase, this always has to be adhered to in accordance with Danish law, the imam explains.

ICCOS works in line with universal 'Islamic standards'. The imam stresses that there are many standards in the global market for halal and ICCOS has to adapt to and be flexible about this kind of diversity. However, Islam is the same all over the world in spite of this variety of halal standards, he concludes. The imam knows this because he often attends halal events in countries such as Saudi Arabia and Kuwait. Yet in recent years pressures have increased and some Muslim groups in Denmark have questioned the work of ICCOS.

Benyones has a Moroccan background, represents the Danish Halal Fund and is a board member of Det Islamiske Trossamfund (www.wakf.com/index.php/da/) (DIT) (literally, Islamic Faith Community). He works as a paramedic and also does volunteer work in DIT with a specific focus on youth work.

Figure 6 The ICCOS halal logo

Benyones argues that the Muslim community in Denmark needs an independent organisation to control the market for halal meat. This call emerged in 2011 when DIT realised that penetrating captive bolt pistols were used to stun animals. While the main halal certifier is ICCOS, DIT and a Muslim umbrella organisation, the Danish Halal Fund, comprising 56 Muslim associations in Denmark and chaired by Benyones, argue that ICCOS supervision and control is inadequate and unclear, and it is this that has resulted in the formation of the Danish Halal Fund. As chairman of the Danish Halal Fund, Benyones bases his argument on visits to abattoirs supervised by ICCOS. It is of particular concern that there is no constant supervision in the abattoirs and that stunning with a captive bolt pistol is being used.

Muslimernes Fællesråd (Muslim Joint Council) (www.mfr.nu/pages) (MFR) similarly decided to break what they consider ICCOS's monopoly on halal certification by developing a monitoring system of their own in consultation with European halal certifiers, on the one hand, and ensuring economic resources to move beyond volunteer halal certification, on the other. On the MFR website the organisation explains that together with HFCE, one of Europe's largest halal certifiers, the organisation carries out halal certification of both animal as well as non-animal products. Thus, both MFR and the Danish Halal Fund are pushing for tighter halal regulation as implemented in the UK by HMC, for example, and in France by A Votre Service. Not surprisingly, neither the Danish Bacon and Meat Council nor ICCOS accepted the critique.

When we discuss the above issues with Benyones he explains that halal has to be based on supervision, control and transparency. Thus, modern halal has to move beyond the traditional relationship of trust between seller and buyer, as has happened in the organic market, for instance. Moreover, in many cases it's still the company itself that is responsible for the halal process, in that they have one or several Muslim employees that make sure halal logos are put on the packaging of products. He explains that more and more companies are approaching DIT to enquire about halal certification because their customers in the Middle East and Southeast Asia are asking about reliable and independent halal certification by third parties: as many producers in Denmark are unsure about halal certification processes, he points out that they thus miss out on lucrative business opportunities. Sometimes DIT are approached by companies that intend to certify 'abstract' things that do not warrant certification in the eyes of Benyones: he argues that halal-certified mineral water, for example, is not necessary and that certifying such products indicates the over-commercialisation of halal.

Benyones believes that draining the blood in connection with ritual slaughter without stunning as well as pork avoidance, including pork gelatine, makes halal consumption healthier. Moreover, he avoids haram E numbers such as E120, found in red sweets. He wonders why halal meat is not more expensive than non-halal meat and he argues that proper certification practices and processes should drive the price up. Ideally, he would like to see a system that is comparable to that in London, within which products, companies and shops are certified by reliable certifiers such as HMC, thus enabling consumers to make more informed choices. While the Halal Fund has challenged the halal establishment in Denmark, it is by no means clear that being strict and fastidious about halal is the mainstream position among Muslims in Denmark.

An example of early Muslim migration to Denmark in the 1950s is the Ahmadiyya mission. Members of this Islamic reform movement founded in India in the 1860s erected the first purpose-built mosque outside Copenhagen, the Nusrat Djahan Mosque, in 1966/67. The group has about 600 members, who are well integrated, but despite its long history and important place in the history of Islam in Denmark, the Ahmadi community is not well researched (Larsson and Björkman 2010: 19). Falah is the Ahmadiyya imam and arrived in Denmark from India in the 1980s. He studied Ahmadiyya theology in London for seven years and is now pursuing his MA in Scandinavian languages and literature. With regard to halal, Falah and Ahmadi more broadly rely on the teachings of the Qur'an and *haddith*. Halal meat is preferred, but since most meat nowadays is produced and slaughtered in the same way as halal meat, even in the West, Ahmadi do not put too much emphasis on buying halal-certified meat.

Conversely, the essence of Ahmadiyya theology and practice is the spiritual and moral relationship between God and man. Consequently, in the eyes of Ahmadi and Falah many Muslims are overly focused on the physical and material side of Islam, while downplaying spirituality, morality, justice, love and the inner search for and development of a relationship between God and man. Looking within is seen to make life easier by lessening the competition evident in the material and shallow forms of religiosity and piety that come to the fore through judgements about the halal/haram consumption practices of others, for example. Thus, even in the major UK market for halal, Ahmadiyya is not involved in animal slaughter or halal certification. What is more, Ahmadiyya does not wish to engage in such business and what are considered to be an overly commercialised form of religion; such practice, it is argued, should be separated from the theological and spiritual aspects of Islam.

In a broader perspective, Ahmadiyya and its congregation are to some extent perplexed by the emergence of material Islam – halal Coca-Cola, wine gums, E numbers and toothpaste are not only seen as unnecessary, but also 'silly' and overly commercial. Issues such as these are never part of Ahmadiyya Friday prayers, whereas spirituality is at the centre of the teachings of the organisation's caliph and imams. In general, the Ahmadiyya organisation is consciously not involved in benefiting from the Islamic economy: the organisation is sustained by donations from the congregation, and it considers itself apolitical – the main purpose of the organisation is its work for the congregation to develop the spiritual bond between God and man. The key point here is that not all Muslims are fastidious about halal. In the eyes of Ahmadi (as we shall see in Chapter 5), halal is currently in the process of being over-commercialised and presented as an unnecessary Muslim dogma.

Discussion: kosher and halal in the UK and Denmark

The market for kosher in the UK has a long history that can be traced back to the nineteenth century: since that time the market for kosher meat has remained steady, and today Manchester is home to one of the largest and fastest-growing Jewish communities in Europe, with some leading *kashrut* organisations. Consequently, this has implications for the Manchester kosher market. Arguably, this market is large and growing because of the growth of a more strictly Orthodox community, competition between the long-established and influential certifier MBD and the continuing popularity of the strictly Orthodox MH. Over the last 100 years or so exports of non-stunned meat to the global kosher market, including Denmark, have steadily increased, but Danish kosher products such as butter are also available in kosher shops in Manchester. Despite the increasingly global nature of work done by MBD through engagement with biotech companies, debates about *shechita* slaughter – which have mirrored social developments over the last two centuries in the UK – continue to generate controversy, all the more so in the context of a rapidly expanding UK Muslim population and a rapidly growing halal market.

Comparatively, the UK halal market developed at a later stage than the kosher market, and it was not until the late 1960s that the market took shape as larger groups of Muslims, many of them from South Asia, settled permanently in the UK. During the 1980s and 1990s debates about slaughter and stunning started to focus on the Muslim community, for example halal in state schools, much as it had around kosher over a century earlier. In the 1990s Muslim political mobilisation intensified and this eventually led to the formation of HFA in 1994 and HMC in 2003, with tension continuing to this day over the authenticity of stunned and non-stunned forms of halal meat and global import and export markets.

The Jewish Community in Denmark and thus the market for kosher is comparatively far smaller than that in the UK. All the kosher meat sold in Denmark's only existing kosher shop is imported and *shechita* has not taken place in Denmark since the 1990s: the Jewish population is small and shrinking and the market for both kosher and kosher consumption has become increasingly secularised among Jewish groups. That said, the Danish market for kosher non-meat products is large, but more aimed at the global market, the UK, US and Israel in particular, rather than the local Jewish market. The Jewish Community in Denmark has traditionally been responsible for national kosher certification, but when Chabad arrived in the mid-1990s (when global kosher was systematically starting to be regulated by the Big Five in particular) this posed a challenge to the established Jewish community and a revival in the focus on kosher regulation and consumption among more Orthodox groups. Chabad, in contradistinction to the Jewish Community, is cooperating with the major global certifiers such as Circle K. Thus, here we see a tension between national forms of kosher understanding and practice between the Danish Rabbinate and the global Big Five certifiers.

Comparatively, the market for halal in Denmark is of more recent origin, reflecting the fact that Muslim migration to Denmark did not start until the 1960s. However, today the local market for halal meat (and chicken in particular) is inseparable from the large and growing global market. Thus, the production of stunned halal meat in Denmark reflects both consumption among local Muslims and Danish exports to Muslim markets. The production of non-stunned meat was banned in 2014 and this accentuated debates among both Jewish and Muslim groups over discrimination and the right to practise their religion. This led several Muslim organisations to argue that established food regulations in Denmark did not represent the requirements of observant Muslims, and eventually, as we have seen, to efforts to import non-stunned meat from the UK and elsewhere. As we shall see, a large part of biotech production in Denmark is both kosher and halal-certified by transnational certification bodies and these processes are not well understood.

These discussions also reflect the broader theoretical and conceptual issues we explore throughout the book. Firstly, the linkages and tensions between different levels of the social scale are evident: local, national and global forms of regulation are in contention and this of course also affects production and consumption. The UK is both a major market in terms of local religious production, trade, regulation and consumption as well being central to the formation of the global market. In Denmark local consumption is not essential, but production and regulation are tightly intertwined with global markets, including the UK, Manchester and London in particular. Uncertainties persist around qualification and requalification (Callon *et al.* 2002) – the processes by which kosher and halal products are contested by divergent actors at different levels of the social scale and in their particular regional settings. Here, the example of qualification can be applied to the contested issue of stunning and non-stunning that has proved to be contentious over the last two centuries in different contexts. The latest phases of kosher/halal regulation on a global scale that took off in the 1990s included non-meat products, but even today the core commodity remains meat and it is to that aspect we will now turn.

2

Manufacturing and selling meat

This chapter explores the manufacture and production of kosher and halal meat (both red meat and poultry) in London and Manchester in the UK and also in Denmark, with specific reference to audits/inspections, legislation, networking, product innovation and certification. The reason for focusing on the UK in particular is, firstly, that the UK has large Jewish and expanding Muslim communities as well as some well-known kosher and halal certification bodies. At the same time this market is far more complex than the market in Denmark. Not only is the market for kosher in Denmark extremely limited, in the UK there is production, regulation and consumption of both kosher and halal meat.

In recent decades kosher and halal meat markets have become increasingly diversified. On the one hand, they have been lifted out of their local religious base in kosher/halal butcher's shops. On the other hand, kosher/halal have become more impersonal in that more meat is now sold in super/hypermarkets where tighter regulation is called for to avoid misuse. To a large extent, Jews and Muslims have similar religious requirements for the manufacture and production of meat, and to understand *how* meat – viewed as an 'economic good' – is transformed into kosher and halal products this chapter draws on the concept of qualification (Callon *et al.* 2002) to investigate how meat acquires the necessary 'qualities' through slaughter, audit, certification and retailing. We explore how different certification bodies and religious authorities define kosher and halal meat through inspection and labelling during manufacture, and how authority and trust emerge in the supply chains through which meat qualifies as kosher and halal. We demonstrate how the attribution of the distinguishing characteristics that qualify meat as kosher and halal starts at the abattoir and finishes only when a product is placed on the counter of a trusted retailer, where it achieves its final kosher and halal qualities. To do this we draw on interviews with kosher and halal certification bodies and other supply chain actors such as butchers and retailers, plus ethnographic fieldwork and observations in London, Manchester and Copenhagen; we also use documentary research to supplement our data where necessary. Our discussion of the qualification of meat in both markets starts in the UK and is followed by a shorter comparative discussion of the Danish context.

The qualification of meat as kosher

The original qualification of meat as kosher emerges from specific passages in the five books of Moses that make up the Torah – specifically Exodus, Leviticus and Deuteronomy – and from texts linked to the Talmud (Hirsch 1962; Campbell *et al.* 2011; Lytton 2013). Pig meat is specifically prohibited and Jews are permitted to consume only the meat of animals that chew their cud and have cloven hooves; for example, cattle, sheep and goats (Lev. 11:3, 11:7). There are also numerous prohibitions against eating birds, with chicken, turkey, duck and goose the most commonly consumed. Meat qualifies as kosher only if the animal of origin is slaughtered using appropriate *shechita* methods as interpreted through rabbinic commentaries and traditional customary practice. As stated in the Introduction to the present book, the key biblical passage concerning animal slaughter as conveyed to Moses by God is contained in the verse: 'You shall not kill of thy herd and thy flock which the Lord hath given you, except as I have commanded you' (Deut. 12:21). Extensive space is also dedicated in the Talmud to issues of eligibility and qualifications for conducting the act of slaughter (Wise 2006).

Three key principles must be followed at all times (Lytton 2013). A qualified Jewish slaughterer – or *shochet* (pl. *shochetim*) – with the necessary skills and understanding of the laws and requirements of *shechita* must conduct the act of slaughter. *Shechita* must also be carried out with a razor-sharp blade on a special knife – a *chalaf* – in order to minimise the risk of damage to the body of the animal being slaughtered. And the knife must be well maintained to avoid bad practice. The Talmud outlines the Hebrew blessing to be recited by the slaughterer prior to the act as: 'Blessed are You, lord our God, King of the Universe, who has sanctified us with his Commandments and commanded us concerning shechita' (see Wise 2006). The act of slaughter – the cut – requires a smooth motion *to* and *fro* across a clearly defined part of the animal's neck; any mistake in the prescribed motion or action and the animal carcass is rendered *treifa* and non-kosher. Animals that have suffered injury, death or illness are strictly prohibited, even if they are slaughtered correctly.

After an animal has been slaughtered, a specially trained expert conducts an inspection – *bedika* – to check the carcass for any signs of illness or injury; *shochetim* are often qualified for this task. As the most commonly damaged organs, the lungs of cattle are inspected for lesions or perforations that would render them *treifa* (the intestines of poultry are checked in a similar way). Initially this involves the carcass being cut open and the inside of the lungs inspected with the hands, before the lungs are removed for a visual inspection. If the lungs are free of injuries the meat is termed *glatt* – a Yiddish word meaning smooth; if they are not, they can still be kosher but not *glatt*. Lytton (2013) argues that this process can be linked back to post-World War II migrants, who clung more closely than previous generations to traditional practices to avoid the threat of fraud, yet the practice can be traced back beyond the industrial period to texts associated with the Talmud. Nevertheless, in the US the qualification *glatt* has gained renewed significance in line with the industrialisation of kosher. As the time commitment underpinning the qualification of *glatt* put rabbis supervising industrial meat production lines under increasing pressure, it became more and more difficult to maintain traditional practice (Lytton 2013) and *glatt* once more became associated with the production of high-quality kosher meat free from the threat of contamination that exists within industrial production systems.

The Torah injunction against eating blood has implications for processing kosher meat, and before it reaches the butcher's counter it must undergo *nikur* or porging to remove veins and forbidden fats. In the front part of the body this process is where meat, viewed as an 'economic good', acquires some of the final qualities that render it a product (Callon *et al.* 2002) in the form of specific kosher cuts, i.e. brisket, shoulder, flank and rib (Lytton 2013). In the hindquarters of the animal this process becomes more difficult and in many diaspora communities this part of the body, which contains the prohibited sciatic nerve, is often sold into non-kosher meat markets (Lytton 2013). Finally, before meat achieves its full kosher quality, all remaining blood must be extracted from the flesh through a process of salting – *melich*; today meat is often koshered in this way by a butcher rather than by the end consumer (KLBD 2015).

Kosher meat in the UK

There are a small number of *kashrut* and *shechita* authorities in London and in towns and cities across the UK, including Manchester. All certify producers, caterers, shops, restaurants and meat, but it is not entirely clear how many oversee *shechita* slaughter. To examine how meat, viewed as an economic good, achieves the qualities it needs to be traded as kosher we focus on two of the largest kosher and *shechita* certifying authorities in the UK, the London Board for Shechita and Manchester Beth Din.

The LBS traces its origins back to 1804. It represents and operates on behalf of the Federation of Synagogues, Spanish and Portuguese Jews' Congregation and the United Synagogues of Great Britain. In the past it owned abattoirs and marketed meat at the local level, but more recently it has focused on providing *shechita* slaughter services more widely. LBS functions as a non-profit organisation and is a registered charity. One of its main functions is to train and license slaughtermen – *shochetim* – through a process of religious and technical training that can take at least five years. *Shochetim* are employed directly by LBS and competing abattoirs and wholesalers buy their services. In contrast to 'conventional' slaughterers, an LBS *shochet* is not paid directly by abattoirs and they thus have a degree of autonomy unusual in the slaughter industry. As well as finding abattoirs that are willing to use *shechita* methods, LBS inspects wholesale, processing and retail premises. Licences are awarded to factories and to butchers considered fit to handle kosher meat and poultry over the counter and/or as pre-packed products. *Shochetim* are accompanied during inspections by teams of aides who check and seal meat and meat products. The LSB also employs food inspectors – *shomrim* – who manage *kashrut* operations at the premises of licensees, particularly the porging and the koshering of meat. Each applicant undergoes a rigorous inspection before it receives a licence that covers the costs of *shechita* and *bedika*, as well as packing and sealing services at the abattoir.

In the UK LBS oversees *shechita* at a small number of licensed premises that work either with cattle or poultry, from where kosher qualified meat is distributed across the UK on a weekly basis. They place great emphasis on the integrity of the supply chain and have stringent processes of quality control. The hindquarters of the cattle are sometimes sold into the conventional market unlabelled and Shechita UK is currently involved in an initiative to overcome this problem, and the theological differences involved, by selling this meat on to the halal market. In 2010 LBS supervised the slaughter of 90,000 cattle, 90,000 sheep and 1.5 million poultry. A list of licensed outlets is available on the organisation's website (see www.shechita.org/licensed-suppliers), but the abattoirs where *shechita* is conducted are not listed because most prefer to remain anonymous.

Processed meat products certified by LBS can be found in a range of kosher retail outlets around the UK, and in other countries, but certified fresh meat and poultry cut at the counter is available only from butchers that have a direct licence from LBS; the licence must be on display for customers at all times. The LBS emphasises the reliability of their licensed retailers and the difference between meat bought from licensed premises and that bought from unsupervised outlets. They caution the public against buying loose, raw, cooked and unpacked meat products from unsupervised outlets, where kosher meat is sometimes mixed with non-kosher meat. The licence acts as a seal of approval through the use of a *hechsher* – a rabbinical product certification visible in the form of a product label or stamp. LBS has always provided two levels of kosher meat, one of which is the higher standard of *glatt* kosher, marketed under the name 'Chalak Beit Yosef'. To qualify as *glatt*, an examination is conducted to check for abrasions on the lungs. Meat that does not achieve the highest standards cannot achieve the *glatt* qualification, but as long as the lungs are completely free of injury the meat of the animal can still be kosher; otherwise it is *treifa* – non-kosher and prohibited.

In an early period of fieldwork we spoke with an informant from a kosher butcher in London supplied with meat from a wholesaler licensed by LBS. Like many kosher butchers, the business had chosen this certification route because it represents a particular tradition of rabbinical authority that they identify with. The process of qualification starts when the retail premises of the butcher are inspected by *shomerim* from LBS, which then occurs on a regular basis, sometimes as often as two or three times a week: these inspectors thus play a crucial role in the process of kosher qualification for LBS-certified products. When meat arrives from the wholesaler an internal *shomer* at the butchers oversees the unloading of the meat and the subsequent inspection of the LBS label and seal; if no *shomer* is present, only the licensee can perform these duties. While a butcher could in theory sell non-kosher meat, our informant explained this was highly unlikely, very rare and very difficult to do in practice. While 'in the old days' inspectors were sometimes 'told off' when they called at a shop unexpectedly, he explained that today *shomerim* turn up whenever they want to and that 'there is no hiding place'.

These high levels of control are reflected in high levels of consumer trust and transparency in kosher production processes throughout the supply chain. Our informant suggested that it is only very rarely that customers ask detailed questions about certification and the origins of kosher meat. While there was a recognition that the number of kosher butchers may be declining, this was seen to be as much a consequence of the new demands placed on butchers as it is about the increase of kosher products in supermarkets. While kosher consumers have always been demanding, our informant argued that kosher butchers now have to provide more specialist services if they are to survive: he also explained that he has customers who consume kosher for health reasons and Muslims who consume kosher because it is similar to halal. As kosher has been lifted out of its traditional religious base it appears that the process of qualification has also become more complex and stringent. These developments are more evident in the operations of MBD.

As we observed in Chapter 1, MBD emerged out of MSB in 1892, prior to which synagogues, acting under individual rabbinical authority, conducted *shechita* and provided *kashrut* services to local communities across the city. Today some of MBD's most important functions revolve around its *kashrut* and *shechita* activities and they license, supervise and certify a large number of local shops, hoteliers, restaurants and delicatessens in the city; licensees can use the MBD *hechsher*. All such activities are viewed as a partnership between MBD and its licensees, the ultimate aim being to provide high-quality products that are kosher, affordable and readily available. These services are also provided, along with *shechita* and *glatt* supervision, for slaughterhouses, manufacturers and butchers. Much like LBS, MBD does not provide a list of abattoirs where they carry out *shechita* and their website indicates only that the slaughter of cattle and lamb is carried out somewhere in Stoke-on-Trent: poultry slaughter and processing is conducted at Tovah Meat in north Manchester. All MBD *shochetim* hold a local authority licence and a licence from the Office of the Chief Rabbi, which combined are seen to act as a guarantee of religious knowledge and technical ability.

While MBD notes a decrease in the number of local kosher butchers in recent years, it is clear that they are expanding their operations, both in the UK and beyond, and this is making the process of qualification more complex in line with different and often competing regulatory practices. Indeed MBD currently conducts *shechita* in Poland, Hungary and Romania and MBD-certified kosher meat is sold and supplied in unprocessed and manufactured forms in a number of European countries, including Denmark, via market intermediaries. The processes of supervision, auditing and inspections involved constitute forms of what we call transnational governmentality (Ferguson and Gupta 2002).

In general MBD inspection and audit processes are similar to those of the LBS. The process of qualification begins when a company is asked to fill out an application where they must declare all the ingredients they use in production, any kosher products that share production lines with non-kosher goods, as well as details about the actualities and time frame of production. After a discussion of the pros and cons of the application, a full audit of the factory is undertaken by a senior *kashrut* consultant or *dayan* of MBD. Any ingredients used in manufacture are checked and any storage and packing areas are inspected. After approval a contract is signed and regular visits are conducted by a *dayan* to ensure compliance with MBD requirements. Strong personal relationships are said to be at the heart of relationships with licensees; the fee structure of MBD is said to be more flexible than other kosher authorities and we heard anecdotal evidence that this allows new companies more scope to enter the kosher market.

A former chief *dayan* at MBD, Rabbi Westheim, made an important distinction between kosher certification and kosher supervision. Certification occurs when a company complies with kosher requirements in all aspects of production at a particular factory. In this situation there will be no non-kosher production on-site and everything produced by the company will be qualified as kosher and therefore certified as such. Alternatively, when a company makes a particular batch of products for the kosher market at a particular factory once or twice a month, this is a supervised relationship. With the former, costs are lower, because after the initial inspection there is no need for a supervisor to be on-site to oversee production. With the latter, there will be a full-time kosher representative on-site the whole time during kosher production and there will also be costs associated with cleaning and cleansing equipment, for example, which will make the overall process of qualification more difficult to navigate and hence more expensive.

As Manchester's Jewish population has expanded and religiosity has increased, the position of MBD has been challenged locally in recent years by certification bodies offering a stricter interpretation of kosher. Paradoxically, while MBD's influence and reputation is growing internationally through processes of transnational governmentality, in Manchester the Machzikei Hadass (Manchester) Board is catering for the increasing number of consumers who are demanding stricter *shechita* standards for meat and poultry. We observed the *hechsher* of MBD and that of MH during a visit to the Jewish community in north Manchester. Walking along Leicester Road in Lower Broughton near the Salford–Manchester border, we encounter a plethora of kosher retail outlets and eateries. Not far from the thriving Cheetham Hill Road, a major thoroughfare dissecting north Manchester's rapidly expanding Muslim community, the Jewish community spreads out neatly down side-streets. We start at the busy Halpern's Kosher Food Store on the corner of Ashbourne Grove, a renowned client of MBD. On the opposite corner of Ashbourne Grove is the prominent and increasingly popular MH Meats (www.mhmeats.co.uk), a licensee of the Machzikei Hadass Kashrut Board prominently displaying the *mehadrin hechsher*. As we move on past the row of shops opposite Mandley Park, we encounter Brackman's Kosher Bakery and Coffee Shop (www.brack-mans-bakery-coffeeshop.co.uk), another MBD licensee, among a variety of kosher shops and cafés, including Tasti Pizza. We then come across another delicatessen and a grocer certified by MBD, before crossing the road to Landaus Grocery Ltd, which has no obvious *hechsher* displayed. We decide to have lunch in the Chef Yum Burger opposite Kings Square, a kosher café displaying the *mehadrin hechsher* on all its menus. We ask a customer where the chicken comes from and we are informed it is all slaughtered locally; for Salford our burgers are surprisingly expensive, at around £7 each. We then move on to Kings Road over the border in Prestwich on the outskirts of Bury in Greater Manchester, which, our guide informs us, is the middle-class part of the community. Walking up Kings Road from Bury New Road we encounter the well-known JS Restaurant and Take-Away (www.jsrestaurant.co.uk), certified by MBD, and Haber's World (www.habersworld.com), another well-known client of MBD. As we proceed up Kings Road we encounter a *glatt* butcher displaying the *mehadrin hechsher* as well as other kosher eateries, bakeries and cafés. At top end of Kings Road, we turn right onto Bury Old Road on our way back to Lower Broughton, where we encounter another *glatt* butcher displaying the *mehadrin hechsher* and a number of kosher shops.

We carry on down Bury New Road towards Manchester city centre and eventually arrive at the Tesco hypermarket on Cheetham Hill Road, which has one of the largest selections of kosher food in the UK. Kosher (and halal) meat is only sold by the major hyper/supermarkets in areas of UK cities with large Jewish (or Muslim) populations. However, while fresh halal meat is available on specialist halal meat counters in these stores (see below), kosher is more standardised and they can only sell pre-packed kosher meat products that have achieved their full kosher qualities elsewhere under the supervision

Figure 7 Tasty Beef Skewers from MH Meat

of particular rabbinical authorities. In Tesco we find rows of vertical freezers and chilled cabinets with numerous branded kosher meat and dairy products under the supervision of national/international rabbinical authorities and certification bodies. There are numerous products from the Israeli company Yarden, which are certified by a number of different bodies and authorities, including the London Beth Din (www.kosher.org.uk) and the Grand Rabbinat of Paris. There is also a range of products that are both kosher and halal certification from Gilbert's Kosher Foods, including diced beef: certification is provided by KF Kosher (www.kfkosher.org) and Halal Consultations (www.halalconsultations.com) to give these products the qualities that allow them to be traded as kosher and halal simultaneously.

Gilbert's Kosher Foods (www.gilbertskosherfoods.co.uk) is one of the major market intermediaries for kosher products in UK hyper/supermarkets. Trading since 1995, the company runs an on-site meat-cutting plant that initially produced a wide range of pre-packed kosher meat products for all the major supermarkets – including Tesco, ASDA, Sainsbury's and Waitrose as well as Harrods and Selfridges; a number of leading food service operatives also work closely with Gilbert's. In the late 1990s Gilbert's were embroiled in a certification controversy with LBS and MBD. An informant explained that Gilbert's were reportedly paying an annual fee of £100,000 to LBS and when MBD agreed to lower the fee considerably Gilbert's switched to the Manchester body. This was extremely controversial and LBS subsequently issued a decree banning Gilbert's 'kosher' qualified products from all their licensed retailers in

Figure 8 Yarden Turkey

Figure 9 Diced beef, kosher- and halal-certified

the London area (see Kossoff 1998). As we can see from this example, market intermediaries such as Gilbert's play a crucial role in the expansion of the market power of rabbinical authorities in the UK, much as they have in the US, by allowing them to work in the conventional market where they can target consumers demographically outside the confines of their traditional religious base whilst maintaining control over the qualification of economic goods as kosher. The non-Jewish owner of a kosher shop in north Manchester explained the significance of these forms of control and standardisation. He pointed out that while Jewish customers will buy pre-packed kosher meat products in his shop, they will not buy fresh meat because he his not certified by a recognised kashrut body.

This situation clearly illustrates the control rabbinical authorities and kosher certification bodies have over the qualification of kosher goods in local, national and international contexts. The process starts with the initial application and continues through processes of supervision, auditing and inspection in a local context within licensed factories, shops and butchers: in the national context through licensed factories, market intermediaries and super/hypermarkets; and also in an international context through emergent forms of transnational governmentality. In all three standardised contexts meat achieves the qualities it requires to be traded as kosher through collective actions that prioritise some characteristics and ignore others through an ongoing 'process of qualification-requalification' (Callon *et al.* 2002: 199).

Kosher meat in Denmark

The number of kosher shops has fallen dramatically in Denmark in recent decades and Copenhagen Kosher, located in the north of the city, is now the only kosher shop in the entire country. The shop relies on ties to the formal Jewish community and has also received subsidies to ensure its survival (Buckser 1999: 199–200). The main commodity in the shop is meat, but wine, cheese, coffee and sweets are also sold: at times, kosher products with the *glatt* qualification are also available. The manager has worked in the shop for 22 years. An Orthodox Jew, he learned his trade from a *menaker* (mentor) and he explains that being fastidious about kosher is necessary in his line of work. Much of the meat in the shop is certified by MBD, and some of it arrives via market intermediaries from factories in Eastern Europe, where *shechita* services are carried out under licence from MBD.

The manager explains that many Jews in Denmark do not keep kosher and that the shop also has competition from kosher bought abroad and over the Internet. Consequently, the clientele is small, but devout and he knows all his customers personally. Because of its limited customer base Copenhagen Kosher can import only limited quantities of pre-packed kosher products and combined with the relatively high VAT in Denmark this drives up prices. The

Figure 10 Copenhagen Kosher

Figure 11 Chicken soup found at Copenhagen Kosher and certified by OU

Figure 12 Olive oil certified by the Rabbinate of the Union of Orthodox Hebrew Congregations, London

shop is under the supervision of the Danish Rabbinate, who conduct regular and unannounced inspections and visits. Interestingly the manager does not consider this to represent 'control' in the sense outlined above in the UK context: likewise, when the Food Safety Authorities visit the manager must demonstrate that products are kosher even though the inspectors do not really understand the meaning of kosher. Qualification in this context is driven by Danish legislation and EU legislation is not considered relevant. Up until 2006, when the only Danish kosher slaughter facility closed, Bent Lexner of the Jewish Community performed kosher sheep slaughter, with the process of qualification continuing in the shop in line with traditional practices. Until the ban in 2014, fresh kosher meat was subsequently imported along with pre-packed kosher meat products.

When we discuss the fact that many companies in Denmark are kosher-certified in order to export to markets where proper kosher certification is a requirement, the manager explains that because the products in the shop are imported and not exported, it is not necessary to rely on certification by certifiers other than the Danish Rabbinate, even if this certification is not recognised by OU or other Big Five US certification bodies, for example. While the Big

Five use state-of-the-art technology and also have almost unlimited resources, making it possible to send inspectors around the world, the manager is content that certification by the Danish Rabbinate is sufficient in the Danish context at the present time. The shop has a small number of Muslim customers who feel that halal is not reliable in Denmark, yet the manager argues that for most Jews halal is unacceptable. As we shall see in subsequent chapters, this is a general tendency among sellers, certifiers and consumers.

The qualification of meat as halal

The original food rulings and dietary laws underpinning the qualification of halal meat emerge from specific passages in the Qur'an (Campbell *et al.* 2011; Fischer 2011). Certain conditions and prohibitions must be observed and practised at all times. Muslims must not consume carrion, blood and pork; such substances are haram – 'unlawful' or 'forbidden'. In all instances, the lawfulness of meat also depends on how it is obtained. As with *shechita*, animals that have suffered injury, death or illness are strictly prohibited as haram.

Prior to *dhabh* animals for slaughter must be clean, healthy, fed and watered, and treated gently; at the time of slaughter they should be calm. A healthy Muslim must conduct the act of slaughter with a cut to the throat that severs the carotid arteries, jugular veins, the oesophagus and the trachea. The knife used must be clean, sharp, free from nicks, regularly inspected, and the slaughterer must recite the 'Tasmiyah' – *Bismillah Allahu Akbar* (God is Great) – over each animal or bird being slaughtered. All blood must be allowed to drain from the body of the animal post-slaughter and death must be caused by exsanguination (bleeding); the slaughtered animal must not be disturbed until it is dead (Mukherjee 2014; MCB 2015). While non-stunning is the universal method practised by Jews during *shechita* slaughter, for Muslims the question of stunning is highly contested and what *dhabh* actually means in practice is under constant negotiation by scholars, imams and consumers, particularly in non-Muslim countries. These disputes originate in debates about the origins of Islam, which Muslims believe are derived from two sources – the Qur'an and *sunnah*. While the Qur'an provides a detailed and for some an infallible source of information about the origins of Islam, the *sunnah* provides an account based on the application of the principles established in the Qur'an through the lived experience of the Prophet Muhammad – as recorded in the *hadiths*. Two prescriptive sets of guidelines for halal slaughter follow from these sources and it is the underlying discourses as they are now interpreted on which current controversy about the authenticity of halal meat stands (Lever and Miele 2012).

The first position is based on an understanding that all 'People of the Book' share common slaughter practices and that Muslims can consume meat from animals reared and slaughtered by Jews and Christians as well as by Muslims.

63

As we observed earlier, this position is aligned with EU legislation that requires all animals to be made unconscious by stunning prior to slaughter. The second position, which emerges from derogation of the above legislation, allows EU member states to grant slaughterhouses an exception from the requirement to stun animals before slaughter in line with human rights legislation that provides minorities with the freedom to practise religion. While all Muslims agree that halal meat must emerge from the act of slaughter, adherents of this position argue that the status of halal meat is linked more directly to Islam through traditional halal practices. On this account, Muslims are permitted to consume the meat of an animal only if the method of stunning is reversible (i.e. animals are unconscious but still alive at the time of slaughter), the animal has been blessed by a Muslim reciting the 'Tasmiyah' prior to slaughter and all blood is allowed to drain from the body completely post-slaughter. The main area of concern for those adhering to this position is with the perceived risk that instead of being made unconscious by stunning animals will suffer or be killed. If this occurs, the meat produced is rendered haram rather than halal (Bergeaud-Blackler 2004, 2007).

To illustrate the complex processes of qualification through which meat acquires the qualities that allow it to be traded as halal we next examine how these competing definitions of halal meat are practiced by the two main halal certification bodies operating in the UK in recent decades –HFA and HMC.

Halal meat in the United Kingdom

We noted in Chapter 1 that HFA emerged in 1994 as result of Muslim agitation for greater rights as British citizens in the mid-1980s. With backing from the Muslim Parliament, a plan was put forward to establish a network of halal butchers to help maintain Islamic practice and the self-identity of British Muslims (Ansari 2009). HFA has successfully maintained authority over halal in the UK for over two decades by successfully straddling the line between the two competing halal discourses outlined above. First and foremost, they argue that animals must be slaughtered in a traditional way in line with clear Islamic principles. They must be alive and healthy at the time of slaughter and the jugular veins, carotid arteries and windpipe must be severed with a razor-sharp knife by a single cut. A fit and healthy licensed Muslim must conduct the act of slaughter, *Bismillah Allahu Akbar* must be pronounced at the time of slaughter and all blood must be allowed to drain from the body completely post-slaughter. If an animal is killed by any other means the meat is haram and thus forbidden for Muslim consumption. This does not mean, however, that non-stunning is HFA's preferred method of slaughter. On the contrary, HFA continues to hold a flexible discursive position within which slaughter and mechanisation are intrinsically linked. While HFA agree that animals should be alive at the time of slaughter, they have a critical approach to stunning and mechanised methods that are considered 'aids' to slaughter in many instances. While HFA prohibited stunning when it first emerged because of the uncertainty surrounding it, this prohibition was eventually lifted through negotiation with slaughterhouses and an understanding that only reversible methods of stunning should be used.

HFA has licensed halal abattoirs and factories for producing certified halal meat and poultry in the UK, Europe and Asia, and informants explained that the procedure for licensing a meat plant is quite straightforward. Once an application is received HFA undertakes an inspection and conducts an audit of the methods of manufacture and the labelling procedure in order to assess a company's compliance with islamic principles and with UK and EU legislation. When this process is complete a fee is paid and the meat plant receives an annual licence and certificate that entitles it to use the HFA logo. As part of the contract, HFA can make a number of unannounced annual inspections in any one-year period. Any change in the manufacture of meat in terms of processing, patenting and marketing must be communicated directly to HFA immediately. HFA has an independent board of scholars and *ulama* providing guidance on certification and recently established an impartiality committee, which has key members from academia and industry (e.g. from the AHDB Beef and Lamb Board (www.beefandlamb.ahdb.org.uk)) to minimise conflicts of interests.

To a large extent, the development of HFA mirrors the development of the UK halal market and their practice has changed in line with the growth of the market and the opportunities on offer. This difficult balancing act has made HFA the target of sustained criticism from some voices within the UK Muslim community over the last decade, particularly those associated with HMC. The main criticism is that stunning and the increased mechanisation of slaughter endorsed by HFA go against the principles laid out in the Qur'an. HFA has also been accused by HMC of providing licences too easily to unreliable and unscrupulous operators, though it should be noted that before the emergence of HMC almost anyone selling halal meat in the UK was seen to hold HFA certification. While HFA accepts that some form of mechanisation is necessary to meet the increasing demand for halal meat, particularly for poultry, informants from HFA pointed out repeatedly during interviews over a number of years that they are categorically against irreversible stunning methods like the captive bolt used on cattle.

Ultimately HFA has been successful by fusing traditional Islamic principles with mainstream concerns about animal welfare in order to attribute a range of qualities (Callon *et al.* 2010) to meat that positions their certified halal products as trustworthy and 'authentic' halal in the eyes of many Muslims (Lever and Miele 2012). Over the last two decades, HFA's percentage share of the UK certification market for halal meat has been regularly estimated at between 80 and 90 per cent, with many mainstream manufacturers and distributors, including most of the UK's major slaughter facilities for poultry, being under their control at some point, including the 2 Sisters Food Group (www.2sfg.com).

Tesco and ASDA first started selling pre-stunned halal red meat and chicken certified by HFA in 2000 and from this point onwards halal was lifted out of local butcher's shops to become part of 'world food' ranges in supermarkets and hypermarkets. At the time, Muslims considered these products relatively expensive but also more questionable than the halal meat that is available in local butcher's shops (Fischer 2011). These processes continued to expand and in 2009 HFA went into partnership with the fast-food giant Kentucky Fried Chicken (KFC). An informant argued that this move was justified as a way of catering for the 'growing demand for halal products' in parts of London and the trial was subsequently expanded to include sites around the country, including Manchester. Many other UK fast-food and restaurant chains now sell halal-certified meat and poultry, yet the pioneering work of HFA has also contributed to increasing public concern and controversy. Today, as a result, HFA does not promote itself openly as a halal brand, preferring instead to stay under the radar by certifying own-label products for supermarkets, food service operators and public institutions in partnership with some of the UK's major meat producers. Indeed, despite growing demand for halal products from Muslim consumers, in recent years supermarkets and food service operators have become more discreet in obtaining and displaying the halal logos of their certification partners (Fazira 2015).

As non-stunned halal meat promoted by HFA's competitors has grown in visibility during this period, public concern about the availability and volume of halal meat in the UK has increased significantly. Many consumers wrongly assume that most halal meat in the UK comes from non-stunned animals (Lever and Miele 2012), when in reality the vast majority still comes from pre-stunned animals (FSA 2012; 2015). Indeed, evidence suggests that the issue of halal slaughter is also wrapped up with wider societal concerns about integration and immigration (Bradley *et al.* 2015). Consequently, as commercial sensitivities have intensified, information has been excluded from quality attribution during the qualification process. In 2014, for instance, imported halal lamb from New Zealand was sold in UK supermarkets without being labelled as such. Concerns over animal welfare and immigration are deeply ingrained in the cultural and social fabric of society and it appears that producers, manufacturers and certification bodies have used information in a limited way to assuage pubic concern and maintain market advantage. A good example of this practice is the self-proclaimed 'No. 1 Halal Brand', Shazans (www.shazans.com), which is owned by 2 Sisters Food Group and sold in Tesco stores without any indication of how the meat is produced or who provides certification. These practices make Muslim as well as non-Muslim consumers uneasy, and as we observe in the next chapter, halal consumers often attribute value through social networks and by drawing on economic as well as moral and religious criteria.

The major global state-led certification and accreditation bodies in Malaysia and Indonesia have recognised HFA for many years. However, despite HFA's position of prominence as the major UK halal certification body, changes in the global market are creating new pressures and challenges as well as opportunities for HFA. As the emergence of new accreditation bodies in places such as United Arab Emirates (UAE) starts to challenge the dominance of Southeast Asia in the global marketplace (Bergeaud-Blackler *et al.* 2015), certification bodies such as HFA are being forced to adapt to changing market demands and requirements.

Although HFA appears committed to pre-stunned halal slaughter, the pressures to move into the non-stunned market have been increasing on a number of fronts. Making the case for this transition, HFA's chief executive, Saqib Mohammed, argues that there is increasing pressure to enter what is referred to as the traditional (non-stun) halal market to overcome the widespread malpractice that is having a negative impact of the halal industry overall. As stated on the HFA website:

> HFA has been accepting traditional halal slaughter since its inception in 1994 but has also been actively supporting and certifying recoverable/reversible stunning. Due to unfortunate events of a series of mal-practices observed and reported for some slaughterhouses that undertake traditional halal slaughtering for Muslims, which has a wider negative effect on the wider halal marketplace, HFA now intends to pro-actively raise standards in this segment of the industry as well. (HFA 2016)

It should also be noted, however, that as the global halal market moves in new directions so the qualities ascribed to meat by HFA may also change. The next stage in this process of quality attribution and requalification will be the development of a second HFA logo for traditional halal slaughter (HFA 2016). While this new logo will sit uneasily alongside the HFA logo for stunned halal meat, in the post-Brexit period it will perhaps open up opportunities to work in new markets through new forms of transnational governmentality.

As this brief account of the work of HFA illustrates, the never-ending process of qualification of meat as halal starts with the attribution of distinguishing halal qualities at an HFA-licensed slaughterhouse or meat plant and only ends when a certified halal product is placed on the counter or shelves of a trusted butcher or retailer. However, as we have also seen, in the context of increasing public concern and moral anxiety over animal welfare, halal slaughter and immigration (Bradley *et al.* 2015), information is often excluded from the process of quality attribution. To a large extent this situation has emerged as a response to the increasing visibility of non-stunned (traditional) halal-slaughtered meat certified by HMC.

Following the longstanding position of kosher-certifying bodies that do not accept pre-slaughter stunning, there has been growing pressure from a small number of halal certifying bodies in the UK in recent years – HMC in particular – to promote non-stunned meat as being of a more 'authentic' and traditional halal quality (Lever and Miele 2012). These groups claim that Muslim consumers are not correctly informed and that mainstream certifying bodies go against the wishes of Muslim consumers by allowing the practice of stunning before slaughter. HMC has been HFA's major UK competitor for well over a decade. Established in 2003 by a group of Muslim scholars and jurists, HMC is a non-profit organisation set up to serve the interests of Muslims. An elected executive committee of volunteers including Islamic scholars oversees HMC's operations and today they claim to have the support of hundreds of mosques across the UK. They argue that both Muslims and non-Muslims abuse the word 'halal' and they claim to understand the difficulties of keeping up with the increasing demand for halal meat whilst respecting halal rules and coping with the problem of trust amongst halal consumers. The major characteristics of 'false' halal meat are seen to revolve around the use of 'mechanical slaughter methods', 'fatal stunning techniques' and a disregard of basic Islamic principles by slaughterers and meat processors.

HMC's definition of halal is based on religious authority, the need to improve consumer trust and discursive practices emphasising a combination of religious compliance and pragmatism about what can be achieved. Stunning is a practice that HMC is clear about rejecting and they base part of their identity on the fact that *all* the meat they certify is from non-stunned animals. The organisation recognises that this is a delicate issue, but they consider stunning to be destructive for reasons of animal welfare, the absence of 'Tasmiyah' and because of the unfit character of the meat obtained. HMC's overall aim is to regulate halal production by monitoring, inspecting and certifying halal products effectively. While they recognise the presence of other halal certification bodies, they do not see them as competitors because they do not recognise their legitimacy. HMC encourages Muslim consumers to do their own research and to work out whether they consider the meat they buy to be halal on the basis of what they know about where it comes from. They believe that the major reason for the current high consumption of stunned and mechanically slaughtered halal meat is that people just don't really know about or have the knowledge to make an informed decision about what they are eating. A scholar summed up the wider approach of HMC during the course our research in the following way: 'I think the biggest achievement of HMC is to make people aware. The awareness of the Muslim community about what is happening in industry comparative to their view before [HMC emerged] is 1000 per cent more.'

HMC have thus made the processes behind halal goods an explicit concern. This process of making visible uses *qualification* as a direct marketing strategy.

By making the *qualities* of their competitors' products explicit (an approach HFA now appears to be mirroring) and placing this in contrast to the qualities of their own products, they attempt to establish their products as more trustworthy and genuine than their competitors'. They have identified problems with the misnaming of halal at all stages of the production process and with existing certification schemes, particularly those that certify stunned and mechanically slaughtered meat as halal, such as HFA. They have established their own criteria for certification based on religious authority, which includes inspections at abattoirs/slaughterhouses, processors and outlets for both red meat and poultry. They encourage certification to ensure the confidence of consumers and they base all their operations on the control, functioning and harnessing of the supply chain with their own label. The aim is to follow the entire route of meat through the supply chain, from abattoirs/slaughterhouses, via the middlemen (processors and distributors) to the retailers (butchers and food outlets).

HMC insists on a personal and physical inspection at all slaughterhouses, and they require and demand access to all areas at all times to inspect manufacturing in its entirety. An initial visit is usually followed by an audit to see if the company's processes are compatible with HMC's certification standard. This involves an examination of their levels of production, what the risk is and an assessment of how many inspectors/inspections will be necessary. This organisation does not simply certify on the basis of information provided by a slaughterhouse; they employ third-party independent inspectors within each slaughterhouse, who work full-time under contract on behalf of HMC. These inspectors check that all the requirements of halal slaughter are met and conducted effectively – that slaughter is carried out by a Muslim, that no stunning equipment is used and that no cross-contamination occurs, but they do not oversee the act of slaughter and the saying of prayers as they do not think that this is appropriate. There are many similarities with the practice of *shechita* in HMC's methods, and another inspector stamps the HMC certification mark on carcasses at the end of the chain before it leaves the factory, which also takes place under the control of HMC. Slaughterhouses are charged for the cost of the inspectors' time, plus a fee for travel expenses, equipment and administration. Alternatively, a flat rate per item fee may also be applied based on levels of production: the HMC website states that their overall system costs the industry less than two pence per chicken or kilo of meat, which they say is a small price to pay for the guarantee they offer. HMC processing plants and retail outlets can only stock and deal with meat products qualified as halal by HMC: once a contract has been signed the licensee receives a certificate to display. Processors and retailers are monitored to ensure they comply with HMC standards.

Certified slaughterhouses and the products certified in them are listed on HMC's website. These lists are also distributed to suppliers, processing plants, butchers, retailers, restaurants and fast-food outlets on request to direct business to HMC-certified products. Shops must allow regular monitoring and access to storage and fridge facilities, and HMC insist that retailers must be aware that in signing up with HMC they will have to change suppliers in order to give consumers confidence that their shop is fully HMC-certified. If a shop accepts non-HMC products their licence is withdrawn and the price of certification goes up; delisted shops are listed on the HMC website. HMC has a label for red meat and another for poultry, and also provides tape and ties with the logo for sealing boxes and bags. The HMC share of the UK market for halal meat has been estimated at between 5 and 10 per cent over the last decade or so, and they supply a number of independent butchers, restaurants, takeaways and caterers in towns and cities across the UK. During this period they have played a key role pushing claims about the authenticity of non-stunned traditional forms of halal meat (Lever and Miele 2012) and their work can thus be aligned with Einstein's (2008) insights about the supply-side theory of religion.

In recent years we have conducted fieldwork in east London and south Manchester to explore the presence of halal certification bodies at the local level. Some years ago in London, we drew a rectangular trajectory on the map, starting at Bethnal Green Tube station, and walked up Bethnal Green Road, before turning onto the famous Brick Lane – the paragon of multicultural London – and continuing to Whitechapel station. As we walked in the direction of Brick Lane we observed numerous fast-food restaurants offering halal chicken. Among these was the popular KFC. The restaurant is full and lines of people from many diverse cultures and backgrounds wait to place an order. A new, quite large HFA logo shines in the front window: 'HFA Approved'. There is a significant difference in marketing between KFC and other fast-food restaurants along Bethnal Green Road, most of which claim to offer halal chicken but do not display any sign of certification. Some do display a certificate with the acronym HFA, which probably dates back beyond the emergence of HMC, while others display no certificate but advertise products with HMC certification.

Bethnal Green Road is also peppered with grocer's shops and many have a halal meat counter. The major certification presence here is HMC, displayed either through a certificate or on hand-written signs worded along the lines of: 'HMC meat sold here'. While this is clearly the certification territory of HFA and HMC, HMC has a stronger presence, both in terms of visibility and by distinguishing itself with a specific 'quality': the claim of assuring 'non-stunned' meat. We interview a butcher at the Halal Meat Corner – whose acronym corresponds to HMC. Situated at a street corner on Bethnal Green Road, the large butcher's shop window gives the impression of transparency and cleanliness. The shop sign is a stylish new banner, clearly stating the 'non-stunned' quality of its meat. We learn that the shop opened in June 2009 and that the largest part of their market is chicken. The butcher at the counter is confident that people are slowly starting to recognise their product as 'HMC chicken'. People are, he claims, increasingly aware of the brand. The butcher chose HMC because of their methods of certification and, in particular, he argues, because of their commitment to non-stunning. We ask how many times they are inspected and we are informed that HMC people visit twice a week to check that everything is in order. We also ask if consumers enquire about certification, and we are assured that if people see an HMC sign this is enough to gain their confidence and trust.

More recently we conducted fieldwork in south Manchester. We set off walking along Ayres Road in Old Trafford, just a few kilometres from the Curry Mile in Rusholme. Starting off at Seymour Grove we walk along Ayres Road in the direction of Withington Road. After passing the Manchester Asian superstore we come across a butchers named Trafford Halal Meat that displays no obvious sign of certification or logo, yet as we walk past the shop a delivery van from Euro Quality Lambs (www.euroqualitylambs.com), a recognised HMC supplier, pulls up outside. We then stumble on the Halal Mosam Bakery. Talking to the owner, we are informed that they bake bread and cakes (notably for special occasions) made only from vegetarian ingredients. Halal meat products certified by HMC are also available, supplied by the aptly named HMC Grocery Store and Butcher's further down Ayres Road. Just before we reach this shop we come across Bismillah Butcher's HMC, which, like the HMC Grocery Store and Butcher's, has the HMC certificate prominently displayed behind the counter. We ask the owner how long he has had HMC certification and he answers that the shop has worked with HMC for a few years, adding that it is 'not possible to do good business in the area without HMC certification these days': he also notes that HMC inspectors visit the shop regularly. We eventually reach Withington Road and decide to explore cafés and takeaways on the return journey to Seymour Grove. We walk into the Red Marrakech Moroccan and Mediterranean Café and Takeaway, which displays an unidentifiable halal logo on its shop front and takeaway menu. We ask the manger if his meat is halal and he replies 'we are Moroccan, all our meat is certified by the HMC'. Another curry house claims to sell halal but again this is not verifiable. We carry on up Seymour Grove on our way to the local Tesco hyper/supermarket on Chester Road, opposite Manchester United's famous stadium. Much like the Tesco in Cheetham Hill it has a fresh halal meat counter overseen by National Halal and HMC.

From 2007 ASDA and from 2010 Tesco began selling halal poultry and red meat from non-stunned animals in a number of independent in-store halal

butchers and specialist world food outlets (Lever and Miele 2012). An informant from ASDA argued that they went down this path because they wanted to
'please all' their customers, but market growth was also a defining factor, with
ASDA's non-stunned halal meat sales having achieved 'year-on-year growth' for
a number of years. Initially the non-stunned meat sold in these hyper/super-
markets was endorsed by the National Halal Food Group (www.nationalhalal.
com) – an established market intermediary – rather than by HMC, which was
widely viewed as being too controversial at the time. In recent years, however, as 2 Sisters Food Group and Tesco have started to position themselves
more strategically in the halal market, thus mirroring the changing strategy of
HFA to some extent, National Halal Food Group as been aligned more closely
with HMC to give both brands added value. While HFA has become *less* visible in recent years, the visibility of HMC has thus increased significantly and
continues to do so. Interestingly, an informant from a major producer and
exporter of non-stunned halal lamb in the UK argued that by ascribing their
own-label brands with stunned halal meat qualities supermarkets create the
space for non-stunned halal alternatives that they can then align with consumer demand and choice to increase their halal offer (White 2014).

There are clearly moves to push the UK halal market to another level by
offering Muslim consumers a greater range of added-value non-stunned halal
products. At Tesco, for example, as we have seen, non-stunned halal meat
is provided through a partnership between National Halal and HMC, while
ASDA offers non-stunned added-value products endorsed by HMC through
the Haji Baba (www.hbhmeats.co.uk) brand and on-line delivery service.
Much as market intermediaries play a central role in the expansion of rabbinical power by facilitating access to the conventional market through an ongoing
process of qualification-and-requalification, so these new market intermediaries allow the major industry players to push the market in new directions.
How much the overall demand for non-stunned halal meat has increased in
the UK in recent years is not clear. While the demand for greater variety and
choice amongst UK Muslims may be increasing in a number of market seg-
ments, as noted by speakers at the HFA Halal Industry Conference in 2016
(www.halalfoodauthority.com/hfa-halal-industry-conference-hhic-2016), the
major supermarkets are also targeting Muslim consumers more openly than
they once did. Despite the intensification of their engagement with the corporate world in recent years, it is also clear that HMC-certified meat has generally acquired its final qualities on the counters of local butchers, restaurants
and takeaways in towns and cities across the UK. As we observe in subsequent
chapters, despite the increasing range and availability of halal-branded products in UK supermarkets, many Muslims continue to shop and show trust in
local butcher's shops, not least because these shops can prepare meat to their
exact specifications in terms of cuts, price and volume. We now turn briefly to
Denmark.

Figure 13 National Halal Centre/HMC-certified non-stunned poultry

Figure 14 National Halal Centre, Tesco Manchester

Figure 15 Shazans halal-certified products

Halal meat in Denmark

The ban on non-stunned slaughter in 2014 seems to have lessened sensitivities about halal slaughter in Denmark. In public discourses the sentiment now seems to be that even if certain groups are not comfortable with Islamic slaughter the issue is, firstly, unrelated to animal welfare now that stunning is mandatory and, secondly, a large percentage of the chicken produced in Denmark is aimed at exports, making this sector not only important for the country's economy (Bradley *et al.* 2015), but also a symbol of national and patriotic sentiment (Fischer 2011).

The slaughter of chickens in Denmark takes place according to the rules of the Justice Department's Declaration for the Slaughter of Animals. All chickens must be stunned prior to slaughter and approximately 99 per cent of all chicken slaughter is conducted at abattoirs approved for proper halal slaughter by the Islamic Cultural Center Scandinavia and/or by the Muslim World League's branch in Copenhagen: this situation is similar to that in the UK, where the vast majority of halal chicken comes from stunned animals certified by HFA in line with mainstream industry practice. The Danish company Danpo (www.danpo.dk), which slaughters about 50 million chickens each year, states on its website that consumers do not pay extra for halal-slaughtered meat because the only difference with non-halal-slaughtered meat is the way that slaughter is monitored:

Under Danish law animal slaughter must be monitored by a slaughterhouse worker to ensure that there is no unnecessary suffering: these workers are Muslims. When slaughter begins, and after there has been a pause in production, a Muslim employee recites a prayer that translated reads: 'In the name of God. Allah is the greatest.' The prayer is what separates the halal method from standard slaughter. Apart from this, slaughter is carried out according to Danish rules: chickens are hung by the legs on a moving shackle line and the head is submerged in an electrified stun bath to make them unconscious before all the major blood vessels and veins in the neck are severed manually or with a rotating knife. The high speed of the production line and the short distance between shackling the birds and the act of killing means that birds die fast and painlessly, in what is regarded as a high welfare system. (www.danpo.dk/en/about-danpo/animal-welfare/halal, accessed 22 January 2016)

Most chicken production in Denmark is halal-certified, although this is not the case with the beef and lamb that some of our informants indicate is their preferred meat. However, imported non-stunned halal chicken is not available in supermarkets, so consumers must go to the many halal butchers' shops that have proliferated in areas of Copenhagen such as Nørrebro in search of fresh meat with the halal qualities that satisfies their needs. However, discussions with butchers in the area established that almost all the fresh meat sold by them is of Danish origin and therefore from stunned animals, as legally required. It was possible to find only one butcher's in which the meat sold was non-stunned and this meat was imported from Ireland.

Even though slaughter without stunning was prohibited in 2014, an informant pointed out that only a few butcher's shops were in fact selling non-stunned meat imported from the UK, France and Poland prior to this. Only one shop actually specialised in selling non-stunned halal meat and this closed because the market was very limited – much as it is in the UK, comparatively. However, the ban on non-stunned meat made more Muslims aware of the underlying issues and consequently more butcher's shops started to advertise their meat as non-stunned. In general, however, the market for non-stunned imported meat is unregulated and distributors and sellers have a hard time checking what qualities the meat they sell has acquired before they receive it. While it is difficult to establish the qualities ascribed to halal meat in supermarkets and food service outlets in the UK because of the commercial sensitivities that have emerged, so is it hard in Denmark to ascertain the specific qualities ascribed to halal meat products in a changing regulatory landscape characterised by standardisation, increasing consumer demand and transnational governmentality.

Discussion

The kosher market in Denmark has been shrinking and there is now only one kosher shop in the entire country: it's also highly standardised and all the meat sold is from non-stunned animals and imported from the UK, France and Poland. Thus, the processes of kosher qualification of meat in Denmark is characterised by the practices of bodies such as MBD, that is, supervision, auditing and inspections that constitute forms of what we called transnational governmentality. Similar processes can be seen in the market for halal meat in Denmark. All the meat we could find in local halal butcher's shops in Copenhagen was advertised and sold as being of Danish origin, meaning that the meat supposedly was of high quality, but also stunned following Danish law. Because almost all of the chicken produced and sold in Denmark is non-stunned this is sold in supermarkets as well as in halal butchers, but for beef and lamb, for example, consumers (as we shall see in Chapter 5) must go to a halal butcher's. As noted, the ban on non-stunned slaughter in Denmark seems to have lessened sensitivities about halal slaughter in the country whilst increasing uncertainty about the qualities of some forms of halal meat.

The processes of qualification underpinning kosher and halal meat manufacture in the UK is more complex. The qualification of kosher meat is similar in both countries in that all the kosher meat sold is certified by recognised rabbinical authorities, but in Denmark the final kosher qualities are ascribed to meat products in other countries. In the single shop in Denmark, and in the plethora of kosher butcher's shops and super/hypermarkets in the UK, kosher meat quality is always confirmed by the *hechsher* of a recognised rabbinical authority or certification body. While the ban on non-stunned slaughter means that all kosher meat in Denmark is pre-packed in other locations, the UK fresh kosher meat is sold in shops and butchers licensed by recognised UK rabbinical authorities. Looking at this in terms of the qualities ascribed through the process of qualification, we can say that for kosher consumers (Chapter 4) in the UK trust is – despite competition between certification bodies – inseparable from licensing and rabbinical authority and from the supervisory processes under which these outlets operate, while in Denmark qualification is more distant and underpinned by transnational governmentality.

The halal market in the UK is similar to the kosher market, yet in this market there are now a number of certifying bodies, notably HFA and HMC, which represent two very different processes of qualification, that is, stunning and non-stunning, and there is thus no centralised standardisation as there is in the kosher market. This market is more complex to navigate than the kosher market due to the fact that much of the halal meat sold in local and national retail outlets across the UK is not marked by halal logos, which is similar to the situation in Denmark but for different if related reasons. To complicate things still further, as religious slaughter without stunning is allowed in the UK (as opposed to Denmark), this presents a complex process of qualification, with intense competition between certification bodies over the qualities ascribed to stunned and non-stunned meat throughout the production and manufacturing process.

In the UK, kosher and non-stunned halal meat products are qualified in much the same way as stunned halal meat within the cultures of particular authorities, yet the kosher market remains more centralised than the halal market: even as the market expands and 'economic goods' qualified as kosher meat become available in mainstream retailers, it appears that the power, authority and organisation of rabbinical authorities allow them to maintain a higher degree of control. In the UK halal market, by way of contrast, corporate control appears to be growing. Large retailers such as ASDA and Tesco are dictating from where and from whom meat qualified as stunned and non-stunned halal can be sourced, and this is constantly pushing the market in new directions. Even if the geographical location of the international accreditation and certification bodies underwriting the work of UK bodies changes, the underlying process of qualification and requalification will remain and perhaps grow in complexity.

To evoke our points on standardisation we can say that the market for both kosher and halal meat is highly standardised in Denmark: all the imported kosher meat is non-stunned, while all the locally produced halal meat is stunned following existing legislation and practices. Conversely, many different halal standards are evident in the UK and this is also to a certain extent true for kosher if we consider the ongoing rise of ultra-Orthodox certification practice. Yet kosher has a longer history of standardisation in the UK, making it more centrally regulated in most cases. Even so, the expansion of kosher and halal into mainstream supermarkets through market intermediates allows less Orthodox kosher consumers to be targeted demographically, thus continuing the process by which these markets are being lifted out of their traditional religious base. In Denmark, by way of contrast, these meat markets are highly standardised and the underlying process of qualification is ultimately dependent on transnational governmentality, as it is through such means that consumers acquire economic goods with qualities that satisfy their needs as kosher and halal consumers.

3

Beyond meat

Within the last couple of decades, the trend in both kosher and halal production is that these globalising religious markets have moved beyond meat to
include enzyme production, for example, as enzymes are part of a wide range
of types of foods and drinks.[1] Thus, in the modern and globalised industry
it is not only for food, but also for biotechnology that a number of requirements must be met, such as those demanded by the injunction to avoid any
substances that may be contaminated with porcine residues (kosher/halal)
or alcohol (halal). These requirements are setting new scientific standards
for production, preparation, handling, storage and certification. This chapter explores how multinational companies that are both kosher- and halal-
certified understand and comply with rising requirements in relation to issues
such as certification, staff policies, science and innovation, for example – and
how non-meat products such as enzymes are produced and qualified as kosher
(Fischer 2015b) and halal (Fischer 2015a).

Before looking into the company studies below we will discuss relevant points made in *Kosher Food Production* (Blech 2008) and *Halal Food
Production* (Riaz and Chaudry 2004), which many companies use as handbooks for kosher and halal production. Micro-organisms or naturally occur-
ring microflora are kosher if such strains are grown on specific nutritional
media that assume kosher status (Blech 2008: 25). Enzymes that derive from
the stomach lining of animals are a potential problem as they cannot be mixed
with dairy products because kosher requires that one does not 'boil a kid in its
mother's milk'. In addition to food, kosher is also widely used to designate the
'rabbinic properness' of a wide range of objects, products, activities, ideas and
institutions. To be able to sell a product as kosher, manufacturers or producers need certification by competent authorities, be this a rabbi or a company
specialised in certification, such as OU, which undertakes the supervision and
auditing of kosher production. The kosher status of a product is the direct
function of the kosher status of the ingredients used in its manufacture, the
equipment on which they are produced and the way in which these aspects are
regulated in terms of certification, supervision and inspection (Blech 2008).
After companies' kosher applications have been approved, an initial inspection

focuses on the verification of the accuracy of the application and ingredient lists submitted and the production system, including the need to undertake a ritual cleansing (kosherisation) of equipment if necessary. Steam or hot water can be of concern if a common system is used in the processing of kosher and non-kosher products (Blech 2008: 13). Many of the above issues are particularly relevant in the case of modern biotech, where fermentation is based on growth of micro-organisms such as bacteria, yeast and moulds.

Enzymes (together with gelatine) are used in a multitude of food and non-food processes, for example in dairy and starch industries. Traditionally, the majority of enzymes used in the food industry were from animal sources, but now there are microbial alternatives. Enzymes from microbial sources or halal-slaughtered animals, it is argued, are halal, whereas an enzyme from a porcine source is haram (Riaz and Chaudry 2004: 21). Alcohol is ubiquitous and naturally present in all biological systems and arguably it does not nullify the halal status of food products. What is more, alcohol in pure form is the best solvent and chemical available for extracting, dissolving and precipitating functions in the food industry. Thus, religious scholars have realised its importance for use in the industry and ingredients made with alcohol or extracted by using alcohol have become acceptable as long as alcohol is evaporated from the final ingredient (Riaz and Chaudry 2004: 24).

Biotechnology and genetically modified organisms (GMO) in particular are contested fields with regard to modern halal. Of course, there is no specific mentioning of (genetically) modified ingredients in the Qur'an because these scientific discoveries are recent (Riaz and Chaudry 2004: 137). Both Jewish and Islamic scholars currently accept products made from simple genetic engineering. However, production conditions in fermenters must still be kosher/halal and so must the ingredients, as well as the processing. The Muslim community is still considering the issue of products with a porcine gene and a final ruling has not been established. The 'leaning' seems to be toward rejecting such materials. Religious leaders of both communities have not yet determined the status of more complex genetic manipulations (Riaz and Chaudry 2004: 162). Enzymes that derive from microbial or biotech sources are acceptable as kosher, halal and vegetarian. Enzymes extracted from kosher-killed animals are accepted as kosher and enzymes extracted form halal-killed animals accepted as halal (Riaz and Chaudry 2004: 164–5). These points are relevant to the companies we now discuss.

This chapter mainly builds on empirical data from Denmark, but also the UK, the US and Asia. Given the relatively limited local markets for kosher and halal food products in Denmark we found it interesting that a small country such as Denmark plays an important role in biotechnology that is compatible with what we call kosher/halal transnational governmentality. As we shall see, Denmark is the leading country in the manufacturing of kosher/halal-certified enzymes globally. Of course, the trend to have biotech production subjected to religious standards (which took off with kosher in the 1990s) is not limited to Denmark, and before moving to the ethnography on Denmark and Asia we outline comparable trends in the UK.

Biocatalysts Ltd (www.biocatalysts.com) is an innovative enzyme producer in South Wales in the UK that is certified by both MBD and HFCE. Biocatalysts recently started manufacturing enzymes and has a bioreactor on-site where they produce and package enzyme blends in line with customer requirements; in effect the company synthesises enzymes to order and ships them out to destinations around the globe. Amongst other things, the company provides enzymes for sugar and salt reduction, colour enhancements, flavours and yeasts. Our contact at Biocatalysts explains that they provide a lot of enzymes for flour in cereal processing and to increase yields during fruit and vegetable processing, but the company also provides enzymes for modified cheese flavours and other products such as oil and butter. The move away from animal enzymes to microbial alternatives has been significant for Biocatalysts and has enabled them to specialise in kosher, halal and vegetarian enzyme applications: they recently produced the first commercial 'pregastric esterase enzyme' to digest fat. The manager of a kosher shop in Manchester explained the significance of these developments when discussing the kosher yogurt and cheese sold in the shop. He pointed out that until 40 or 50 years ago there was no mass production of yoghurts and that producers just let milk go off and eventually it became yoghurt or cheese. Today, however, he notes that some producers simply buy yeast off the self and that as far as kosher is concerned the question is no longer 'what is the source of the product?', but rather 'what's it grown on?'. Rabbis from MBD have been overseeing the production of kosher enzymes at Biocatalysts for over three decades and an informant from the Manchester body explains that having a rabbi on-site ensures that the enzymes produced are fit and proper and can be used in kosher food production.

An informant with a supervisor from HFCE noted that he often works alongside rabbis from MBD at companies such as Biocatalysts. Stressing the similarities and differences in what is involved and how kosher and halal audits and certification processes work, he notes that halal and kosher supervisors 'conduct audits independently, we work together, we ask similar sort of information, we look at sort of similar things, you know we get on'. Despite the similarities between kosher and halal supervision, our informant also pointed to a number of differences, the primary one being that rabbis are always present when equipment is being cleaned and cleansed, when a blessing is given and also, in some cases, during the production of certain enzymes. It should also be recognised at this juncture that in both the case of kosher and also in that of halal, cooperation between competing certification bodies can be difficult, simply because they often do not recognise each other and/or because they have different understandings of what is and is not acceptable.

When a company such as Biocatalysts applies for halal certification our contact points out that HFCE sends out an application form to ascertain what ingredients are being used, what their source is, what industry the company is selling in and what the manufacturing process is. The company's HSCCP (Hazard Analysis and Critical Control Points) plan and food safety programme are examined and the destination countries of the final products are explored in depth. This is particularly significant in the halal market, we are informed, not least because different regions and markets have different halal requirements and different bodies have to be consulted. As our informant states: 'Yes, it's one religion, but in that there are subtleties or differences in the market.' Because HFCE doesn't have any halal guidelines or standards of its own, as a third-party certification body they certify in line with the demands of importing countries and we are informed that occasionally this can present problems. As far as Biocatalysts are concerned, however, understanding the requirements of religious accreditation has been beneficial and allowed the company to be recognised as one of the world's leading speciality enzyme manufacturers.

For a long time kosher and halal production was seen as specialist production and it could only be carried out when a rabbi from MBD or an HFCE supervisor or inspector was on-site. However, the ongoing growth of kosher and halal markets globally over recent years has brought new demands and Biocatalysts recently applied for and achieved kosher accreditation from MBD for a new manufacturing facility in South Wales. This was done in a relatively short period of time and customers no longer need to order enzymes from Biocatalysts in advance because kosher enzymes can now be produced without a rabbi being present. All enzymes produced at the new facility, for individual customers and for the general market, can be kosher, halal or vegetarian, and the company claims that this offers customers a strong competitive advantage. As the marketing and customer services manager confirms: 'Biocatalysts are now considered as experienced and knowledgeable in the aspect of religious accreditation and we are delighted to share this knowledge with our customers, guaranteeing problem free product compliance' (Biocatalysts 2015).

Novozymes

Novozymes is the leading enzyme manufacturer globally. The company's history starts with Nordisk, founded in 1923, and Novo, founded in 1925. These were merged into Novo Nordisk in 1989 and Novozymes was founded as a result of a demerger in 2000. The company has enzyme plants in six countries, three in Denmark, two in the US, two in China, two in India, one in Brazil, and one in Canada. Novozymes has more than 6,000 employees and in 2013 annual revenues were about US$2 billion. The company makes around

900 enzyme products purchased by many different industries manufacturing detergents, foods, beverages, textiles, biofuel and animal feed, among other things. Novozymes started undergoing auditing for *kashrut* compliance in the late 1980s and is certified by OU. In order to comply with divergent halal requirements set by Islamic organisations globally, the company's products are certified by three different certifiers: IFANCA, HFCE and MUI. Previously, Halal Control, a German halal certification body, also certified the company. Hence, in order to ensure global coverage and strengthen transnational governmentality, more than one certifier is needed. In 2000, the position of global halal and kosher coordinator was created. This individual has been with Novozymes for many years and has been involved in quality assurance and several other areas of enzyme production. Novozymes is a good example of a company that takes global kosher and halal challenges seriously and this has impacted on certification, staff policies and innovation in the company. Practically, all of the company's food-grade enzymes are kosher- and halal-certified. Comparatively more enzymes are kosher-certified because some of these are for the production of alcoholic beverages only, that is, halal certification is irrelevant.

Novozymes started replacing the limited number of animal ingredients in production about 20 years ago as a result of BSE and rising kosher requirements. Both factors made animal ingredients undesirable. Novozymes' coordinator provides a specific example of the way in which the company complies with such kosher standards: these necessitated a change in ingredients and production processes in connection with replacing porcine gelatine with fish gelatine to produce an immobilised lipase for edible oils. These transformations signify the move towards kosher standardisation. The replacement of animal ingredients by other ingredients was not only resource-demanding and costly, it also generated forms of innovation that benefit the company today. In many ways non-animal ingredients are more unproblematic in the globalised market in an era of food scares and rising religious requirements. Thus, over the last two decades religious principles have played an important role in shaping knowledge, work processes and practices in an organisation such as Novozymes. Formalised standardisation in the form of certification and auditing/inspections by an identifiable certifier such as OU marked the start of systematic kosher regulation.

Novozymes trains all staff involved in kosher production, that is, basic rules/regulations, approved ingredients/raw materials, as well as handling and certification procedures. These sessions start with a general introduction followed by detailed instructions about the rules that specifically apply to that audience. Occasionally, the OU rabbinic field supervisor who is also responsible for training Novozymes' employees around the world knows that they can contact the coordinator if they have any questions about kosher certifica-tion and compliance. The coordinator is responsible for such training and also participates in training arranged by OU, for example. Novozymes' training of staff takes place at different levels at the company's sites around the world. The coordinator functions as the company's overall authority on kosher globally, but at each of Novozymes' sites one member of staff is appointed local coordi-nator responsible for kosher. Worldwide, the company has seven local coordi-nators, one per site. Consequently, training takes place centrally in Denmark and at local sites of production in each country. This point shows that stand-ardisation is also about persons (employees and inspectors), who each in their way possesses standardised skills to produce and regulate kosher products, but also transmits kosher knowledge in order to avoid divergent types of clas-sifications globally. Training itself can be seen as a standardising process in which learning and disciplining meet. Kosher training is a way to increase workers' employment value, depending on their skills. Skills terms, especially 'communication', 'team' and 'leadership', formulate aspects of personhood and modes of sociality as productive labour. Ideally, team members complement each other's capacities and collaborate fluidly. Team training is seen to prom-ise optimal labour coordination, resulting in higher productivity and personal transformation (Urciuoli 2008: 222).

When kosher became more and more important in the 1990s, Novozymes' coordinator assumed that there would be a textbook that could tell him all he needed to know, but the only books he could find were written for Jewish housewives and not for production engineers. Consequently, he had to pick up the necessary information from frequent meetings with OU representatives, including the rabbinic field supervisor or inspector. As noted above, another source of information is *Kosher Food Production* (Blech 2008), which many companies use as a handbook for kosher production. This type of manual is important in standardising kosher principles, audits/inspections and their translation into practice – and is also a text that helps to shape uniform global governmentality.

In principle, the coordinator could manage Novozymes' kosher compliance without knowing very much about kosher apart from what he could find in this book, as well as OU requirements set out in the contract between the cer-tification body and Novozymes, especially keeping in mind possible restric-tions on Schedule A – a listing of kosher ingredients that are acceptable for use in certified as well as non-certified products. However, there have been situations where these two texts together did not give the whole story. In such situations, knowledge about kosher rules can prevent violations before they arise. Furthermore, when training other people in kosher rules and compli-ance, it is helpful to have a greater knowledge and this also makes the job as a kosher coordinator more interesting, he reasons. This knowledge also enables him to better understand the OU's decisions and to find applicable solutions in discussions with rabbis. However, from his desk in Novozymes' headquarters the coordinator cannot ensure compliance at all plants in Denmark, India, Brazil, the US and China. It is therefore critical to translate the requirements into standardised systems and terminology that can be understood by all Novozymes' employees who are involved on a daily basis in kosher compliance. This is done by formulating a set of global procedures for kosher compliance that work as centralised and standardised procedures for practice. Once kosher principles are translated into practice they are unlikely to be rolled back, even if consumer demand should drop. Thus, standardisation processes and inspections tend to take on lives of their own. In other words, the history of kosher compliance in an organisation such as Novozymes shows that the move towards formalised standardisation between certifier and certified is an extremely powerful one that shapes and disciplines a whole range of everyday practices.

When we participated in a kosher inspection in 2010, the OU inspector was particularly interested to know about changes in production processes, but as Novozymes' raw materials are generally unproblematic, this is not really an issue. The OU inspector visits several times each year and has done so for many years, pointing to the routinisation and standardisation inspections have undergone. Over the years the inspector and the coordinator have developed a personal relationship and there is mutual professional respect between them. Almost all inspections are announced, but in principle unannounced inspections are possible. Other companies we have worked with that use more problematic ingredients, or also produce non-kosher products, simultaneously experienced unannounced inspections. The fact that inspections are announced and routinised minimises tensions between kosher principles and practices.

An example of such standardised practice is kosherisation or ritual cleansing. In some cases, kosher inspectors perform kosherisation of equipment in addition to the cleaning the company does itself. At Novozymes, kosherisation is done after producing the only product that contains milk-based ingredients subject to special kosher rules. The ritual cleansing involves leaving the equipment inactive for 24 hours prior to thorough cleansing with hot water or steam under the supervision of the OU inspector. When researchers took part in inspections in 2010 there was no need to perform kosherisation. Kosherisation is an example of the compatibility of kosher principles and practices, that is, the principle and practice of this ritual is shared by certifier and company.

The coordinator mostly accompanies the OU inspector on the big annual inspection, while other Novozymes staff trained in kosher compliance are responsible for many of the other inspections. The kosher inspector is the only inspector to carry out inspections at Novozymes Denmark and this helps personalise the relationship between the Novozymes coordinator and the inspector. All Novozymes' factories in India, Brazil, US and China have main kosher inspections at least once a year and frequent follow-up visits. Novozymes' coordinator explains that even though inspections always complicate planning slightly, thanks to the familiarity between the inspector and the coordinator, these can be 'cosy' and 'fun', he explains. More generally, as long as inspectors are well qualified in the area of biotechnology and relevant areas of expertise, inspections can be interesting for companies. They are an opportunity for a company such as Novozymes to demonstrate how they comply with complex religious requirements and to establish and maintain a personalised relationship between staff and inspectors. This is important, because in the eyes of a company such as Novozymes kosher compliance in the form of certification and standardisation is considered value-added in competition with other companies that are not kosher-certified.

In 2010 OU and its inspector announced that the yearly inspection would take place in May and Novozymes' management agreed that researchers could participate after signing a confidential closure and sampling agreement. An inspection takes place over two days in several of Novozymes' facilities such as factories and warehouses across Denmark. Before such an inspection starts, the coordinator informs teams of employees to be prepared for receiving the inspector at specific times in the different locations. These teams also receive inspectors from local and international authorities as well as customer audits: in a way, the pervasiveness and intensity of audit culture standardise inspections in the eyes of companies. The OU inspector responsible for inspecting Novozymes is senior European rabbinic field representative, but he also does inspections in countries such as India and Japan. The inspector is in his seventies, and he grew up in the UK and holds degrees in chemical engineering from the US, where he discovered Judaism. When the inspection starts at one of Novozymes' plants in Copenhagen, the OU inspector wears the traditional black hat and dress of Orthodox Jews: he also has long hair and a big beard. The researchers could not help wondering about the seeming incongruity between these markers of Orthodoxy and the setting of the enzyme-producing plant. However, as the inspection starts the inspection team, including the researchers, is soon covered in protective plastic suits that have to be put on and taken off each time we stop at a particular site. At these sites, members of teams are ready to receive the inspection group and they are also wearing the protective suits.

The second day starts at the same time and we initially go to a warehouse. Then we drive to fermentation, have lunch and then on to environmental operations, recovery, standardisation and finally granulation. It is not only the route of the inspection that is mapped and standardised. In kosher inspections, flowcharts play an important role in giving inspectors a quick overview. Often during inspections, the inspector together with the coordinator and the employee or team of employees responsible for the individual production processes look at and discuss flowcharts. If changes in production have taken place, these can be indicated on the flowchart.

During the kosher inspection, the OU inspector is thorough, inquisitive, talkative and joking. Staff told us that they enjoyed the inspector's humour and that this made kosher inspections something special. Obviously, there is a personalised relationship between the inspector, coordinator and team members we meet as we move along production areas and laboratories. The inspector explains about his work and the purpose of the inspection and how a company such as Novozymes best complies with kosher principles. For example, in the warehouse of another company he once found 'piggy things' that are clearly prohibited from being stored among products that are designated kosher. This is a rare example of how kosher rules can be broken and the sacred can be polluted by the profane. However, as 99 per cent of raw materials in Novozymes are already OU-approved, his main focus here is on potential cross-contamination and pollution relating to the complex kosher rules in biotechnology, on the one hand, and auditing in connection with accompanying documents and certificates, on the other.

More specifically, he looks for 'loose labels' that can be signs of improper or unreliable kosher certification by other kosher certifiers. In general, there is competition and also mistrust between many kosher certifiers. Hence, kosher inspectors often consider products certified by other smaller certifiers or individual rabbis to be unstandardised and thus unreliable because these do not have the resources or authority to properly regulate products and processes. Conversely, large certifiers are seen to be more reliable and their certification is recognised while they are also main competitors in the global market.

Much of the inspection work and practices focus on looking for proper kosher logos on products and raw materials and the trajectories of these, that is, where they are produced, by whom and how they ended up in Novozymes' production or stored in a warehouse. Hence, in several cases he wants to have specific files sent to him for checking at a later stage. This type of documentation and traceability is at the heart of audit culture. Another related question is about a list that covers incoming goods to the Novozymes warehouse within the last month. Many of these questions are central not only to kosher, but also more broadly to issues such as quality assurance and the ways in which Novozymes plan and run production. A specific question among many others that arises in the production area we are in relates to the use of milk powder in production, as milk is traditionally a sensitive issue in kosher. Thus, milk powder is an example of a substance that is kosher as long as it is not mixed with animal ingredients.

The inspector acknowledges that as kosher is proliferating, more and more product types are subject to religious requirements, including non-food products. Kosher-certified detergent, for instance, may not be essential for OU and its inspectors, but if the demand is there, as in the case of North America,

producers and certifiers meet these demands. Consequently, inspection practices must address work processes and ingredients that go into the production
of kosher detergent. Another issue during inspections is potential changes in
Novozymes' guidelines for production. These questions are often of a highly
technical and complex nature and OU inspectors debate these issues among
themselves to reach final solutions or decisions that can been seen as rabbinic
standards companies can follow. While Novozymes is solely certified by OU,
both the inspector and the coordinator acknowledge that kosher understanding varies from inspector to inspector – even within OU. Consequently, a
longer and personalised relationship is important when negotiating proper
kosher practice between inspectors and coordinators, and this is mainly developed during inspections, but also through training.

When we stop at granulate mixing, the inspector looks at containers with
OU logos and wonders about transportation details: 'How do raw materials arrive? What are the delivery details? Who owns containers or are they
rented? Who cleans these containers and how? Are there any papers on the
tank truck?', he asks. These questions crop up in a specific part of a production
area that is fully kosher; it does not produce anything that is not kosher so
questions target proper handling during transportation and how this can be
documented. Standardisation of proper handling and transport are challenging not only for Novozymes, but also for companies that supply containers, for
example, and again documentation and traceability become essential in making kosher production auditable.

Thus, traceability in connection with ingredients is of particular importance during kosher inspections. These ingredients have travelled far, taking
complex 'secular' routes, and they therefore pose a specific concern for OU.
Hence, proper labelling with kosher logos by OU or one of the OU-recognised
certification bodies together with labels that detail contents are essential
for traceability. Batch numbers and barcodes are also inspected in order to
determine traceability. In general, the further a product has travelled along
complex routes between suppliers, middlemen and companies, the more they
can be seen as problematic and in need of proper certification and labelling.
These points also vary from raw material to raw material seen to require different kosher status – some products must be certified as kosher, while this is
not essential for others, so there are grades of kosherness to consider during
inspections.

The inspector explains that there are four basic groups of ingredients with
different kosher status: the first is ingredients that can be bought from anyone
without documentation; the second is ingredients that must be bought from a
certain supplier; the third group is ingredients that should be checked by labels
or batch certificate signatures; and the last group of ingredients are acceptable
to have in a factory, but not in kosher products. This classification is important for OU-standardised understanding of what kosher is and it also guides

inspectors when they do inspections. All this necessitates in-depth knowledge of classifications among companies and appropriate documentation that can be translated into standards. The inspector now looks at a raw material that is made by another multinational biotech company. For a number of reasons this raw material does not carry a kosher logo and the inspector wants to know if a batch-specific kosher certificate exists. The Novozymes coordinator contends that such a certificate exists in the relevant office for the inspector to check afterwards.

The inspector notes that in many cases enzymes that should be kept separate are mixed in complex ways. This trend is also an effect of the intensified globalisation of the trade of enzymes, in which more and more 'secular' middlemen handle kosher in divergent ways. According to the OU inspector, an example of this is 'individual and unreliable rabbis' who want to make easy money without possessing the necessary knowledge or resources to handle kosher properly. In this 'incestuous world of enzymes', logos and labelling are an essential sign of standardisation that can say something about 'the other side of the logo', that is, the kosherness of products is not easily verifiable without these logos on products or certificates.

While we wait in a production area for a certificate for a particular product to be recovered from the nearby office, the inspector reasons that while more and more attention is paid to how certification and proper logos on products can give producers, certifiers and consumers assurance, the relabelling of products and the ongoing process of qualification and requalification entailed complicates things significantly (Callon *et al.* 2002). Many products are relabelled one or more times as they move from production to consumption and attain new qualities. Sometimes, the inspector complains that labels are ripped off during transport, which and this makes kosher status verification impossible. However, no matter how detailed the label on products may be, kosher rules cover ingredients and processes that cannot be covered by a secular declaration alone, and this point necessitates the marking of correct status with a logo.

As we move around, several less convincing kosher logos come to the attention of the inspector – for example a big logo by a French kosher-certifying body the inspector considers reliable, but he dislikes the design. We also encounter an example of a raw material the Novozymes coordinator is not quite sure how to document on-site as kosher. The OU inspector suggests that Novozymes can have a picture taken of its batch number and barcode so that paperwork and a certificate can accompany the product. This shows that audit culture practices can determine whether a product is kosher or not. This procedure is becoming more and more common in such situations. When exploring the fermentation process the inspector wants to know if any changes over the last two months and changes more generally have taken place. Potential changes in production are a concern of kosher inspectors in general, as these challenge standardised methods of practice in ways that have implications for kosher principles. If companies can provide detailed information about changes, it is easier to determine how kosher status is affected, so this is often one of the first questions inspectors ask and one that companies are prepared to answer. Another specific question is about raw materials for different types of production. Other questions asked by the inspector relate to changes in particular processes since the last inspection – for example, new suppliers of raw materials. We now reach recovery and the inspector again asks if there have been any changes in this process since his last visit. The coordinator can answer these questions to the satisfaction of the inspector, and the specialised teams we meet at different steps of production are prepared to elaborate in their particular field of expertise.

In a specific part of a production area the inspector is enquiring into the potential risk for contamination in relation to a product that is stored in a state-of-the-art steel tank. The researchers could not help asking how a modern steel tank can be suspected of causing contamination. The inspector answers that this is 'Because there were traditionally holes in metal containers and theological reasons.' As noted, another example of these historical or theological aspects is the inspector's questions and concern with steam as a potential media of contamination in connection with pigs and other pollutants – steam or hot water issues pose a concern if a common steam or hot-water system is used in the processing of kosher and non-kosher products. Concerns with contamination risks in steel containers and steam show the extent to which historical/theological kosher principles condition kosher production practices. However, as long as companies can comply with these requirements through standardised practices they are not concerned. The training of staff, in particular where the OU inspector also participates, provides a framework for inspections that makes kosher compliance smoother. Even if kosher inspections are only one type of inspection among many others, employees generally consider kosher regulation different from other standards and regulations due to its divine origin. The ethnography shows that not only are inspections standardised and routinised, but they also serve the purpose of establishing personalised relationships between inspectors and coordinators that help to ensure smooth cooperation and the translation of kosher principles into practice. After the two days of inspection the inspector moves on to the next company before returning to Novozymes in due course.

Although Novozymes has complied with steadily growing kosher requirements since the 1980s, the coordinator explains that enquiries about halal certification from Southeast Asia, especially Malaysia, Singapore and Indonesia, culminated in new practices in 2001 following a food scandal in Indonesia (Fischer 2008a).

However, already before this food scandal there was increasing interest in halal, and Novozymes and the coordinator started to learn about halal and its similarities to and differences from kosher – also in terms of locating and ultimately choosing certifiers. In the eyes of the coordinator there is not too much difference in handling kosher and halal: pork avoidance is similar in both systems, but most importantly there are similarities with respect to the understanding and practices surrounding the approval of raw materials, product certification and audits/inspections. Alcohol is allowed in kosher and more generally kosher is more complex in terms of avoiding cross-contamination. Consequently, kosher inspections are often more detailed, as we shall see below.

In order to comply with divergent halal requirements set by Islamic organisations globally the company's products are certified by three different certifiers, among them HFCE. When we discuss standards and standardisation the coordinator contends that halal standards similar to those of the International Standards Organization (ISO) would be desirable. It is confusing that different halal certifiers compete and have different halal understandings and practices resulting in tensions and a constant uncertainty about recognition and misrecognition between certifiers. However, despite calls for such standards by certifiers and companies, there is no sign that actual halal standardisation is being institutionalised on a global scale. Such standards could ideally also include inspections and this would perhaps lessen different certifiers' scepticism about the inspection qualifications, competences and capabilities of other certifiers that can lead to a certifier being misrecognised.

Novozymes trains all staff involved in halal production, that is, basic rules/regulations, approved ingredients/raw materials and their handling, and certification procedures. As with kosher, the Novozymes coordinator trains staff involved in every aspect of halal production and also participates in training arranged by MUI, for example. Moreover, training also addresses communicative aspects such as how to cooperate with halal certifiers and especially their specific requirements when getting products and production processes through the certification process. An important question in this respect is how these recognised certifiers understand and practise MUI requirements.

According to the coordinator training is also important because during the breaks issues such as certification and recognition can be discussed and potentially negotiated. Companies such as Novozymes participate in quite a number of these events and here they learn about other companies' experiences with halal challenges. Novozymes together with other multinationals in biotech, dairy and food ingredient production, for example, have formed a network that at regular meetings and electronically share experiences with both kosher and halal. This network started as a kosher experience network about ten years ago, but now also includes halal. These companies have appointed kosher and halal coordinators in order to comply with rising requirements, and this network gives them an opportunity to meet and exchange experiences with religious requirements in their particular types of companies. These 'alliance structures' or intercorporate alliances are forms of institutionalised relationships among firms based on localised networks of exchange collective action (Gerlach 1992: 3).

In Novozymes the researcher found halal logos from various certifiers on certificates for raw materials. Certificates state that the products are properly certified and contain all necessarily product information. Logos on products themselves are not very common, as it is not a formal requirement to put logos on packaging or boxes. When logos can actually be found on product boxes or packaging, this is mostly because customers wish to display the logo and thus make it a part of the company's branding (Fischer 2012). In general, Novozymes' customers are not too interested in pursuing the option of having logos on products themselves – the certificate that accompanies products is the central form of documentation and hence qualification.

We were given the opportunity to carry out participant observation at a halal inspection in Novozymes. The halal inspector is the chairman of HFCE. He is also vice-president of the influential halal certification body IFANCA, based in Chicago; HFCE can be seen as a kind of subsidiary organisation of IFANCA in Europe. The inspector was born in Malaysia, where he worked with JAKIM and has been involved in setting up Malaysia's state-regulated form of halal certification since the early 1980s. The mission and objectives of HFCE are to promote the concept of halal globally in the interfaces between Islamic organisations and scholars, Muslim consumers and companies, research and training.

When a company is requesting halal certification an audit/inspection of the production facility is done to review the production processes, ingredients and sanitation aspects of the facility, and this was also the case in Novozymes. Companies must provide necessary documentation and information pertaining to specification sheets, labels, flowcharts, cleaning/sanitation procedures and other production details. A contract is signed between HFCE and the company when there agreement by both parties. HFCE is recognised by JAKIM, MUIS and MUI. It is essential for Novozymes to be certified by a body that enjoys the most widely recognised type of certification. Even if HFCE and IFANCA cooperate closely, they carry out independent inspections at Novozymes. For example, Novozymes' factory at its headquarters in Denmark only has inspections from HFCE, while the company's factory in China is inspected by both MUI and IFANCA. The HFCE inspector explains that kosher is a term similar to halal, but there are many differences; while Islam prohibits all intoxicants, Judaism regards alcohol, among other things, as kosher.

The regular inspections of Novozymes by HFCE take one to two days, during which the HFCE inspector explores the production process. The inspector does not concentrate on the biotechnological details as much as on hygiene in the production process to ensure that no cross-contamination with haram substances occurs. Similar to kosher, these inspections are resource-demanding for Novozymes. However, they allow the company to develop and refine their production methods to comply with increasing religious requirements. For example, Novozymes does not introduce new ingredients or production processes without consulting its halal certifiers about the overall process of qualification. Consequently, these organisations influence the innovation process within the biotechnology industry. Unannounced inspections are allowed, but unsurprisingly Novozymes and other companies prefer announced inspections that they can prepare for and schedule.

The HFCE inspector is more focused on visual aspects of the production processes as well as scrutinising logos, certificates and accompanying documents. The HFCE inspector is well aware that Novozymes has been fully kosher-certified for many years, which limits his main concern to alcohol, and that Novozymes also has very few ingredients and production processes that can be considered problematic. Occasionally, ritual cleansing of equipment in addition to the sterilisation the company does itself is performed.

Similar to what we shall see in the case of Nestlé below, Novozymes is a global and leading company in its field that has chosen to fully comply with both kosher and halal. However, the company has not developed its halal policies and practices in close cooperation with JAKIM, and in the context of ethnic politics and Islamic revivalism in Malaysia this is a main difference between these two multinationals. Kosher certification has helped Novozymes comply with rising halal requirements and the company's coordinator equally divides his time between halal and kosher. The coordinator puts a lot of effort into ensuring that the rising requirements of not only Southeast Asian halal certifiers such as MUI and JAKIM, but also their recognised halal certification bodies in other parts of the world are met. As a global company, Novozymes must generate in-depth knowledge about halal in divergent settings. This point is different from kosher and certification by OU, in that a company such as Novozymes works directly with this organisation and not with any recognised kosher bodies; qualification (how non-meat products become kosher and halal) in the form of certification, standards, staff policies, training and networking meet in this company. Obviously, religion and regulation with a particular emphasis on audit culture is central to the company's history of halal standardisation.

Kosher and halal biotech: food ingredients, enzymes and bio-based solutions

In an industrial estate in Malaysia we visited a European multinational company that produces food ingredients, enzymes and bio-based solutions. The company has specialised in offering manufacturers new opportunities to meet growing consumer demand for halal-labelled products and halal certification plays a key role in this. The company is halal-certified by JAKIM and kosher-certified by OU and therefore OU frequently visits. Inspections often target the introduction of new raw materials and their religious status. For inspections the tendency is that they have changed from being announced to unannounced and this study shows that companies use many resources in order to be constantly prepared for many types of audits and inspections. Kosher regulation in this company is not standardised, that is, frequency and content of inspections are not standardised and the same goes for audit processes in general. Consequently, for a company such as this one it is more complex to translate kosher principles into auditable practices. This brief example shows that kosher is a truly globalised and expanding market and that kosher products, ingredients, technologies, inspectors and ideas travel further and further along not only 'secular' routes, but also in Muslim contexts such as Malaysia. All the company's raw materials comply with halal requirements and thus the certification process was relatively uncomplicated. This is a company in which the application of Islamic audit culture is essential, that is, the way in which this company as a social organisation understands and practises halal.

We are discussing halal in the work of the company with two representatives from the halal committee that is mandatory for halal-approved companies to set up.[2] The first representative is a man who has been working for the company for 19 years. He is a chemistry graduate who was initially involved in production and then shifted to work on implementing system requirements on safety and health and ISO standards on environmental management. The company chose to focus on good manufacturing practices and food safety, which is internationally recognised, instead of the local Malaysian standard for halal, MS 1500 (production, preparation, handling and storage of halal food). The halal committee member is responsible for managing halal compliance and certification, including application for and renewal of certificates with JAKIM. Encouraged by JAKIM, he has also participated in training to enhance knowledge of halal technology and management. In his own words, he is the plant's 'halal manager'. His colleague is a woman who has worked for the company for 13 years: she handles JAKIM halal online registration and certification as well as quality control, product services, product specification and customers' requirements.

JAKIM inspectors visit the company regularly. As in the case of kosher, inspections often target the introduction of new raw materials and their religious status. Unannounced halal inspections that in most cases take about a couple of hours almost exclusively occur when halal certificates are about to expire and renewal is due. A standard inspection or audit is not very detailed, but far stricter if a new raw material or ingredient is animal based. Hygiene and containing risk of cross-contamination is another aspect looked into during inspections. Before or during inspections the company provides JAKIM with documentation in the form of production flowcharts and lists of ingredients used and combined. Flowcharts play an important role in giving inspectors a quick overview. They are important technologies for communicating about halal processes in different stages of production.

When we discuss the company's halal committee, we are informed that it comprises five Malay Muslims, who are 'appointed from executive level'. JAKIM informs the company about training seminars and halal committee staff members have attended a few, but mostly they do not. The focus in most of these seminars is on the process of application for halal certification and the company has more than 18 years of experience with this. The cost of certification has been stable over the years.

One of the major challenges for a company such as this one is that it takes 'too long' for JAKIM to process an application, approximately four to six months. When a new product is introduced, the company has to wait another four to six months to obtain the halal certificate for that new product, the halal committee members explain. Another crucial aspect is to control the halalness of raw materials from a wide range of suppliers. Using the same supplier for longer periods of time simplifies things and ensures the process of qualification runs as smoothly and quickly as possible. The company is faced with two groups of officers from JAKIM: firstly, a group specialising in technical knowledge with particular reference to food. Secondly, another group with an Islamic background is more focused on religious aspects such as the binary halal–haram. In connection with inspections or more informal visits, these two groups accompany each other and divide tasks between them. One of the halal committee members is occasionally invited by JAKIM to discuss technical developments with regard to flavours and emulsifiers, for example. In this way JAKIM tries to keep up with industry innovation and companies can discuss potential innovations with JAKIM before these are finally implemented in production. An important aspect is that company representatives and JAKIM officers not only exchange knowledge, but also develop rapport that helps to facilitate smooth cooperation.

JAKIM's halal logo can be found on boxes and bags with raw materials around the plant. Because of requirements from MUI and other halal certification bodies, it is compulsory to put the halal logo on product labels. To sum up, a company such as this one is, on the one hand, subjected to increasingly strict halal requirements by OU and JAKIM, but they also develop more refined processes to comply with such requirements. Even if the underlying principle behind kosher and halal remains a system of religious precepts and beliefs, religious audit culture is a privileged domain that highlights the interplay and compatibility of varying degrees of standardised forms of kosher and halal compliance, for example with regard to training, establishing the halal committee and raw materials traceability.

A leader in kosher and halal food

Nestlé Malaysia exports its products to more than 50 countries worldwide and the company was the first multinational to voluntarily request halal certification of all its food products when it was first introduced in 1994. This does not imply that Nestlé products in Malaysia were not halal prior to that. The certified halal status for all Nestlé Malaysia products provides assurance that Nestlé products are manufactured, imported and distributed under the strictest hygienic and sanitary conditions in accordance to the Islamic faith. Products and premises for manufacturing have been inspected and have earned halal certification by recognised Islamic bodies. The halal logo on the company's packaging indicates that the products are prepared according to stringent Islamic requirements, whilst assuring that production adheres to the strictest quality and that non-Muslims will also appreciate the high standards (www.nestle.com.my/AboutUs/Nestle_in_Malaysia/Pages/halal_policy.aspx). This empirical study of Nestlé mainly focuses on halal in Malaysia, but kosher is also important to the company.

Nestlé recognised that the OU symbol is the most widely accepted kosher symbol. Nestlé USA and OU have a longstanding relationship that dates back to the Nestlé Foods Corporation that opened in the United States in 1900. Kosher was a priority for Nestlé's initial confections business and established a close relationship with OU. An important aspect of the cooperation between OU and Nestlé is the submission of new ingredients and products for approval to OU office and this office also addresses issues raised during routine inspections with the plant managers. These processes are monitored by Nestlé corporate offices elsewhere in the US in recognition of the importance of monitoring the maintenance of the kosher programme in its plants. To ensure that ingredient and labelling issues are properly handled, correspondence is copied to both the plant and corporate levels. The primary kosher responsibilities of the corporate managers include supervising the implementation of kosher policy at Nestlé, addressing significant production issues, day-to-day management of certified co-packing plants and financial management. The handling of production issues at the plants is a prime example of the importance of good communication between the Nestlé corporate offices, plants and the OU office. Nestlé USA's kosher programme requires significant teamwork and the kosher status for each product is coordinated among many people, including ingredient suppliers, factories, marketing, technical services, quality assurance, legal and regulatory affairs. Each of these groups is responsible for a piece of the process, and their expertise is essential for delivering the appropriately manufactured and labelled kosher product (Orthodox Union 2004).

Advertisements for Nestlé halal products are ubiquitous not only in Malaysia, but also globally. For example, a Nestlé advertisement in 2010 shows a Muslim woman wearing a *tudung* (long headscarf) eating a KitKat chocolate bar in front of a computer in her office with London's Big Ben and the Houses of Parliament in the background. The heading reads, 'Bringing Peace of Mind around the World'. The text states that halal 'benefits everyone' and since the 1980s Nestlé Malaysia has been manufacturing products according to guidelines on halal. This has earned Nestlé Malaysia the recognition as the halal centre of excellence for the Nestlé Group worldwide. Following the text is a clear image of the JAKIM halal logo. An important insight from Nestlé's engagement with halal is that with regard to food, global capitalism has made peace with cultural diversity (Wilk 2006: 197).

In March 2010 the researcher was in the audience for the Fourth International Halal Food Conference held at the Sheraton Hotel in Brussels, Belgium, arranged by HFCE. Islamic organisations, halal certifiers and companies from around the world were in attendance for a conference entitled 'Establishing a Halal Quality Assurance System'. In his Brussels speech, the committee chairman of the Nestlé halal committee (regulatory affairs) explains that the company has come a long way, having taken halal to its global position today. He joined the company in 1988 and has worked there since. He is educated in food technology from Universiti Putra Malaysia and started in the production of noodles and moved on to research and development at the company's headquarters in Switzerland to learn about pasta.

Nestlé established its halal policy in 1992 in close cooperation with the Malaysian state represented by JAKIM. Prior to state institutionalisation of halal in Malaysia, a plethora of Islamic revivalist groups produced halal products without a proper certification process, the committee chairman argues. Islamic revivalism and Malay ethnicity in Malaysia since the 1970s have been major factors behind pushing halal to become a global market force, which Nestlé has a deep knowledge of and expertise in marketing. The committee chairman recalls that he visited Pusat Islam or the Islamic Center in Kuala Lumpur (set up primarily to reduce vice and upgrade Muslim morality rather than regulating halal in a systematic manner) to ask for halal certification.

As a 'human company' with 'social responsibility', Nestlé started to produce halal seriously on a global scale. In 1997 the company implemented a plan that would give customers 'global access' to halal. Nestlé has 86 halal-certified factories globally, the committee chairman shows on his slides, and several standards are in place and to be implemented to increase halal reliability. The company also set up its halal committee comprising senior Muslim executives from various disciplines to be responsible for all matters pertaining to halal certification and training workers on complying with halal standards and auditing Nestlé factories worldwide. What is more, over 1,200 small and medium-sized companies have enrolled in a Nestlé corporate social responsibility mentoring programme that aims to build halal knowledge and skills of productivity, marketing, quality assurance and efficiency measurement. The company's production is certified by JAKIM in Malaysia, while other credible halal certification bodies certify products manufactured outside Malaysia.

The committee chairman explains that 'knowledge' is key in Nestlé's handling of halal and that the following aspects are essential: cooperation with JAKIM; learning from global experience in settings such as the UK; commitment and sincerity; knowledge of raw materials and ingredients; utensils; sanitation/hygiene; food safety; cross contamination; critical Muslim consumers and consumer groups in Malaysia that claim their rights; as well as training of non-Muslims involved in halal. The committee chairman ends by stating that third-party assurance or certification is essential concerning all the points he raised. As a Muslim he always checks labels for halal logos and if no proper logo is to be found on products in shops, especially outside Malaysia, he looks for 'sensitive' ingredients on the labels. All this testifies to how Nestlé as a multinational company has helped shape halal as a global assemblage. Simultaneously, it is also clear how Nestlé as an organisation adapted to rising halal requirements historically, that is, the story of standardisation in this particular company.

After the committee chairman's presentation, a company representative in the audience wanted to know if it was advisable to have logos printed on raw materials. The committee chairman answered that it is often a good idea in order to avoid contamination, especially in connection with the certification of batch production. He passed this question on to the JAKIM representative in the audience, as he would perhaps be better qualified to answer. Halal logos are the visual manifestation of the company's history of certification and standardisation. Another company representative asked why there was no global harmonisation of halal standards. The representative suggested that a harmonisation of standards would make it easier for his company to comply with often conflicting or overlapping understandings of halal. The committee chairman answered that future harmonisation could become a key element, but that it was not yet possible because of multiple approaches to halal understanding and practice. A last question concerned the accepted level of alcohol in industrial processes. The committee chairman replied that alcoholic beverages are not allowed at all and if a company needs to use ethanol only as a processing aid (for example to extract flavour) it must not come from alcoholic beverages. Based on scientific evidence and techniques from labs in Malaysia, the residual limit must not exceed 0.5 per cent and as a 'best practice' Nestlé Malaysia does not use alcohol in its products.

During fieldwork in Malaysia the researcher visited Nestlé's headquarters, which is located in a suburban setting about 15 kilometres west of Kuala Lumpur. We discuss Nestlé's involvement in halal with the committee chairman and a staff member who works in halal production. He was educated in food science in Malaysia and joined the company in 2000. Since his appointment he has been sitting on the halal committee and he is currently involved in developing new halal chocolate products. One of the topics we discuss is the halal committee. It is a requirement for halal product manufacturers to set up a committee and this one comprises 16 Muslim staff representing various departments in the company, including the factories and supply chains. Besides the fact that now this committee has become a legal requirement, it predominantly acts as a focus for sharing halal knowledge and commitment enhancing halal practices within the manufacturing sites. The two representatives explain that the company set up the halal committee on its own initiative long before it became mandatory. Similarly, Nestlé also developed its halal policy before other companies, which gave the company a global advantage.

Nestlé is pleased with the Halal Act, which came into being on 1 November 2011 and contained amendments to the Trade Descriptions Act 1972, providing stiffer penalties for those using fake halal certificates or logos. The representatives argue that in the global market for halal the old Trade Descriptions Act of 1972 is far from effective in protecting halal integrity and that is it unsatisfactory that 'anyone' can declare that their products are halal without serious legal regulation and enforcement. Because Nestlé has such a long history of halal policy and compliance, the company also possesses in-depth knowledge about how the state, and JAKIM in particular, have understood halal over the years, that is, how the leadership has stressed the importance and possibilities in promoting Malaysia as a 'halal hub' on a global scale. The former Prime Minister, Tun Abdullah Haji Ahmad Badawi, for example, was the driving force behind promoting Malaysian halal more generally. In collaboration with stakeholders, Nestlé's status as a leader in halal globally has made the company more resilient. The present Prime Minister, Datuk Seri Najib Tun Razak, has taken halal to greater heights with the establishment of halal parks creating initiatives for industries and especially small and medium-sized enterprises to grow.

Around the world, consumers can find Nestlé products with halal logos on them and the company's design department has great influence on how the JAKIM logo fits in with the design of packaging of products. JAKIM is very flexible about the placement of the logo and its colour, as long as it is put in a 'proper place', that is, where consumers can easily notice it. The logo should not exceed the 'minimum size' and not be placed in any 'obscene' contexts. Over the years, there have been many versions of the JAKIM logo and this has followed more general trends in the design of wrappings for the vast number of Nestlé products. Nestlé's design department also considers how the JAKIM logo fits together with other types of logos on individual wrappings.

Nestlé is experienced when it comes to handling inspections by JAKIM. These inspections, in line with tightened regulation of halal in Malaysia, take place 'very frequently' at the company's factories and each one lasts for up to a day. Inspectors and JAKIM have the 'power to do what they find necessary during inspections', that is, there is not really a standard route inspectors might take. 'We are open and have nothing to hide', the committee chairman says. Normally there is rotation of new inspectors who visit Nestlé so there is no 'personal relationship' between the company and inspectors. Nestlé maintains good collaboration and ongoing work with JAKIM directly or via the Federation of Malaysian Manufacturers and other Malaysian government agencies to further improve the certification process.

What is more, for each application to have a new product certified there is an inspection. While inspections were previously unannounced, they are now 'moving to announced' status. However, what the Chairman calls unannounced 'enforcement audits' occasionally take place. The Nestlé representatives approve of this form of audit culture and they explain that it exists because of a general lack of halal understanding among companies and specific instances where companies purposely or accidentally have failed to comply with halal regulation. This, in turn, has created a form of 'surveillance audit' culture that should be in place, the representatives argue, for companies that have limited knowledge of halal. Conversely, Nestlé as a 'respected' and 'trusted' company that has 'internal halal assurance, logistics management, and a halal committee' has 'disciplined' the company to be 'outstanding' in 'instilling' halal 'discipline' within the company.

Nestlé is a good example of a global company that has adapted to increasing halal requirements in Malaysia and then taken these experiences to a global level. Nestlé's history of standards and certification is also the history of the emergence and consolidation of halal as a global assemblage. So since 1992 Nestlé has not only standardised halal production through JAKIM certification, the company has also itself been rationalised, systematised and differentiated to adapt to modern halal production and regulation. In Malaysia, the state certifies Nestlé's production; imported products produced by Nestlé are certified by IFANCA. These certifying bodies are competitors in the global market for halal certification, and a company such as Nestlé is meticulous about selecting certification that is acceptable in particular regional, national and local markets. We will now discuss halal understanding and practice of companies based in Europe that are certified by JAKIM-recognised bodies. JAKIM cannot possibly certify companies around the world, so it 'outsources' regulation to smaller certifiers such as IFANCA or HFCE. In effect, these smaller bodies are themselves regulated by JAKIM, and as we shall see, this form of 'indirect' certification poses challenges to companies.

Halal biotech: food, health, and animal feed

At the conference in Brussels the researcher met the halal and kosher coordinator of a company that is a global supplier of bioscience-based ingredients to food, health and animal feed industries. More specifically, the company produces cultures and dairy enzymes, probiotics and natural colours. The company is certified by several kosher bodies and halal-certified by HFCE, IFANCA and the Halal Feed and Food Inspection Authority (HFFIA), based in the Netherlands. The company has offices around the world, including Malaysia and Singapore. In the eyes of the company's halal and kosher coordinator and his assistant, kosher certification and regulation is 'extremely efficient' and 'modern'. The company chose to be kosher-certified by OU and also by OK Kosher (Circle K), another leading kosher certifier, as these were seen to be the most reliable choices. For certification of individual kosher products around the world, the company is also certified by Star K, yet another leading kosher certifier. Even if these certifiers are competitors they recognise each other's certificates and this is a big advantage for both companies and kosher organisations and their inspectors. Hence, when inspectors do inspections they can easily spot and approve raw materials, ingredients and products that are certified by these organisations.

The cost of kosher certification is outlined in a contract that was written up when an agreement on certification came into effect. The company pays an annual fee that includes annual routine inspections and there are extra costs in connection with additional inspections. Altogether the company receives four types of auditors/inspectors from ISO and customers, as well as local and foreign authorities. Hence, kosher audits/inspections are only one category among a whole range of others and not really considered to be that different. The main thing for companies is that requirements and regulations are clear so that they can comply with these in order to obtain certificates they can show to their customers. Kosher inspectors from the major certifiers are for the most part properly educated to undertake inspections and oversee the process of qualification.

In this company, most kosher logos are to be found on accompanying documents and certificates and not so much on products themselves. Consequently, audits are at least as important as inspections, as most of the documentation is found in offices or electronically. Some kosher requirements can be 'negotiated'. For example, kosher principles stipulate that if you have produced in a non-kosher manner and will produce kosher afterwards you have to kosherise equipment and leave this inactive for 24 hours before a final scald of the equipment. Unsurprisingly, a multinational company like this one is uninterested in leaving equipment inactive for 24 hours, as this is inefficient and expensive. Hence, the company negotiated alternatives with the rabbinic supervisor from the kosher certification body in question and an alternative and more 'suitable' solution was found. This type of negotiation is often premised on the degree to which the kosher inspector, on the one hand, and the company and its coordinator, on the other, have a personalised relationship. If it is the first time a new inspector has come to the company, the coordinator is not sure whether one can negotiate or not. However, in most cases a suitable compromise is found, 'because inspectors are also businessmen'. An example of such as compromise was when the German certification body Halal Control visited the company and discussed ritual cleansing after the manufacturing of a haram product. The halal inspector suggested that 'clay detergent' was applied to perform the cleansing of the production equipment. The company's engineer protested and argued that clay would definitely damage the equipment. Hence, a compromise had to be worked out: the company now applies standard cleaning to the equipment.

A final example from this company stands out: the kosherness of products is not easily verifiable. The company's coordinator gives evidence that when the OU and OK Kosher rabbinic supervisors visit the factory, they perform the following test: he tastes water in a steam boiler that contains traces of non-kosher material to make sure that it has a bitter and unpleasant taste. This he does to make sure that a bitter substance such as Bitrex (the most bitter substance known) has been added to make the boiler water unpalatable to humans. This type of test can only be done during an inspection and it testifies to the significance of scientific practices that take place on these occasions.

During work with kosher certifiers and companies the researcher found this to be one of the few examples of a test or scientific practice that can verify, and thus move beyond historical/theological principles to determining whether a substance is acceptable or not. A few other tests actually exist that can be used to detect the presence of unwanted ingredients. A polymerase chain reaction (PCR) analysis is an example of such a test. This type of analysis can be used to detect traces of porcine material. Kosher principles and practice in these two companies are comparable to that of Novozymes, that is, companies find it relatively unproblematic to comply with kosher requirements and inspections once they choose to fully comply and transform production accordingly.

Halal certification is essential for this company as a result of demands from customers. The coordinator explained that MUI had 'uplifted' itself to become a form of global authority on halal, in fierce competition with JAKIM and others. More specifically, this means that if the halal certifying bodies that certify the company's production are not on MUI's or JAKIM's list of recognised bodies, the company will have problems in Asian markets in particular. On a number of occasions, MUI has temporarily taken European certification bodies off its list of recognised bodies and this led to a 'tsunami' of concerned requests to the company from customers in Asia. JAKIM is also essential for the company's sales, but mainly in Malaysia, where JAKIM has uncontested authority. Comparatively, MUI's authority is more widespread in Asia and this is why MUI above all is important to the company.

Since the researcher first met the company's senior chemist in Brussels, who is also halal and kosher coordinator, many developments in the area of halal had taken place, especially with regard to the misrecognition of halal certification bodies. During fieldwork at the company's factory the coordinator and a colleague of his also involved in halal and kosher explain that the work with halal started a few years back. When requirements from customers 'escalated', the company discussed two possible halal strategies or approaches: firstly, an ad hoc or 'take it as it comes' approach that included a relaxed attitude towards halal requirements, that is, having individual products certified and not the whole production process. Secondly, a 'once and for all' approach that was ultimately chosen and included having all possible products and production processes halal-certified, in the same way that the company approached kosher. This transition was not overly resource-demanding as only a few raw materials and ingredients were haram and had to be replaced. Being kosher-certified also smoothed this process, as alcohol was the only real concern.

The company has been halal-certified by HFCE, IFANCA and HFFIA, as well as MUI, for some years, but the German certification body Halal Control was also considered for a shorter period of time. This happened when MUI stopped recognising HFCE when the organisation faced internal problems. The company then needed an alternative plan for certification and chose Halal Control as a viable option. When HFCE yet again appeared on MUI's list, the company reverted to HFCE certification for production in Europe and IFANCA certification for US production. As noted, the company is also certified by the Netherlands-based HFFIA for some enzyme products, as some local customers require this. These customers argue that MUI recognises this certifier, the coordinator explains. However, at one point the HFFIA was also de-listed by MUI, but then recognised again at a later stage. The coordinator thinks this is strange as HFCE is also on MUI's list of recognised bodies, and speculates that this is a question of 'market shares and authority' in the global market for halal.

When the workload involved in halal became heavier, more staff became involved in this area. A colleague in the company assists the coordinator and she explains to us that she cooperates with the coordinator and specifically looks into documentation in connection with the large amount of products that need certification. What is more, she tries to 'streamline' and 'optimise' procedures surrounding halal application processes – for example, retrieving product certificates from certifiers and a lot of other 'practical' issues. More generally, staff policies in the company changed when the focus on halal intensified within the last decade or so. The company management, and the marketing manager in particular, needed to make strategic decisions about the cost of transforming production and hiring and training staff to meet halal requirements. It took much more work than they ever dreamt of and this is still the case. As we saw above, the company decided on a wholehearted approach, having as many products and production processes as possible halal-certified, that is, all that could possibly be halal was certified as such. This also meant that locating and choosing certifiers, organising inspections and ordering appropriate documentation were needed. The company also made sure that halal fits into the overall production processes.

Working with halal certification is similar across different types of products. To maintain efficiency it is important that the same approach and procedures can be used in different applications such as dairy production and cultures for salamis, which are in big demand among Muslim consumers in Germany, for example. 'Doing everything in the same way', the halal coordinator explains, is not only easier, it also makes it possible to avoid doing ritual cleansing that takes up valuable production time when halal and non-halal production meet. What is more, complying with halal in a concerted way standardises halal production procedures and this is a general trend in highly specialised pro-duction processes where halal is only one question among many others, such as avoiding allergens. This is an important point because it shows that when companies such as this one go wholeheartedly into halal, they actually set halal standards that are not based on requirements from consumers or certifiers.

The coordinator and his assistant made it explicit to the various halal certi-fiers that requirement for Muslims to be involved in the production processes would not necessarily be the met. Instead, the company argued that ISO stand-ards and quality assurance ensured that production meets halal requirements. In response, the company was offered a one-day training course by Halal Control in Frankfurt, Germany, on how to handle halal as a non-Muslim com-pany. The company accepted the offer and participated in the training, which proved to be educational for both certifier and company. From companies and certifiers the researcher learned that there is now a common understanding that outside Southeast Asia certifiers are well aware that requirements about employing Muslims are sensitive and even illegal. This is an example of the way in which certifiers and companies negotiate important issues in the glo-balised market for halal – and that training can play an important role in this.

When the company was first halal-certified and awaited its first halal audit/ inspection, the inspector asked if the company was kosher-certified. When the coordinator confirmed that this was the case, the inspector was pleased because, as he explained, there are so many similarities between halal and kosher. Actually, halal certifiers often see the Jewish system of kosher certi-fication as a model for the institutionalisation, standardisation and certifica-tion of halal. In the eyes of the coordinator and his assistant there is a major difference between working with kosher and halal certifiers. Kosher certification and regulation is 'extremely efficient' and 'modern'. Efficiency for the company, for example, means that Circle K's kosher communication is digitalised so that on Circle K's website the company can list the product that contains this or that raw material. Circle K then sends the certificate electronically the following day. This makes this process unproblematic as Circle K knows about all the company's raw materials. What is more, Circle K also updates certificates once a year and contacts the company's suppliers so that all raw material lists are fully updated. Conversely, halal certification is less efficient. Several of the certifiers the company has worked with are slow to respond to important enquiries about acceptance of new raw materials for instance, and there are often errors in their processing. The coordinator explains that other companies face similar problems. He knows this from discussions in the kosher/halal network, where discussions about religious requirements in their type of production take place.

When the HFCE inspector inspects the company he is most of all interested in any changes in production that may involve non-halal products or ingredients. There is a big difference between halal inspectors and the way in which they inspect – some are thorough and systematic, while others seem unqualified and focused on issues that do not have anything to do with halal. The general tendency is that when inspectors are not educated in food technology or biotechnology they tend to focus on 'standard' issues instead of the particular production process. Kosher inspectors from the major certifiers are for the most part properly educated to do inspections. Normally, a halal inspection takes about half a day and it is always announced, but in principle it could be unannounced. This means that the company is highly prepared for these announced inspections and during the researcher's stay at the company's factory he was given the tour that inspectors normally take. During inspections ingredients lists covering acceptable ingredients are also discussed. These lists are normally valid for one to two years.

Until MUI started regulating, halal requirements were 'fluffy' to say the least. Before the company was halal-certified and could get a standardised certificate from a certifying body it would send out a simple questionnaire for suppliers to fill in, which asked questions about ethanol, gelatine and raw materials. At the time, the answers given by suppliers were sufficient, but this was far from the case when halal 'standardisation' emerged. Now MUI 'outsources' the regulation of standards to its recognised halal bodies in Europe. Comparatively, there are more kosher logos than halal logos to be found in this company.

The material from this company shows how religion, science and technology are fully compatible in the market for biotech products. The difference, however, is that while halal is being promoted by the state in Malaysia, a European company such as this one must set up its own forms of self-control to live up to halal requirements that originate in Southeast Asia. These requirements are then outsourced to European halal certification bodies to enforce in connection with production in Europe and this complicates processes of certification, standardisation and hence qualification. The ethnography from this company shows that not only is kosher important for halal understanding and practice, kosher is also seen as a model or ideal in terms of efficiency that some halal certifiers could benefit from being inspired by.

Discussion

Even if global kosher and halal production has been regulated since the 1990s, the need for human oversight remains essential and standardised inspections and auditing show that principles and practices only become compatible during inspections. Besides the obvious theological underpinnings, modern kosher and halal principles are also about traditions that are handed down irrespective of technological development. Kosher and halal qualification takes many forms and it is premised on complex understandings and practices of certification and standardisation in a variety of overlapping and divergent contexts. Logos help to personalise kosher and halal exchange or transaction, that is, ideally the producer, trader and consumer all share the symbolic content of the kosher logo that emerges through qualification processes. Certifying bodies not only claim authority in these transactions but also try to instil in companies the naturalness and reasonableness of the instituted rules. Thus, companies and their procedures have become more auditable and in practical terms this involves formalised procedures of application and negotiation with a certifier, for example. Auditors and inspectors collect and analyse evidence in order to form conclusions, but evidence is always relative to the rules of acceptance for particular communities, as we have seen it in the case of personalised relationships between inspectors and coordinators. Standardised practices put in place to comply with kosher principles are to a large extent applicable in the context of halal regulation. The more kosher and halal proliferate as globalised religious markets, the more scientific modes and methods of production and traceability become important for producers, traders, certifiers and consumers. The increased focus on such methods to verify commodities as kosher and halal constantly expands the requirements to cover new types of commodities and practices. Both religious authorities and companies are increasingly relying on scientific evidence in the regulation, innovation and proliferation of kosher. The empirical material shows that in the eyes of companies the proper education and qualifications of inspectors are more important that religious authority. A central aspect of audit culture is the pushing of control and self-control further into companies to satisfy the need to connect internal organisational arrangements to public ideals through ongoing processes of qualification and requalification. Many companies argue that even if requirements and control have intensified, halal is more professionally regulated and standardised today compared to the unclear and confusing requirements of the past, and that this trend is comparable to kosher regulation.

It is clear from the above that a multitude of divergent kosher and halal understandings are now being overshadowed by processes of standardisation, and that companies themselves are rationalised to deal with these challenges. Kosher and halal as religious injunctions influence the social organisation of business, that is, how companies understand and practise halal requirements as social organisations. We have explored kosher and halal in the histories and cultures of companies and also webs of interpersonal networks linking different people in different constellations for different intents and purposes. To conclude, in relation to transnational governmentality we need to distinguish between Denmark, the UK, the US and Asia in the empirical examples above. In Denmark religious enzyme production fully relies on forms of standardised transnational governmentality, with certification and supervision solely carried out by transnational certifiers such as OU and HFCE. For other non-meat products, we saw in Chapter 2 that the Jewish Community/Danish Rabbinate and Chabad are involved in supervision and certification. For kosher, the UK non-meat market is regulated by both local organisations such as MBD and transnational certifiers, whereas the halal non-meat market in the UK has not yet seen the same level of attention from national certifiers and instead these activities are carried out by transnational organisations such as HFCE and IFANCA.[3] The Malaysian case study shows that for kosher this area can be regulated by OU in that no or few local Jewish organisations are operating in Muslim-majority Malaysia, but for halal this is fully regulated by JAKIM. In sum, we can say that with respect to non-meat kosher and halal manufacturing by multinational companies, an expanding system of transnational governmentality with complex processes of qualification has developed over the last two decades or so.

Notes

1 An enzyme is 'a substance that acts as a catalyst in living organisms, regulating the rate at which chemical reactions proceed without itself being altered in the process'. Enzymes also have valuable industrial and medical applications, for example the fermenting of wine, leavening of bread, curdling of cheese and brewing of beer are reactions understood to be the result of the catalytic activity of enzymes. Enzymes have assumed an increasing importance in industrial processes that involve organic chemical reactions (*Encyclopedia Britannica Online*, Academic Edition).

2 The purpose of this committee is not only to ensure the halalness of products, but also to reduce the risk of non-halal contamination, that is, the committee is a form of standardised Muslim risk management (Fischer 2015b).

3 IFANCA was founded in Illinois in 1982 with the objective of increasing awareness and understanding of Muslim dietary requirements; standards and regulation; scientific research related to food; and nutrition and health. It provides halal supervision and certification for many companies worldwide.

4

Kosher consumers

In this chapter we explore how Jewish consumers in the UK and Denmark understand and practice kosher consumption in their everyday lives. As we noted in Chapter 1, several studies deal with how diverse groups of Jews in the global diaspora negotiate kosher principles and practices. For example, dietary practices provide a common symbolic system through which the increasingly heterogeneous notions of Jewish identity in Denmark can be expressed, and one way to reinforce one's Jewish identity is by keeping kosher (Buckser 1999). Similarly, for Jews in suburban Canada keeping kosher signifies the creation of a Jewish lifestyle, building religious observances and practices (Diamond 2000, 2002). Among Jews in Brazil kosher observance and practices help maintain identity vis-à-vis other ethnic groups, but kosher is also a contested question that marks the diversity present in the Jewish community (Klein 2012). These studies show that many Jewish groups are fastidious about their everyday kosher consumption and this point has reinforced regulation of global kosher production and regulation. It is this literature that this study feeds into.

A specific focus in this chapter is how consumers make sense of the issues raised in previous chapters, that is, buying/eating meat and non-meat products in a changing global context. Another important theme explored is how Jewish consumers understand and practise their everyday (kosher) food consumption in our two case countries: as we have seen, the market in the UK is not only large and expanding, but also more integrated into the global market for kosher. This is different from the case in Denmark, where there is only one kosher shop in the entire country and where the purchase of kosher products on the Internet or bringing food back from abroad has greater significance. Among our mostly middle-class informants we explore to what extent they are focused on kosher as specific forms of standardised 'qualities' in their everyday lives (Callon *et al.* 2002). We also explore how 'compound practice' (Warde 2016) links eating with issues such as health and spirituality, for example, and with the influence of secularism and ritual. It soon becomes clear that all our consumers are acutely aware that they living in a world where kosher markets are globalising. Even the most 'secular' of these consumers must relate to and negotiate the larger issues we explore in this book: kosher as formative of distinctions between individuals and groups in everyday life; the specific national and local contexts that frame their lives and 'kosher globalisation'; including how transnational governmentality (Ferguson and Gupta 2002) frames their everyday choices and how they must practice more self-discipline when deciding what is and is not acceptable (Wouters 2008).

This chapter and the following one on halal consumers are organised so that in each chapter we start out by discussing consumers who are very observant about kosher/halal, moving gradually towards the less observant or relaxed consumers at the other end of the spectrum. The first part of the chapter explores kosher consumption in the Jewish community in Manchester in the UK before we turn to Denmark. All our empirical material from interviews, informal conversations and participant observation was obtained in these locations.

Kosher consumers in the UK

Yaakov, now in his early sixties, was brought up in a traditional, middle-of-the-road, Jewish family from Manchester and Salford in the 1950s and 60s. He lives alone in north Manchester. As a student in London in the 1970s he left the Jewish community and became totally non-observant, but that after divorce from his first wife in his late twenties his mother sent him to Israel to study Hebrew and he became Orthodox again. He then attended Yeshivat Aish Hatorah ('Fire of the Torah') school in Jerusalem and became extremely Orthodox. Today Yaakov is a well-known Jewish historian, lecturer and public relations consultant, with a PhD in Jewish history from the University of Manchester.

Kosher, for Yaakov, means that animals have to be what the Torah accepts as kosher, so cows, sheep, goats and poultry, for example; kosher fish have to have fins *and* removable scales. The processing of food also has to be kosher, he points out, and kosher is not just about raw materials. Yaakov notes the 'complicated Jewish legal' rule of 'nullified in 60', *battel b'shishim* in Hebrew, to illustrate the problem of unacceptable ingredients. He explains, for example, that if one drop of milk is accidently dropped into a huge pot of chicken soup, as long as there is more than 60 times the volume of soup than milk the soup is fine. However, this rule does not apply in production, as Yaakov states; 'If you know in advance that there is a mixture of non-kosher to kosher or milk to meat, then the rule does not apply.' It only applies 'ex post facto', if the event occurs by accident rather than by intent. Discussing enzymes, Yaakov points out that every single food additive has to be listed before a product can attain kosher certification. He has heard that there is now a global database shared by all the *kashrut* authorities worldwide, which lists all accepted additives and enzymes; consequently, if something comes up during production that is not in the database, it has to be replaced with something that is it fit for use.

In the mid-1980s Yaakov worked as the first Orthodox Jewish race relations adviser in local government for Hackney Council in London. He provides a brief anecdote of his work training the council's 'Home Help' service to illustrate the nature of kosher shopping skills. During the training he would visit a kosher grocery store in Stamford Hill in North London and take things off the shelf to show his trainees acceptable products certified by rabbinical authorities or any of the major *kashrut* organisations. He would also point out that going to Tesco, for example, required more attention, and that if a product didn't have an appropriate seal or *hechsher* a customer or client might refuse it; in this sense, he argues that being a kosher shopper is 'a bit like being a detective'.

Yaakov eats meat at least twice on Shabbos [The Sabbath] and on Jewish festivals (*yom tov*) such as Passover. On a typical Friday night and Saturday evening he might have a fish course, chopped liver or chicken soup, followed by a main course of chicken or meat (lamb or beef), followed by a pudding or something non-dairy; depending on his income at the time he might have meat again during the week. However, he only eats *glatt* kosher, including that from MH, as most of their meat is *glatt* by default; he points out that *glatt* chickens are called 'split-back chickens', which refers to the process of cutting open the carcass to facilitate a more comprehensive salting to remove any traces of blood, which is forbidden in the Torah.

Diseases such as foot and mouth, he argues, only effect older male animals, and as kosher slaughtering in the UK is not carried out with animals more than two years old it's highly unlikely that any BSE or foot and mouth problems would arise in kosher-slaughtered animals. He doesn't agree with the way geese are treated to make *foie gras* and here he stresses the ethical laws of Judaism – *tsar baalei chaim* – another biblical commandment not to cause unnecessary pain or distress to animals. He tends not to eat veal because of the way young animals are forced fed to produce white veal; he also buys free-range eggs.

Health is a different matter and Yaakov notes that there is an expression in Yiddish – *chazer b'halacha* – that roughly translates as 'he's a pig within the laws of *kashrut*'. The implication, he points out, is that while one can eat kosher food every day one might still be eating the wrong things. Health thus has nothing to do with kosher on this understanding, but he quickly counters this with the recognition that if you have an allergy to some kind of dairy product, for example, or a nut allergy or sensitivity, then kosher regulatory practice is actually very helpful. When kosher says its *pareve*, he states that there will definitely be no meat or dairy in it. For Yaakov, non-Jewish consumers such as vegetarians and vegans thus form a big part of the kosher market.

Yaakov eats out very occasionally and he points out that there is now a good choice of kosher restaurants in Manchester. When he first moved back from London in 1991, there was only one kosher restaurant and one 'dodgy takeaway', which said it was kosher but wasn't actually supervised; today there are probably around ten supervised kosher restaurants, cafés and takeaways, as well as the many shops and butchers. To some extent he suggests that this is because the community has grown, but he notes that younger generations seem to have more money and tend to like dining out more than older people did; he also points out that this is part of the trend towards middle-class sub-urbanisation, even within the strictly Orthodox community.

Because the observant sector of the community is becoming more strictly Orthodox, Yaakov contends that the number of kosher customers is growing. However, he contrasts this with the argument that the less observant section of the community is less concerned than they once were about kosher, and thirdly that because regulation, production and inspection are all better than they once were it is much easier to get the required information.

Peter is an accountant in his thirties living in Prestwich in north Manchester. Married with three children, he attends a local synagogue. He was educated at a prominent Jewish school in London and moved to Manchester with his parents after he left school. He then spent two years in Israel before studying for a degree in history and philosophy at the University of Manchester, where he met his future wife. Peter argues that food is kosher only if it complies with the Jewish dietary laws of *kashrut*. The family applies this in the home, where they have a kosher kitchen with two sinks, two dishwashers and two ovens to keep it 'neutral for meat and milk', and also outside the house when they go to a restaurant. All the places they eat must have a certificate stating that the food is formally kosher, and *kashrut* is thus central to their everyday food practice.

Peter thinks the laws of kosher and *kashrut* have always been the same and that if you are brought up in an strict Orthodox family you know what it is by default; he also acknowledges that some Jewish people will say they 'keep kosher', but will be nowhere near as strict as he is. Some people will, he points out, eat fish at non-kosher restaurants and avoid any meat-based items to cover themselves. As Peter states, 'being a bit more Orthodox, for us it's important that the restaurant actually has to be kosher'. To the same extent, he notes that some people only keep kosher on the Sabbath. For Peter, however, kosher is all-encompassing. When he organises family events, for example, or entertains clients at work, he always orders the food from prominent kosher restaurants in his own neighbourhood. Having children also reinforced his desire to pass knowledge of kosher on to the next generation.

While at one time understandings of food were quite simple, 'you know, meat was meat, bread was bread', Peter suggests that today food products have so many ingredients that production is more associated with science and biotechnology than at any time previously. He argues that this has in turn increased the risk that people consume products containing unacceptable ingredients, as is the case with certain E numbers; it follows that people attempting to 'keep kosher' thus have to be more careful than they once were. Science is thus much more important in food production than it once was, he claims, and young people are stricter 'than they were 50, 60 years ago'.

Peter thinks that kosher meat is less susceptible to problems that emerge from food scares such as the horsemeat scandal and he states that 'If it's kosher it's kosher.' Certification is more important with meat than any other kosher food, he argues, primarily because meat has high status and also because of what it symbolises. Stunning, he suggests, is non-negotiable and meat has to be produced 'the Jewish way or no way'; the family's favourite meat is chicken and mincemeat. Bread is also seen to be important and Peter notes people washing before they have bread and saying special blessings, especially at Passover.

He also points out that it is much easier to check what is kosher these days than it once was and therefore much easier to shop kosher. Peter gives the example of the kosher guide from the London Beth Din, as well as iPad and iPhone apps, where he can check a product instantly. He suggests that with over 95 per cent of the products the family buy, they either know what they are because they check them in this way first, or because they buy them from a kosher shop; this is central element of their everyday practice and a skill set that is developing all the time. Peter occasionally shops for kosher food at supermarkets, where some acceptable products, bottles of grapefruit juice, for example, which has ritual status, are much cheaper. He doesn't believe it's essential for kosher products to be produced by Jews, just so 'long as it's got the right stamps on it', it's OK. To the same extent, Peter indicates that as an Ashkenazi Jew, he eats Sephardi food and that it is the overall process of production rather than the actual producer that is important.

When they eat out with friends that are not as strictly religious as they are, he notes that they are always understanding and will go to a kosher restaurant. However, while there is great availability of kosher food in Manchester, Peter argues that the only sphere where kosher is limited compared to London is when eating out, particularly in the city centre. He argues that in London the choice is much better and that people demand better quality; he identifies kosher Indian, kosher Chinese and kosher Portuguese restaurants in London, and suggests that New York is also on a higher level than London when it comes to choice.

While traditional Jewish food isn't the healthiest, Peter says it is difficult to summarise because a lot of Jewish people eat Sephardi foods that are much healthier and contain lots of rice and vegetables. He has never bought halal food unless it is also kosher-certified. The family sometimes buy organic and they know that 'kosher organic' is available in America, and perhaps in the UK as well. His likes Ashkenazi-type dishes such as chicken soup and stews, which people often have on a Friday evening with bread, but says his favourite kosher dish is either steak or Chinese sweet and sour chicken.

Food consumption, for Peter, is a direct reflection of piety: 'I think it's a very important part of it actually … people say blessings before we have the foods, you know. You shouldn't be sort of gluttonous.' This is a big part of the community and he notes that a lot of Jewish events are based around food. Nevertheless, Peter thinks that kosher is far too expensive, over-commercialised in a sense, and that a lot of people make a lot of money out of it because it's a massive market. He links this to the politics of certification and suggests that cost is often about specialisation. As noted, he sometimes shops at supermarkets, particularly at Hanukkah and Passover, when he finds that they undercut kosher shops on some items. In general Peter suggests that when it comes to religiosity, some people get more religious as they get older, whiles others become less so. He notes that a lot of people also become more religious because of worldly concerns, which he recognises as a current trend within Judaism, including in Manchester.

Leonard is in his early sixties and lives in the Jewish community in north Manchester. Brought up in a non-religious background in Gateshead, he notes that his early life had no religious component. Although his family attended a local synagogue, he describes himself in his early years a 'three times a year Jew'. This changed when he met his wife 30 years ago. Her family were Palestinian Jews and Leonard's future father-in-law was very strict, taking animals to a *shochet* personally to observe that they were slaughtered cor-rectly. From this point onwards Leonard became religiously observant, and once married he moved to Manchester with his new wife. After a short spell in Israel, they moved back to Manchester, where they have lived for the last 25 years with their 23-year-old daughter. Today Leonard attends a local syna-gogue three times a day, or as often as work permits. He believes that the fam-ily is the major route for knowledge of kosher to be passed on and maintained across generations.

When it comes to kosher, Leonard describes himself as fairly Orthodox. He keeps Shabbos and a kosher household, but suggests he is 'sensible' in his dealings with people in the outside world; while he doesn't hide his Yiddish identity, he doesn't thrust it upon other people either. For Leonard, kosher food often includes products that are not certified as kosher, but which are on 'a list' of acceptable products overseen by organisations such as MBD. As well as uncertified products found in local Jewish shops, this can include natural foods like fruit and vegetables. Processed foods are seen as the big-gest threat to 'keeping kosher' because of the variety of ingredients and addi-tives involved, which is why 'the list' is so important. He gives Kellogg's Corn Flakes and Walkers crisps as examples, but counters this with recognition that some people he knows will only eat cornflakes and crisps from a Jewish manufacturer. He believes that all major food and most household products include things that are kosher and things that are problematic. Leonard recognises that enzymes can pose problems if they are of animal origin, though he argues that medicines made from gelatine are often so far removed from their original state that it may no longer matter; he counters this with the suggestion that his rabbi would be better placed to speak about these issues than he is. The key to 'keeping kosher', he argues, is to keep oneself abreast of current developments.

Leonard believes kosher supervisors in food-processing factories are effectively responsible scientists conducting *halachic* work to prevent spiritual contamination and maintain the boundaries of the permissible. While it is permissible to eat food cooked by non-Jews, he argues that food should really only be prepared by a Jew, and that meat is the key kosher food because of its status. He eats a little chicken, though not too much because of health considerations, and some fish every week. He notes that questions are often raised about what kinds of fish are allowed and that the number of kosher vegetarians is increasing, even within Orthodox Jewish circles. This can be because of health concerns, he argues, but also because the cost of meat can be prohibitive, particularly in restaurants. Consequently, while vegetarian products don't usually have certification, he believes that they should be checked in the same way as meat.

Leonard mentions a number of different certification bodies in north Manchester, including Shefa Mehadrin, Badatz Igud Rabbonim and MBD, but suggests that many strictly Orthodox families will not go near these bodies and prefer MH in Manchester or Kedassia in London. Leonard notes that kosher is a massive business and he thus often takes the political claims of each certification body 'with pinch of a salt'. Whilst recognising that kosher certification and consumption can be taken to extremes, and be over-commercialised in some instances, he argues that you cannot be 'too kosher' when it comes to meat and processed foods. When friends invite each other out for Shabbos meals he points out that in extreme cases some people will only attend if the meat is certified by MH or Kedassia. As far as he is concerned, however, 'kosher is kosher'.

He believes that *shechita* is the most effective way of slaughtering animals and he is not surprised that the current political situation has led to bans in some parts of Europe. While he has kept kosher in the same way since he met his wife 30 years ago, he believes political affiliations are growing and becoming stronger within the community overall. Discussing the complex state of kosher certification in Israel, he suggests concerns over kosher certification are more about 'social groupings' than anything else. Here he makes reference to different ethnic groups, how Sephardi Jews, for example, are permitted to eat certain type of locusts, but that as an Ashkenazi Jew he is not. He argues that

114

this is because historically Sephardi Jews are closer to 'the source' of Judaism than Ashkenazi Jews. Despite these differences, he says that with meat it generally 'just comes down to the *kosher* authority', and that this 'can be illogical sometimes'.

Since the horsemeat scandal in 2013, Leonard has noticed an increase in the number of non-Jewish people buying kosher meat, even though it's much more expensive; he believes this is because they see kosher as more trustworthy and because 'it is what it says on the tin'. He has also noticed Muslims buying kosher and argues that halal production is probably less strict than kosher production. While Orthodox Jews would never consume halal, he suggests that what he calls 'middle-of-the-road' Jews might, depending on the circumstances. Leonard recognises that his own strictness has often led to a bad diet, particularly when travelling and working away from home, and that this may have led to personal health problems. Also, while kosher food can be a healthier food option, he notes that lots of sugar is used and that making food 'kosher' does not necessarily make it healthier; his family eat organic 'fruit and veg' if available.

There are a couple of kosher restaurants in north Manchester that Leonard takes his wife to occasionally, primarily because he trusts the people running them and because they have a good reputation. He also mentions a kosher-certified Chinese restaurant and the availability of kosher pizza in north Manchester; his favourite food is fish and chips. Leonard believes that public institutions in Manchester are generally well catered for. He gives the example of North Manchester General Hospital, which provides certified, packaged kosher meals (supervised by the Manchester and London Beth Din, and Kedassia approved), and Salford Hope Hospital, which has a Shabbos room. There are also numerous Jewish schools in north Manchester, he points out, which provide their own kosher catering. On the Sabbath, because cooking is forbidden, a meat stew called *cholent* is kept warm on a low flame from Friday evening onwards; this stew, he opines, which can also be vegetarian, is a stereotypical Jewish food. Leonard associates kosher with what is permissible to eat according to Jewish law, but also thinks that 'life is meant to be kosher all the way through no matter what you do'. Overall he suggests that 'the whole kosher thing is about trust and supervision'.

Adina is in her twenties and comes from a Sephardic background; her mother's family come from Greece and her husband's family from Syria. Married with two children aged five and three, she works part-time as a teacher in a local infants' school in Prestwich in north Manchester. She moved to Manchester from London when she was six months old. Because she believes that one can always 'grow' as a person in Judaism in all areas of life, Adina states that she tries to do her best at all times and to be to be 'observant' as she can whenever she can, which she argues can be challenging. She gives the example of when she is out and about in 'town' feeling hungry, smelling tempting food, knowing that she will have to wait until she gets home to eat. Reflecting on this, she says that she feels privileged and lucky that she can 'keep kosher': 'I do look at it in a way that it's good for me and improves my quality of life, my spiritual quality of life. So some people buy organic foods or the more expensive options of foods to improve their quality of life, so I'm looking at kosher in that sort of way that is good for me.' She also recognises that some people are a lot stricter than she is. While Adina buys a lot of food that doesn't have kosher certification, including things like rice and tinned products, if she's not sure about something she asks her rabbi or contacts MBD to get a trustworthy opinion.

Kosher, for Adina, refers simply to food that meets the requirements of the Torah. She says that she doesn't know all the requirements because she's not a rabbi, but that the family tries to 'keep kosher' as far as possible. They have a kosher kitchen, which means that they don't mix meat with milk, and don't cook or eat them together. She recognises kosher animals and non-kosher animals and gives the example of the pig as non-kosher, because although it has 'split hooves' it doesn't 'chew the cud'. In Judaism she says this situation is not and cannot be contested, and that she trusts and relies on certain rabbis and community leaders in Manchester for information, which would be the same wherever she lived; she recently phoned the helpline at MBD to check whether a fruit bar was kosher. Adina thinks that school is important for learning about kosher, but that there are now also useful helplines and websites. However, she tries to get by without using the Internet. She adds that just because something says that it's kosher on the label doesn't necessarily mean that she will eat it. Manchester is well catered for when it comes to kosher food and she thinks the range and choice is increasing.

Adina buys fresh kosher meat at the Shefa Mehadrin Super Deli on Bury New Road in Prestwich and believes that all meat must come from animals slaughtered by Jews. She thinks kosher meat is safer than non-kosher meat and she has never really been influenced by food scares or scandals. The family eat chicken once or twice a week and maybe some beef; lamb is kept for special occasions and they try to maintain a healthy diet by avoiding fatty meat and foods with too much sugar. She doesn't look for organic or Fairtrade products, but every now and then she buys Fairtrade bananas because they're being sold and also because she thinks that 'fair' trade 'sounds like a good idea'. The family sometimes buys 'Chalak Beit Yosef' – a type of 'glatt' kosher meat – from a butcher's on Leicester Road, which has to be pre-ordered from London: the LBS introduced Chalak Beit Yosef about 25 year ago to replace the Machzikei Hadas brand, and while it was initially associated with Sephardic Jews it is now bought more widely. The family also shop at Halpern's on Leicester Road in Broughton because it has a wide range of kosher food, including fruit and vegetables, which are all kosher; at this point, Adina's five-year-old daughter, present throughout our interview, states that Daddy has just gone to Halpern's. The family often avoid fruit and vegetables from Israel when they can't be sure that the law of *shmita*, which requires the land of Israel to be left fallow every seven years, is being followed. Adina doesn't avoid products from Israel necessarily, but she prefers kosher products from America; dealing with these issues requires a certain level of skill and understanding of the market.

Adina trusts the kosher brands and the meat certification at the places where she shops, but indicates that there are kosher brands at other shops that she is far more wary of; price is also an important consideration in her everyday kosher practice. She notes that the local Sainsbury's and Tesco supermarkets both have an isle of kosher food and a isle for halal food, both in Prestwich and in nearby Cheetham Hill; they also have fridges with kosher cheese, milk, falafel and smoked salmon, but Adina rarely shops at these places. She thinks that Muslims who keep halal will eat kosher, but that many Jews will not eat halal, though she suggests that this probably depends on availability and so works by degrees. She also recognises that kosher food is more expensive than other foods, but argues that 'you get what you pay for'. When she goes to a supermarket and sees the price of non-kosher food products she points out that she sometimes thinks 'wow, that looks so cheap compared to what I pick'. Whilst recognising that for some people kosher is about more than food, for her it's just about the things the family consumes. She buys kosher-certified Colgate toothpaste and while she understands that some people may find this excessive, she thinks that 'some people just prefer it'.

Adina will eat food that is not cooked and prepared by a Jew just as long as a Jew oversees the overall process. She does most of the cooking and she believes men and women are equally interested in kosher. The family only 'eat out' at friends' houses they trust 'kosher-wise', and who accept that they are very careful about what they eat. While there are some great kosher restaurants in north Manchester, she indicates that the choice is not endless and that the family don't eat out that often; when they do they might go to Milky Dreams on Bury Road or JS on Kings Road, which is certified by MBD; when they eat out, 'value for money' is one of the most important considerations. Their children's school is kosher and Adina says when she's been in St Mary's Hospital in Manchester pre-packed kosher meals produced by Hermolis (which she has also had on British Airways) have been available. Salford Royal Hospital also has Jewish rooms and provides kosher food. Adina thinks kosher is something you learn at an early age through your family, but recognises that some people, including her parents, learn about kosher during their lifetime and thus start to keep kosher as they get older; she feels lucky that she was born into it and has always kept kosher.

Simon was born in London in the late 1960s and brought up in an Orthodox family. His father was born in London and his mother was born in Antwerp in Belgium; he is married with five children. He spent most of the formative years in London and only came to Manchester when he was 16. He then did a did a couple of years at medical college and two years at a college in Israel, before getting married and finally settling Manchester about 15 years ago; he now works as a manager in a kosher shop in the community.

For Simon, kosher literally means befitting, so something that's not kosher would be something that's not fit to use or eat in line with the commandments and stipulations laid down in the Bible for different types of foods. The best-known stipulation, he argues, is that Jews are not allowed to eat pork, but he points out kosher dietary laws also do not permit the mixing of meat and milk, for example, which is a less well-known Jewish practice. He also notes that today kosher is much more complex than it once was. Up until 40 or 50 years ago, he points out, production processes were far simpler, primarily because there was no mass production of things like yogurts, for example. Back then 'you let your milk go off … and it became yoghurt. Today, scrap that, you know there's no natural yeast in it and the problem then becomes, from a kosher perspective, what's the source of the yeast, what's it grown on', for example.

The shop where Simon works sells unsupervised milk and he notes that this provides a good example of understandings about different levels of kosher practice and observance; while some people think that milk from Sainsbury's is acceptable, others don't. This is because there are certain things that are perfectly acceptable in English law but which perhaps aren't so in Jewish law. In English law, for example, antibiotics make the milk-producing animal healthy and, once the antibiotics have cleared, the milk is safe, while in Jewish law the cow is now considered seriously ill at this stage. Relating this back to observance, he claims your level of observance depends on what you want to consume and what your level of acceptance is. He points out that while on his last family holiday to Scotland they took milk, frozen raw meat and their our own bread machine, some people will only go on holiday to places where there are kosher shops, often because they've got a number of children and they're worried about how they are going to feed them when they're 'away from civilisation'. Other people just go to Israel, or to places like Florida or California, he suggests, where there are fully kosher hotels.

When we discuss food scares, Simon points out that cows in kosher production are much younger for a number of reasons, including the fact that because all meat is salted it is tougher and producers must therefore start with younger animals; he argues that to some extent this practice protects kosher consumers from some of the problems that occur in the food chain, from BSE for example, which only develops in older animals. Of course, there are other complexities with kosher production, he argues, and as a consumer he has to make his choice, like everyone else, on the certified agency stamp on the package he is looking at. For Simon, these choices lie at the heart of all kosher food practice.

Simon points out that things get very complicated at Passover, when people seem to make a slightly larger effort to keep kosher. This has implications for the shop, as there are often complications between what European Jews and those of Sephardi origin can eat at this time, particularly around rice and vegetables. In the same way, he notes that certain brands appear only around Passover and that most people's diets at this time are basically gluten-free. He also identifies a move away from smaller UK brands to a preference for mass-produced American brands, but suggests it's hard to tell what people really want, why they consume the way they do, and what motivates their practice overall; people have complex motivations and complex shopping skills.

Simon and his family don't eat much meat. This isn't for any philosophical reasons, he argues, just because the family find it 'very heavy'; occasionally they will eat chicken. He argues that workers needed to eat meat in the past because they required a lot of strength for manual labour, but that because we now live relatively sedentary lifestyles we no longer need the same amount of meat, or the calories it provides. He points out that customers in the shop often ask for free-range eggs and that this presents a complex set of issues; when it comes to animal welfare, for example, from a kosher perspective, the whole point of practising kosher comes to the fore, as an animal will not be accepted as kosher 'if it has a broken bone or a bruise'. To some extent, he argues that this issue is therefore illustrative of the influence of a growing market for animal welfare-friendly products in the UK and beyond.

While food was supportive of the community in the Middle Ages, when 'people were not allowed to buy meat from another town', Simon argues that today this type of practice occurs in only very small villages, the implication being that kosher has to a large extent moved away from its traditional base as a Jewish community practice.

Elizabeth and David have lived in Didsbury in south Manchester all their lives. They are both in their late sixties and have been married for 37 years; they have five children, who have all moved away from Manchester. They believe that in general, knowledge of kosher is passed on in the home, or at school, and they explain that their children have all experienced different degrees of 'keeping kosher' in the families of their new husbands and wives, from strict Orthodox to not very observant. The couple have always kept a kosher home and indicate that they are 'pretty observant' or 'Orthodox', particularly when it comes to food. They separate meat and milk and use separate sets of crockery and cutlery for each. They eat lots of fruit and vegetables and suggest that they have noticed a slight increase in kosher vegetarians in recent years, primarily they think because the price of meat is so high, but also because it's easier to be that way. They try to avoid food containing too much fat or sugar and while they realise that kosher is now seen as a healthy food option, they also recognise that this is often not the case with traditional kosher foods, particularly those favoured by older generations. In general, they don't eat any meat outside the house unless they are absolutely sure where it comes from, although they accept that some people are 'more diligent' than they are; with non-meat items they are careful outside the house to different degrees, depending on the occasion.

To the south of Manchester, kosher meat is available only in Cheadle and the couple generally shop in the north of the city, where there is more choice and competition between kosher businesses; south Manchester is said to be 'more expensive' because there is less choice. The bigger community in north Manchester, with its kosher establishments, restaurants and shops, is seen as the foundational part of the Manchester Jewish community. Some years ago, a south Manchester rabbi told them about a butcher in 'the north' who sold less expensive, independently certified meat and they have been buying meat from this butcher ever since; such insight is central to their everyday practice and it allows the couple to observe and practice kosher as they see fit. They don't eat a lot of meat, but they usually have chicken and beef (sometimes steak) on the Sabbath on Friday evening or Saturday lunchtime; lamb is more of a treat and they sometimes have fish. In general they see meat as 'a bit of a luxury' and because it's expensive they don't eat huge amounts; they indicate that meat has the highest status of all kosher foods. David indicates that certification is critical for meat because it confirms that an animal has been killed and treated in the right way. They accept *shechita* as a given practice, but insist that they don't want to know more than they do about animals being killed.

While kosher means different things to different people, they suggest that in south Manchester when people say they 'eat kosher' it usually means they only 'buy kosher meat'. They argue that in general people aren't as Orthodox in south Manchester as they are in the north and that when it comes to food other than meat it all comes down to individual choice and what people have concerns about; they give the example of chocolate and state that this type of product doesn't have to be supervised as far as they are concerned, but that for those with a stricter understanding of *kashrut* it might have to be. As long as food is vegetarian most people in south Manchester think it's safe to eat. At the same time, however, they note that if they are entertaining 'very religious people' they tend to go down 'the very kosher route'. They also draw a distinction between Sephardi Jews, with Middle Eastern origins – who prepare meat with pulses and vegetables, for example, to make it go a long way – and Ashkenazi Jews, who eat more European meat cuts.

If the couple want to eat out, they occasionally go to JS, a kosher restaurant in Prestwich in north Manchester where they can 'eat in peace' without being overly concerned about things like gelatine; they also note the availability of kosher sushi and pizza in north Manchester. While the distinction between Sephardi and Ashkenazi is not as strong as it once was in south Manchester, they point out that the kosher market in Manchester is still segmented in line with the different requirements of different Jewish groups.

Elizabeth thinks products with very small amounts of questionable ingredients are fine, but states that she avoids products where certain e-numbers are listed. The couple don't mind who produces kosher food as long it has appropriate certification and they often buy such products from Tesco in north Manchester; they also look out for 'kosher bargains' in Tesco, though admit they don't find many – a recent bargain was kosher-certified margarine. They opine that in north Manchester the Jewish community is expanding because of an influx of 'big Orthodox families' from London looking for 'affordable property'. With more children going to Jewish schools these days than previously, they also suggest that many Jews are becoming more influenced by their children than they once were; because Jewish people are frightened that they might be assimilated and lose their identity, Jewish education is becoming much more important than it once was, with children influencing their parents' attitudes to kosher indirectly. They often encounter stricter people at weddings and other events and state that guests often won't eat the meat provided by kosher catering companies for various reasons, including because 'it's not "glatt"'.

They also mention what they call 'kosher-style' food, which is not kosher-certified but is acceptable because it is the 'sort of food that Jewish people eat'. They suggest that this type of food is often more available in London and America, and they give the example of chicken soup, or something that you 'might make at home' as being 'kosher-style'. Kosher-style food is often available at parties and events where people can't afford to go down the full kosher route, with the people who attend usually knowing and accepting this in advance. They think that the politics of kosher certification can get a bit tiring, particularly when things change every year; they give they example of the Chocolate Mars Bar, which at one time was acceptable in London but not in Manchester. They also refer to 'kosher wars' and suggest that things get very intense around Passover, when different groups get very particular about kosher supervision and prices increase 'wildly'. In general, Elizabeth and David associate kosher with good supervision, 'with food that has "biblical authority"'. They suggest that products can be checked with organisations such as the London Beth Bin if there is any doubt, but that what is and is not acceptable changes all the time because 'the food industry is so complicated'.

Marc is in his late sixties. A retired photojournalist of Sephardi stock, he was 'born and bred' in Manchester and is married with two children. He attends a local Orthodox synagogue in Didsbury three times on the Sabbath and also on holidays and during festivals. He was brought up in a kosher home and suggests that he still tries to keep as much of the tradition as he can, but that he has to a large extent gradually been assimilated; he describes himself as 'pretty relaxed'. The family do not run a kosher household, he points out, primarily because his wife is secular and against any type of religious dogma; he also states that it would have been impossible to lead a harmonious married life if he 'kicked up a fuss about kosher food all the time'. Once or twice a year he visits his sister's home nearby, usually during holidays and festivals, to eat in a 'completely kosher household'. In an ideal world he thinks that knowledge of kosher is passed on in the home, through Jewish newspapers and at the synagogue under the influence of local clergy. As he states: 'You know, if you live within a Jewish community it's part of your life, like growing up, it's like talking.'

For Marc, kosher food is that which is produced in accordance with 'halachic' or Jewish law under the supervision of an individual from an organisation such as MBD, the local Jewish court of law. He states that this is a very complicated process that he is not 'fully versed' in, but that he does know the basics. While Jewish law never changes, he argues that definitions or interpretations of the law does sometimes change. Marc personally does not eat pork or shellfish, either in the house or at a restaurant, although he accompanies this with the statement that he is 'not concerned' whether he eats in a kosher or a non-kosher restaurant; occasionally he might visit the kosher restaurant JS in Prestwich, north Manchester, if he 'really feels like kosher food'. In general he notes that most Jewish areas will have a Jewish butcher, a Jewish baker and/or maybe a 'full-on Jewish grocery store' where kosher products are available. However, in south Manchester he points out that most Jewish-owned shops and family businesses have closed, whereas in north Manchester there is never a problem getting kosher food. Shops are supported by communities and if there was strong enough support for a kosher food in Didsbury he suggests that there would still be 'one or two shops open as there used to be 20 or 30 years ago'.

While there are different levels of observance amongst Jews, Marc thinks that there is common understanding about kosher wherever you are in the world, and that if people keep kosher they are Orthodox to some extent; as he understands the edicts of ruling authorities, a product cannot be kosher if it contains even a minute quantity of a questionable ingredient. Kosher he argues is all about tradition, but it has also proved itself to scientifically sound in a lot or areas, he believes, including hygiene and animal slaughter. Kosher food does not have to be produced by Jews, just in the right way, as Marc states: 'I don't think it makes any difference if they're employing gentile workers to do the work as long as the work is done according to the law.' Shopping for kosher is done in line with different levels of observance of what is and is not considered kosher, and he suggests that for him there is no difference buying something like butter or margarine from a regular shop or from a kosher shop with all the kosher guarantees in place, notwithstanding the price. If he eats with Jewish friends who are observant and have kosher households he will eat the kosher food that's on offer, while his gentile friends don't prepare anything for him that has pork, shellfish or crustaceans in it.

Marc's wife buys meat from a variety of sources and although he isn't a big meat eater, he prefers chicken and steak. Certification of meat does not come into the equation, simply because his wife does not keep a kosher household.

Although people argue that to stun an animal before slaughter alleviates some of the pain, he argues that the whole process is over very quickly whichever way it is done. While he doesn't consider himself an 'absolute moral idealist', he suggests nonetheless that his meat-eating habit and all that follows from it does mean that he thinks about such issues; he doesn't want animals to go through any unnecessary suffering and, when 'all's said and done', the traditional Hebrew way of dispatching livestock is the quickest and most humane method he believes. Whilst food scares affect us all, Marc argues that the kosher market is somewhat isolated from other supplies of farm animals, but he thinks problems probably occur somewhere.

When Marc was a schoolboy in north Manchester, at lunchtime he was taken by bus to a kosher canteen in Higher Broughton that fed Jewish pupils from schools all over north Manchester, primarily, he argues, because there was no thought of providing special foods in schools as they do today. While there are more special and state-funded Jewish schools today than there were then, Marc still thinks that there could be more provision for Jewish pupils in state schools. In general he thinks that kosher food tends to be fresher and not so pre-packed; he points out that observant Jews will not be seen eating in McDonald's or Burger King, that most will buy their food locally and that it will therefore be fresher, but not exclusively so. Most kosher food is by definition organic, he argues, but he is not sure about the additives that go into it. While kosher food is always more expensive, he argues that in general you get what you pay for and that kosher is often good quality, though not always.

His favourite food is a 'good 24-hour stew' and occasional pastries. Although he is very relaxed about kosher, Marc is very clear that kosher food is a reflection of both piety and community: 'If you've got a community that is a Jewish community it's got to have kosher food. Kosher food can't exist without the community.' He reiterates the points that this has now changed in south Manchester and that unless one goes to north Manchester for kosher products, the nearest shops to Didsbury are a little bit further out from the city in Cheadle and Hale in Cheshire. He suggests that most families who attend his synagogue today and consider themselves Orthodox generally don't follow kosher food laws, and that in south Manchester the Orthodox Jewish community is shrinking and cannot therefore support kosher shops any longer. Although not politically active, Marc supports Israel publicly on marches and demonstrations if he feels the need, or if he receives an e-mail from the Zionist Federation to protest against something.

Kosher consumers in Denmark

Naomi is a woman in her mid-fifties who lives with her husband near Copenhagen. She has a son and a daughter and is currently self-employed. Naomi grew up in Israel and moved to Denmark in the early 1980s when she married her first husband. Her parents were born in Palestine within a family originating from Eastern Europe. While her mother's family was Orthodox, her father was a communist and Naomi 'navigated' these two worlds and eventually chose to sympathise with the Orthodox religious side because it 'felt right' in terms of kosher food, songs, spirituality, rituals and family traditions. Naomi recalls that as a child her grandmother would stress that a contaminated teaspoon should be buried in the garden in order to kosherise it. Experiences and memories like these reflect Naomi's belief that the physical world, including food and drink, is symbolic in that it represents something bigger and more spiritual. Naomi thus says a blessing before consuming food and drink, acknowledging that these practices are just as much about spirituality as they are about everyday nutrition, and a prayer of thanks after consuming a certain amount of food or drink. With specific reference to kosher, Naomi considers herself Orthodox and fastidious, but not 'extreme', arguing that she accepts many types of kosher logos and that this would not be the case for ultra-Orthodox individuals and groups. Most of all, Naomi recognises kosher certification by Badatz (a major Jewish rabbinical court). She is a vegan and this fact makes her everyday food consumption in Denmark easier.

At the age of 12 Naomi started to identify with her grandmother's family and to stringently keep kosher. This posed a challenge for her mother, who 'expressed love and affection through food'. Moreover, the family purchased plates made of glass – such plates have a hard and impenetrable surface that can easily be cleaned. She kept the kosher rules the best she could: waiting six hours after eating meat before consuming dairy products. At the age of 17 Naomi moved to Paris for one year and even though she went to a Jewish school that served kosher food she stopped keeping kosher in this quite different context. She moved to Denmark at the age of 22 in connection with marrying her first husband. She quickly adapted, undertook higher education and lived a regular Danish life, though always with spirituality as a basic core. Five years ago she started studying Kabbalah (Jewish spirituality and cosmology). After six months she realised that these studies are meaningless without physical practice. Thus, Naomi embraced Orthodox Judaism and started observing all the Jewish living instructions, including keeping kosher. Keeping kosher in the Danish context was reinforced by a stress on Jewish culture, religion and consciousness.

Studying Jewish theology and *halacha*, as well as Kabbalah, Naomi realised that spirituality was at least as important as her secular education. In a broader perspective, Naomi argues that while the Jewish Community in Denmark is focused on identity and not so much on religion and kosher observance, Machzike Hadass, Copenhagen's Orthodox Jewish Community, represents true Orthodox values. Chabad cooperates with both communities and is physically situated near Machzike Hadas. Thus, Naomi's reorientation also included contact with Chabad and its rabbi, Yitzi, whom Naomi knew through her Orthodox son. Yitzi helped Naomi set up her kosher kitchens: one is for milk cooking and the other for meat. These two kitchens also have separate sets of utensils. Because Naomi is a vegan, Yitzi stated that this was the easiest kosherisation he had ever performed. More generally, Naomi consults her son or the Internet, if she is in doubt about products and ingredients.

Naomi explains that in her everyday shopping for food in Denmark certain skills are essential. Most of all she looks for proper kosher logos such as that of Circle K on chocolate. Moreover, there's a list of approved products and ingredients issued by the Jewish Community in Denmark. In addition to this list, which Naomi does not always agree with, she uses apps and googles specific products and ingredients to find them on other lists around the world. Again, being a vegan makes this process easier. There are not many kosher logos to be found in shops in Denmark, so Naomi looks for E numbers that can tell her about the acceptability of products. She states that in Judaism insects are considered to be even more problematic than pork. Hence, E120 (a colouring agent called carmine extracted from an insect found on cactus in Mexico that adds a ruby-red colour to drinks, for example) is completely unacceptable. Occasionally, she will go to the Copenhagen Kosher & Deli to buy things like chewing-gum and Mentos, but also to support the business.

She refers to the dogma *bishul akum* (literally, food cooked by a person not required by the Torah to keep kosher) when arguing that in general observant Jews are not allowed to consume food prepared by non-Jews. However, certain raw foodstuffs such as fruits and greens are allowed even if they are cooked by a non-Jew. Because wine and grape juice have a ritual status in Judaism she is careful when buying them and does so either at Copenhagen Kosher & Deli or via the website www.kosher4u.eu, where a wide variety of kosher products are available at reasonable prices. This is also where she buys grape juice and bread for Passover. Even as a vegan she feels that ritual slaughter is acceptable and that it's more humane than industrially slaughtered stunned meat.

In terms of home cooking, Naomi, like most other Orthodox Jewish women, she argues, is responsible for shopping and cooking. More generally, every new kitchen item must have a hard surface and if a non-Jew produces it must be kosherised. This is done in a *mikveh* (a bath used for the purpose of ritual immersion in Judaism) that can be found under the little synagogue of Machzikei Hadass in central Copenhagen, which is under strict *halachic* supervision. There is one more *mikveh* in the Jewish House at the major synagogue on Krystalgade and ritual immersion in the sea will also suffice. Naomi tries to avoid genetically modified (GM) products and she doesn't really go out to eat or drink in restaurants because there are no kosher eateries in Denmark. She once took her own kosherised cup to a café as this allowed her to have tea there. When visiting Jewish friends and family, she accepts the food when she's reassured about their knowledge of keeping kosher.

Naomi believes that keeping kosher is healthier not only spiritually, but also physically: for example, she states that drinking milk separately from and before eating meat lowers the risk of colon cancer. Naomi contends that enzymes should be kosher in order for processed food products to be kosher. She also believes that some products manufactured by Muslims are acceptable, that *bishul akum* is not compromised in this sense, especially when kosher is unavailable, but she states that such products must be controlled and must not contain meat or milk.

Sara is a woman in her thirties who lives with her husband and two children in Copenhagen. She studied social work and now works as a team coordinator. Her husband is not Jewish, but he is a vegan, which makes food preparation and consumption easier in the household. As a child, Sara's mother, originally from Germany, taught her about keeping kosher. Sara describes herself as being quite observant about kosher: to keep kosher and avoid *treifa* (non-kosher). For the 'meat side' she keeps regular kosher and for the 'dairy side' she also keeps *chalav Israel* (dairy products supervised by observant Jews) and thinks it's important to do so. The difference between *chalav Israel* milk and regular milk from a kosher animal is that the former is supervised by an observant Jew while the latter is not, even if both are kosher according to *halacha* (Jewish law), she explains. In the eyes of Sara, keeping *chalav Israel* is a good thing, it's an extra stringency, but not keeping it does not mean you are eating something *treifa* (non-kosher). *Chalev Israel* products are not available in Denmark, so Sara buys long-life milk in bulk at www.kosher4u.eu. Sara only eats bread and cakes on a kosher list issued by a Jewish community.

As a child, Sara ate what was served at school, but as her mother stressed that she could eat only a vegetarian diet she never ate meat with other children. As Sara got older and started to earn a living herself she became increasingly focused on keeping kosher. When we discuss the sources of Sara's kosher knowledge she explains that she grew up with a relatively strict kosher understanding; when she embraced vegetarianism in her twenties, she suggests, everyday shopping and consumption became a lot easier. Keeping kosher was reinforced during her studies at a religious school in Israel, where she learned a lot about keeping kosher and becoming more observant.

Sara's children eat meat from Copenhagen Kosher & Deli and they bring their own food to school. Sarah states that this type of observance becomes complex when her kids are invited to birthdays and other occasions with their friends: even if the parents of their friends are aware of their kosher dietary requirements and seek knowledge about this, Sara normally arranges for her kids to bring their own food. Similarly, the kids will bring their own sweets to celebrations and these are normally bought via www.kosher4u.eu like many other products. Even if halal sweets were more readily available in Denmark, Sara would not buy them. She also has concerns about vegetables and the risk of insect infestation and checks and rinses vegetables thoroughly.

Central to Sara's kosher understanding and practice is the availability of authentic kosher logos and she is willing to pay extra for products bearing such logos. To Sara, food items can be kosher even if they do not have a *hechsher* (kosher certification). The selection of certified kosher products is better in Swedish supermarkets compared to Denmark, although kosher-certified Heinz ketchup and peanut butter are available in Danish supermarkets. Sara explains that going shopping in Denmark in particular requires knowledge of E numbers such as E120 and she feels that the selection of products carrying proper kosher logos could be better. Because of their kosher observance, Sara and her family do not frequent restaurants. With regard to takeaways, Sara feels that this could also be better, although the delicatessen has started such a service. Everyday meat consumption in the family is modest and mostly consists of sausages and chicken. With regard to the question of stunning, Sara relies on the authority of kosher certifiers, that is, meat can only be kosher if kosher slaughtered without stunning. Sara and her husband both cook, but because her husband is a vegan she's in charge of meat preparation.

Sara has designed a kosher kitchen in the family home, a small flat. The kitchen has limited space so this required careful planning: the main part of the kitchen is for milk and there is a small area for meat. The main part consists of a sink, a countertop and a cooker. The cooker has a built-in oven, but this is used only for food that is *pareve*. So if Sara cooks a potato dish in the oven it can be eaten with a meat or dairy side dish since the potato dish itself is neither dairy nor meat and can be used for both; fish is not eaten with meat, though. The meat area has one countertop and one cabinet for utensils. In addition, Sara has a small oven that is used for cooking chicken, for example, and a set of separate burners for cooking meat. They also have separate utensils used only for meat. This design accommodates both kosher and vegan sensibilities. None of the food her husband eats is cooked with the utensils used for meat preparation.

Sara considers kosher healthier for these reasons: divine rules in the Torah signify health even if these are beyond human comprehension; it's better for animals to be kosher-slaughtered because stunning prolongs the process; and, thus, kosher slaughter makes meat fresher. Organic kosher meat is difficult to find, but for vegetables Sara prefers and buys organic produce as a healthier alternative. Even if halal slaughter is comparable to kosher, Sara does not consider halal-slaughtered meat acceptable or healthier because *shechita* (slaughter according to Jewish law) rules are somewhat different. If vegetarian processed products such as falafel are not kosher-certified she prefers certification by the Vegan Society to halal certification, which she has limited knowledge of because it's another 'religion-based criterion'; she also notes that some brands of falafel can be on kosher lists even if they don't have a *hechsher* on the package.

When we discuss whether enzyme production should be kosher-certified, Sara states that even if she didn't know that a large part of enzyme production has been kosher-certified since the 1990s she fully supports this development. With regard to non-food products such as leather she does not believe that pig leather, for example, warrants kosher certification, as leather is not eaten and one is allowed to derive benefit from some things even if they aren't kosher – as is the case with leather. However, one should not derive benefit from something that is a mixture of meat and milk. Consequently, while it is possible to wear a leather jacket made from pig leather, Sara suggests that pets such as dogs should not be fed a dish of mixed meat and milk. Sara stresses that the family uses a brand of toothpaste that is on a kosher list. For Pesach (Passover) she will buy a new toothbrush and only use toothpaste that has a reliable *hechsher* on the package, though she notes that other families are not as strict as this.

Hannah and *Benjamin* are a couple in their mid-sixties who live in a flat in Copenhagen. They have three children in the US and Israel. Benjamin was educated in civil engineering and Hannah as a pharmacist. They keep kosher as much as they can, based on their knowledge, and have done so since childhood. Benjamin explains that you either keep kosher or you don't – there's no easy option. The couple go about their everyday shopping for food in several shops, including the kosher delicatessen, and also at supermarkets, where they look carefully at labels. Benjamin feels that it's helpful that proper labels are statutory in Denmark and can easily be checked and that 'there's no excuse for not keeping kosher'. In particular the couple look for animal contents and potential new ingredients and also consult the list of approved products issued by the Jewish Community in Denmark, even if it's not always updated. Hannah is lactose intolerant and this makes her more alert when shopping for food and drinks. The couple recall an incident in a local supermarket when they looked at the label of a wine produced in South America and were surprised to find that it contained milk, which also surprised the rabbi they consulted. Generally, as long as the Jewish Community rabbi approves E numbers, the couple rely on this decision.

Meat is bought only at the local delicatessen and they explain that their children in the US and Israel have an easier time shopping for meat in markets with much better availability compared to Denmark. They consider only non-stunned meat kosher and this can be found only in the delicatessen, where they also buy cheese. However, they bring cheese back from the US or Israel when visiting their children. They also accept the cream cheese Philadelphia that is produced using microbial technology and not rennet (a complex of enzymes).

All available kosher logos are accepted in the delicatessen and the couple do not prefer particular logos to others; they have no issues with vegetables as long as they are washed thoroughly. At Passover 'everything' is bought at the delicatessen, even if prices are higher there. Because of relatively high prices and the restricted availability of kosher, their meat consumption is limited: meat is mostly eaten at weekends and when guests are over. It's mostly Hannah who shops and cooks, but they both possess knowledge of E numbers, for example, that can also be looked up on smartphones over the Internet. In general, the couple explain that they rely on the judgement of the rabbi of the Jewish Community as well as experiences of other Jews in Denmark.

They feel that it would be convenient to have more kosher availability in Denmark – for example, frozen foods at the nearby supermarket. Even if halal products are widely available in nearby shops these in no way present an alternative to kosher. Benjamin argues that generally 'the kosher slaughter is halal, but not the other way around', and Hannah recalls a Muslim boy in their son's school whose father was an imam who accepted kosher. In the eyes of Benjamin and Hannah kosher is an expression of religious observance and not 'political' support of Jews or Israel.

Both Benjamin and Hannah think that keeping kosher is met with understanding in Denmark – for example, when Hannah is meeting up with her old schoolmates the menu is sent to her beforehand and she is always offered fish. In their workplaces kosher dietary requirements are also taken into consideration. Going out to restaurants is far more complex, and when they do go out to eat they usually have boiled fish, as Benjamin explains: 'We would not accept barbecued fish because you never know what's been on the grill before.' However, they do accept the eating utensils when they go out to eat, and Hannah explains that if they didn't 'they could never go out'. In their kosher kitchen there are five sets of utensils: one for guests; a set for milk and meat respectively; and an identical double set for Passover. Jokingly, Benjamin explains that installing two dishwashers was confusing to the plumber.

When discussing whether keeping kosher is healthier, the couple make the case that they keep kosher out of belief and not because of health concerns. However, they feel that kosher may actually be healthier and that this point has been backed up by scientific evidence recently. Benjamin: 'I'm not sure whether this is based on facts or not … At sports competitions in hot climates athletes do not eat molluscs such as snails or shrimps to avoid the danger of food poisoning.'

With regard to the relationship between food and non-food products, the couple has one dish brush for milk, one for meat and one for *pareve*. All brushes should have nylon bristles and not bristles of animal origin. Similarly, hand soap without any animal ingredients is used. At Passover kosher toothpaste is brought home from the US or Israel after visiting children. However, when we discuss the necessity of San Pellegrino mineral water being kosher, Benjamin and Hannah agree that this is not really necessary. They speculate that if living in the UK, for example, they would probably accept and thus buy a wider variety of kosher products – also because prices are generally lower in the UK. They are familiar with the UK kosher market because Benjamin's sister lives there.

The couple are relatively pragmatic when it comes to the significance of having enzymes kosher-certified and they point out that very small quantities of unknown substances are generally seen to be acceptable; but Benjamin also states that when it comes to medication gelatine is not essential. When we discuss the limited nature of the kosher market in Denmark compared to the huge and growing global market, Benjamin is quite knowledgeable, as he once conducted kosher supervision for one of the major Danish multinational companies. However, the couple note that in countries such as China, which they have visited as tourists, there is still very limited kosher availability; when they were in Shanghai they therefore relied on the local Chabad chapter's hospitality.

Theo is a man in his early eighties who lives with his wife in central Copenhagen. He worked as a researcher until his retirement. He has also researched the relationship between ethics and Jewish law. His family is originally from Poland and migrated to Denmark in the early twentieth, whereas his wife's family is from Denmark. He explains that quite a number of Jews live in this area of Copenhagen because it's within walking distance of the synagogue and that Jews who keep kosher are also those that go to the synagogue and observe Shabbat. In terms of self-description, he would classify himself as Orthodox when it comes to kosher observance. Conversely, his grown children who live in Israel with their families are far more fastidious when it comes to kosher and they will only consume *glatt* kosher. His children would never simply buy food in a regular shop, and when they visit the family home in Copenhagen they might bring their own milk, for example. Theo's parents did not keep kosher and his personal observance of kosher only developed when he was about 40 and his children started Jewish school in Copenhagen. Before that time kosher was mainly about pork avoidance.

He drinks milk produced in Denmark, whereas local cheese is more problematic: he only buys kosher cheese from the local kosher delicatessen. Rennet (a complex of enzymes) is an essential part of cheese production and traditionally rennet was produced in calf stomachs, but today this can be produced artificially using microbial technology in laboratories. Consequently, kosher cheese is produced using kosher rennet catering for Jewish consumers like him and his wife. In general the couple agree that enzymes for food production should be kosher and they thus support kosher certification of companies such as Novozymes. Theo explains that there's little actual knowledge about the ethics of schechting, that is, to what extent scientific knowledge can help address the question whether religious slaughter without stunning can be considered humane to animals. He fully trusts the local rabbi's position that emphasises that only non-stunned meat can be considered kosher. With regard to seafood, the couple would never eat Atlantic wolffish or shellfish, for example, while it is not quite clear whether turbot is acceptable because of its spike.

Even if there are next to no kosher-certified products in Danish supermarkets, he trusts milk and butter without kosher logos. Food production should ideally be supervised by a rabbi to ensure that products do not contain pork or any other unwanted ingredients; ice cream, for example, can be problematic because of whey. Vegetables can also be of concern because insects can be hiding inside: insects are 'absolutely' not kosher except for a particular species of grasshopper; he speculates that this exception has to do with food scarcity at the time Jewish food laws came into existence. When the children visited the family home recently a dish with salmon, Greenland halibut and green asparagus was served, but the children felt insecure about this because of the asparagus.

In general, Theo's kosher consumption relies on Jewish law and not on the support of Jewish producers. However, because there is only one kosher shop in Denmark, Theo and his wife buy all their kosher products there and they also recognise the need to support this shop. He argues that it does not help matters when Jewish consumers start importing meat on their own or buy it over the Internet; even if prices are high, so is the quality, and he acknowledges that you always have to pay for quality products. In general, kosher from the delicatessen is to be enjoyed at the weekend and when friends and family are around.

He argues that as a Jewish consumer in Denmark you definitely have to develop certain shopping skills: 'Suddenly there's gelatine in rye bread and E120 in Fanta', he explains. You have to know about E numbers such as E471 that can be produced from natural fatty acids and E120. The Jewish Community in Denmark has developed a list of kosher and non-kosher products and ingredients and he notes that the Internet is a valuable tool for looking up E numbers. He rarely asks for advice from local rabbis, as he wants to take responsibility for his own choices and preferences. The basic Jewish food laws laid out in the Torah and *halacha* are 'crystal clear so there's nothing to discuss', as he puts it.

All the meat eaten in the home is bought at the local delicatessen – mainly chicken, veal, beef and minced meat. It's mostly his wife who is responsible for cooking in the couple's 'kosher kitchen', only certified kosher food is allowed in the house and the entire kitchen, eating areas, dishes and utensils are kosher. The couple has three sets of utensils: one for milk and milk-based dishes, one for meat and some tools for *pareve* (which cannot be considered neither meat nor milk). Similar sets are used specifically for Passover.

For celebrations and religious festivals in particular, kosher has greater importance – not only because of the religious festivals themselves, but also because at these occasions friends and family gather. When the children visit from Israel they used to serve food on paper or plastic plates to accommodate their standards. At times, the children are not in agreement about kosher requirements and Theo explains that this is where he draws the line and calls for compromise.

Occasionally, the couple go to restaurants and when they do so they have fish or vegetarian dishes. They make sure that food is served on proper plates and not on a wooden plate, for example. Plates must have hard and impenetrable surfaces so that non-kosher content cannot have caused pollution. There are no proper kosher restaurants in Denmark, but the congregation in Copenhagen employs a cook that prepares kosher food in the community centre next to the synagogue. The couple are well aware that they have been 'difficult' over the years in relation to their food and social life with non-Jewish friends. Typically, friends serve fish in their homes and do their best to accommodate kosher requirements, and when friends want to bring 'unspecified food' to their home they explain that this is not really acceptable in a kosher kitchen. In this case, the couple have to balance 'food and friends', but challenges are always worked out. The couple always took their own food to work.

As to whether kosher food is healthier than non-kosher, Theo states that the food of Eastern European Jews tends to be fatty and unhealthy – proper, but unhealthy, kosher food. As a child Theo had that kind of food, but since then the couple have changed their diet and it is now more 'green' and 'lean' with less meat; they have introduced a day each week where porridge is on the menu.

Theo envisions a difficult future for the kosher market in Denmark and eventually the availability of kosher food for the Jewish community may decline, with Orthodox Jews being 'driven' out of Denmark because of limited availability. There were once many kosher shops in Denmark after the waves of Jewish of migration in the early nineteenth century and in the 1970s, but there is now only one shop left in the entire country. When buying meat in this shop the couple are not particularly concerned with kosher logos – everything in the shop is acceptable to them. Generally they buy only meat there, but around Passover 'everything' has to be kosher, and even instant coffee is available at the shop. It is also at this shop that they can buy sweets for the children.

When we discuss kosher in connection with non-food products, Theo explains that this is not really important, except perhaps for toothpaste during religious festivals, but if they were stricter he suggests it would be wiser to live in Israel, the US or the UK. Another example of the importance of non-food products is that toothbrushes and dish brushes should have nylon and not animal bristles. He does not accept halal for the simple reasons that the prayers pronounced during kosher and halal slaughter are different and kosher slaughter must be performed by a *shochet*. In his eyes there are 'basic' differences between kosher and halal, but he is of the opinion that most Muslims would accept kosher.

Rosa is a woman in her forties who works in a private company. She is married to a non-Jewish husband and has two children who attend the Jewish

132

school. Rosa moved to Denmark 17 years ago from Eastern Europe and describes herself as a 'convenient Jew', that is, in the eyes of Rosa 'kosher is an individual and flexible choice' mainly focused on pork avoidance. Having children at school increased the family's focus on 'kosher life'. Her son takes kosher seriously and strictly avoids pork and for this reason Rosa stopped eating shrimp and mussels herself – she knew this was important for her son and she respects his preferences. However, ritual slaughter and the question of stunning is not important to the family. Thus, Rosa to a large extent experiences 'kosher living', and the fact that this is expensive in Denmark, through her children. Moreover, because of their special preferences the kids will bring their own food to the Jewish school.

Rosa recalls a conversation with a Jewish friend that puts her own kosher priorities into perspective: the friend told her that her son wanted to taste pork and that she was strongly opposed to this. However, being a 'convenient Jew' Rosa did not impose her views and fully accepts that everybody should follow their own path without dogmatism: choosing 'super-Orthodox kosher living' can only apply to oneself and others must find their own way. She states that in Denmark most Jews are flexible, while a smaller group prefer 'kosher forever', which can be a complex choice in the Danish context: kosher is expensive, hard to come by and kitchens and fridges are not designed for kosher, for example. When her son's strict friend visits their home food is served on a paper plate and the friend enquires about 'what's in this or that dish?' or 'what's been in the oven previously?'.

Even if Rosa sees herself as a 'convenient Jew', the idea of supporting Israel through shopping or consumption appeals to her. For example, once she noticed Jaffa oranges in a shop and she felt that it was natural to buy these in support of Israel, even if this is not a consistent choice in her everyday life. Rosa's flexibility with regard to kosher is also apparent in that she often goes to particular supermarkets to buy organic and non-kosher meat – it is virtually impossible to find organic kosher meat in Denmark and she also goes to halal butchers if these have been recommended by Muslim friends. In general, Rosa prefers organic produce to kosher. Rosa recognises that there are many similarities between kosher and halal and the family also accepts halal sweets if they can find them. This flexibility also means that she does not really think that being a Jewish consumer in Denmark requires certain skills.

More generally, Rosa explains that the majority of the Jewish community has been 'assimilated'. If Jews in Denmark send their children to Carolineskolen you're part of that community even if you do not go to the synagogue or Chabad. Rosa once attended a kosher cooking class at the Chabad house, which she found really interesting. The course, taught by Yitzi's wife, gave her an insight into the 'kosher lives' of others and refamiliarised her with Jewish dishes such as chicken soup. Even if Chabad represents dogmatic and ultra-Orthodox Hasidism for Rosa, taking the cooking class made sense.

If the family wants to buy specific kosher products such as wine gums that are not available in ordinary stores, the brand Goody Good Stuff can be bought at 7-Eleven; for products that are unavailable in Denmark they use www. kosher4u.eu. In general, shopping and cooking is divided between Rosa and her husband. If the family has a celebration Rosa or her husband will ask Jewish guests about specific food preferences beforehand, but she will cook fish at these occasions rather than buy kosher meat at the delicatessen. Being flexible about kosher also allows the family to go to restaurants in Denmark, and Rosa explains that if she was stricter about kosher she couldn't do the job she does, which involves extensive travel – often on the Sabbath.

Rosa believes that separating milk and meat makes kosher healthier and that this is a principle that applies to diets in general: protein and milk should be separated as they naturally represent separate chemical processes, yet she states this does not apply to eating steak and cheese together. Rosa does think kosher enzyme certification is significant, and the same goes for non-food products such as leather that may come from pigs.

Rafi is a man in his thirties who has lived in Denmark for 13 years and now works in IT. He moved to Denmark from Israel, where he met his non-Jewish Danish wife in a kibbutz. Rafi explains that he is not very fastidious about kosher as he grew up in a secular family related to Mizrahi (groups descending from Middle Eastern Jewish communities) and Sephardi (groups of Jews that historically formed communities in the Iberian Peninsula). Traditionally, these groups would be flexible about their religion and they would go to the synagogue, light candles and avoid work at religious festivals, but accept watching television during the weekend, for example. Rafi's family would keep kosher even if they did not have a kosher kitchen. His mother still keeps kosher, and when she visits the family in Denmark Rafi is more focused on kosher and goes to the delicatessen or serves fish/vegetarian dishes.

When Rafi was a teenager he would eat cheeseburgers, but to this day 'when I see a colleague of mine eat a burger with a glass of milk it seems strange. I can eat a cheeseburger, but drinking milk and eating meat is strange.' Thus, even if Rafi sees himself as a flexible Jew the overt mixing of milk and meat that is so common in Denmark is unfamiliar. With regard to meat the family prefers beef, but occasionally pork is also eaten. The situation in Denmark is radically different from Israel: when Rafi was in the army everything was kosher and the approach to kosher here he sees as dogmatic and representative of unwelcome Orthodoxy. As a teenager he started breaking kosher rules, for example eating cheeseburgers, to rebel against his father and authorities. Rafi's own children 'eat what they are served', but at the Jewish school they keep kosher. His daughter wanted to keep kosher at home after couple of years at school, but regretted this decision when realising that she then couldn't have spaghetti carbonara. In general, Rafi feels that too many groups within Judaism take kosher to extremes. Orthodox Rabbis reinforce dated traditions to claim authority in a way that was never intended. Kosher enzymes is an example of this in the eyes of Rafi. Orthodoxy and over-interpretation infuse the market and regulation of kosher rather than common sense. To Rafi, what makes sense in Judaism is a form of cultural heritage created over generations, and kosher rules may have made sense historically when there were no fridges, but today they seem dated and unnecessary.

When we discuss whether kosher is healthier or not Rafi argues that many Danes regularly eat pork, so there must be limits to how harmful to health pork actually is. In the eyes of Rafi it makes sense that kosher is regulated to avoid horsemeat or sick animals, and kosher may therefore be considered healthier. Conversely, he does not consider the separation of milk and meat healthier and the same goes for avoiding shellfish, but he wouldn't eat shrimp in Israel in August.

The family mostly goes about their everyday shopping in supermarkets, and although they live close to the delicatessen Rafi only goes there when his mother or observant Jews are visiting: personally, Rafi prefers meat that is fresh and not frozen and expensive, as is the case in the delicatessen. In the case of oranges and avocados, Rafi would buy those produced in Israel to support local produce, but he does not in the same way support kosher.

The family does not have a kosher kitchen, and this becomes particularly important when celebrating children's birthdays, for example. Rafi stresses that this is an occasion when he makes sure that all guests are treated well and that visiting children do not have to bring their own food. Thus, he would go to Chabad to bake kosher rolls, only use kosher butter and serve everything on paper plates. For these occasions the family have also bought sweets in bulk when visiting relatives in Israel to bring back to Denmark. Rafi's family is flexible about going out to restaurants and at work he has no problems eating the food that is served in the canteen. The family also accepts halal meat and products more generally, whereas they think organic products are too expensive.

Hagai was born in Israel, grew up in a kibbutz and has now lived with his Danish wife and three children in Denmark for six years. Hagai was educated as a cook and now pursues further studies in Copenhagen. Although Hagai sees himself as 'ultra-secular' like his parents, and kosher has 'absolutely no significance' in the family's everyday life, his children attend the Jewish school in Copenhagen. Overall, however, he sees kosher as a kind of unwanted political ideology that should not be allowed to dictate everyday practice, not least because it represents state and religious power, economic gain and manipulation.

Hagai's background is influenced by his secular upbringing in Israel, and when attending a secular school he looked for non-kosher foods and pork to protest. In the Israeli army everybody must fit in so everything is kosher to cater for ultra-Orthodox groups, and the same goes for hospitals and schools. It was this system that Hagai rebelled against. These institutions are under rabbinate supervision and kosher logos are ubiquitous and thus controlled by authorities that Hagai challenges. Most of Hagai's friends are likeminded, but he does have more Orthodox friends. In his children's school several of the other kids are far more fastidious about kosher and this can be challenging. Some Jewish families in Denmark keep kosher at home while being flexible in public, but others are also observant in public – celebrating a child's birthday, for example, is an event where kosher becomes important in order to accommodate all guests. In this instance, Hagai goes to the delicatessen to make sure he caters for the more Orthodox guests. Another challenge is when socialising with Orthodox friends or family in Israel that focus on the separation of milk and meat and pork avoidance.

Hagai's family basically eats 'anything', but avoids pork because of animal cruelty. They are far more focused on buying organic and wholesome products. Another aspect of the family's food preferences is to cook typical Danish dishes such as meatballs (*frikadeller*) as well as falafel, humus and tahini that represent Israeli and Middle Eastern cuisine. To Hagai it's important that his kids learn about these two food cultures. He explains that he does not believe that kosher is healthier in any way, but that kosher has a different taste because it's salted and dried. Hagai believes that there are many similarities between kosher and halal and that the family has no problem buying halal meat. Regarding meat, the main principle is the taste and quality, on the one hand, and making sure that no animal cruelty is involved in producing the meat, on the other.

Discussion

In Manchester we can see the differences between Orthodox and more secular consumer understandings and kosher practices. To a large extent, these differences can be explained through the demographics of the Jewish population in Manchester, in the split between the increasingly Orthodox communities and bounded neighbourhoods to the north of the city and the secularising suburban sprawl to the south. The kosher market, particularly to the north of the city, is characterised by extreme availability: here you can find a wide variety of meat, non-meat and even non-food products such as toothpaste and care products certified by a range of local, national and transnational certification bodies. What is more, many of these products are produced and sold by Jews, and they are even available in mainstream super/hypermarkets, though at the same time there is also a trend towards more strict Orthodxy and what are seen to be more rigorous kosher standards and requirements.

These tendencies are visible in the empirical data discussed in this and previous chapters: firstly, informants are knowledgeable, well informed and conversant about what kosher is or ought to be. Differences and divisions evident in the empirical material are most openly expressed through reflections on debates over proper kosher understanding and practice among divergent Jewish groups and communities, rather than over limited availability, as it the case in Denmark. Meat and its qualification remains at the centre of kosher understanding and practice even if awareness of non-meat kosher consumption in the form medication is evident and growing. Kosher meat is widely available and the price level goes up according to the strictness of the qualities ascribed to products by supervising bodies and rabbinical authorities (Callon *et al.* 2002); yet while there are differences in levels of observance, all our informants argue that stunning animals before slaughter is unacceptable. Notably, in relation to *glatt* kosher we can say that the process of qualification is characterised by a more strict selection based on expertise about what is permissible.

Kosher food provision is evident in public institutions such as hospitals and schools across Manchester, though perhaps not to the same extent as halal food. While there is a growing awareness of the benefits of healthy eating, for many of our informants this relates to the spiritual as much as the physical realm; some make the case that Sephardi food is healthier than Ashkenazi food because it reflects the culinary traditions of the Mediterranean and is more vegetable- and less meat-based. In all such cases, it is clear that kosher is a compound practice (Warde 2016) made up of a wide range of practices involving family, friends and communities, notably around health and spirituality. Some informants, Yaakov and Peter, for example, argue that it is easier to keep kosher today than it was for previous generations, not least because of the variety of ways that consumers can now check the qualities of kosher products (Callon *et al.* 2002), using social media for example. Yet as was pointed out, the increasing complexity of food production, and the vast number of ingredients now used in a single food item, often makes it more difficult to know what to eat, with judgement and justification becoming ever more complex and difficult to negotiate (Wouters 2008). As a number of our informants suggest, simply because an economic good acquires a set of qualities that allow it to be marketed and traded as kosher does not mean that it is fit for consumption.

In the Danish context the Jewish population is small and shrinking and this is also reflected in the market. More specifically, the small size of the Jewish community and the fact that there is only one kosher shop in the entire country frames the everyday understanding and practice of kosher in Denmark: kosher meat is hard to come by and expensive. That said, all informants are acutely aware that the global market for kosher is huge and expanding, on the one hand, and certification by the Big Five is a global and lucrative business, on the other. This is good news for the more Orthodox groups, who appreciate increased regulation, while more relaxed groups find this excessive and unnecessary.

Among the most Orthodox informants, such as Naomi and Sara, kosher is inseparable from religious ritual life, when, for example, using a *mikveh* or setting

137

up a kosher kitchen. Conversely, more secular informants either describe themselves as 'convenient Jews' or being ideologically against kosher as an expression of a dogmatic and capitalist, and thus unwanted form, of religion. However, more relaxed Jews also send their kids to the Jewish school, where vegetarian kosher food is served, and many explain that to a large extent kosher is only about their own preferences and those of their family. Several informants who are either relaxed about or explicitly critical of kosher explain that at children's birthdays, for example, they go to the kosher shop or consult Chabad in order to make sure that kids from more Orthodox families feel welcome. Many informants rely on a kosher list covering acceptable foods published by the Jewish Community in Denmark, while others consult Chabad or look up products/ingredients on the Internet. Quite a number of the children from more Orthodox families have moved to Israel, the US or the UK – and quite a lot of the meat imported into Denmark comes from the UK. Several informants also explain that they themselves, their children or friends bring meat back from these countries. Because the kosher market is so limited in Denmark, all informants go to ordinary shops for the everyday shopping, and for the Orthodox group this entails in-depth knowledge of E numbers, for example. Several informants explain that they are often surprised to see that suddenly a product they have been buying over many years may now contains a new, questionable and often unwanted ingredient. While some informants argue that keeping kosher is healthier, for example avoiding blood and separating milk and meat, it is again clear that judgement about what to do in a given context can be extremely complex (Wouters 2008); Hannah and Benjamin make this point well, stating that if they didn't use the utensils provided in eating establishments in Denmark they would probably never go out. Thus, kosher knowledge defines not only Jewish group identity in Denmark, but also family and everyday life through compound practice (Warde 2016).

Very few of our informants in either the UK or Denmark were aware that enzyme production has undergone kosher supervision and certification in recent decades but the majority thought it was a good idea. However, this supports the argument that modern forms of transnational governmentality or religious audit culture tend to take on a life of their own: the relationship and cooperation between producers, sellers and certifiers is intensifying to such an extent that most consumers are unaware of these trends and processes. As these processes become more evident over time it will arguably become more difficult for kosher consumers to know what to eat, where to eat and, ultimately – even if it is easier to find information than it once was – how to judge what is and is not acceptable.

More generally, Jewish consumers in the UK are reassured about the processes of kosher qualification (availability, certification and trusted Jewish retailers) than they are in Denmark, where the market is extremely limited. Comparatively, in Denmark, availability, certification and trust in local retailers with knowledge of kosher are uncertain and limited, a situation that leads the group of Jewish consumers to focus more on the proper handling of food that they do not feel completely at ease with. More specifically, these consumers ritualise not only the buying and consumption of food, but also more contextual compound practice through the use of items such as utensils that they purify by various means. In other words, this form of everyday ritualisation is aimed at strategically distinguishing kosher consumers from the impurity of the secular context, its hegemonic preferences and unpalatable alternatives (Warde 2016). Two of the Danish informants are vegetarians/ vegans and this can also be seen as response to particularities of the Danish context. In the UK, consumers only occasionally refrain from eating meat, particularly when going to restaurants, notably when they feel that the price is excessive and/or the quality of the food is poor.

5

Halal consumers

In this chapter we explore how Muslim consumers in the UK and Denmark understand and practice halal consumption in their everyday lives. Following on from Chapters 3 and 4, the specific focus is how consumers make sense of buying/eating meat and non-meat products. As in the previous chapter, another important theme explored is how Muslim consumers understand and practice everyday (halal) food consumption in the UK and Denmark. We build on but also move beyond existing research on halal consumption in the everyday lives of Muslims in a globalised market (Gillette 2000; Navaro-Yashin 2002; Bergeaud-Blackler 2004, 2005, 2007; Fischer 2008b, 2011; Bergeaud-Blackler and Bernard 2010; Lever and Miele 2012; Lever 2013) to show how halal understanding and practice among Muslims should be explored in the context of halal as a globalising, but also increasingly regulated market characterised by what we refer to as transnational governmentality. .

As in the previous chapter, the geographical focus of this chapter is on Manchester and Copenhagen and all our latest empirical material was obtained in these locations. We again start off by discussing consumers who are very observant about halal and move towards the less observant or more relaxed consumers. However, it is not as easy to make a clear-cut distinction between orthodox and relaxed halal consumers as it is with kosher, particularly in the UK. While some Muslims are very strict about their preference for halal meat this might be in relation to either stunned or non-stunned halal meat and their overall practice might be quite different. Others have a more wide-ranging understanding of halal that moves beyond food consumption to consider everyday (halal) actions alongside more relaxed opinions about certification and/or stunning. This makes the process of defining levels of observance more difficult and open to interpretation than it is in the case of kosher consumers. Yet as with kosher consumers, compound practice (Warde 2016) is evident in relation to health and spiritually, for example, and the changing nature of food production, all of which require more self-discipline of consumers in deciding what is and is not acceptable in different social contexts (Wouters 2008).

Halal consumers in the UK

Khadija moved to the UK from Nigeria in 2001. In her mid-thirties, she is married with three children and works in public health as a pharmacist in Manchester. For Khadija, halal, haram and *makrooh* (or *mashbooh*) determine her everyday consumption. Primarily, halal food has to be 'wholesome'. Animal products must come from certain types of animals that have been treated well, slaughtered in the right way with a sharp knife, with the *bismillah* recited at the time of slaughter. Khadija explains halal practices to her children in terms of what they can and cannot eat, and why; she is a regular meat-eater and she prefers white meat and poultry because it's better for her children. Because of the question mark over stunning she buys meat certified by the stricter HMC, primarily because she thinks they scrutinise stunning more than other certification bodies, particularly when it comes to small animals such as chickens. Her husband usually buys meat from Hulme in central Manchester, from shops near their local mosque. A lot of the restaurants Khadija frequents are also HMC-certified: if she goes to a place that isn't, she will ask if the meat is halal and if it is she states that this usually fine too; she notes that in some restaurants chicken is halal while beef isn't and that she thus makes her choices accordingly. Khadija also believes that kosher meat is halal because of the way animals are slaughtered and prepared for slaughter.

Khadija argues that halal is also about much more than food. Islam, she states, is a complete way of life with a prescribed way of doing everything. When anything questionable comes into the equation she states that you just 'have to apply it to what you know' and make appropriate decisions: here she gives the example of gambling as always being wrong. While some Muslims think that using alcohol to cook and produce food is acceptable, Khadija believes this is always wrong and she states that she wouldn't do it because she would never have alcohol in the house; nor would she eat food in a restaurant if alcohol had been used or served. However, when it comes to medicine, if there's no alternative, Khadija argues that this is different. If she needs a particular medicine urgently and there's alcohol in it she will always take it because 'preserving life in Islam is the most important thing'. Likewise, she explains that in her work she might sometimes have to use alcohol to wash her hands. Khadija isn't aware of kosher and halal enzyme certification.

Khadija recognises that halal can be more expensive at times of celebration, at Eid for example, but she argues that this is just because there is increased demand and more marketing involved. She believes that halal tourism is increasing because Muslims have more disposable income than they once did, and also because there are completely segregated beaches where Muslim women can sit around in a bikini without any concerns. She reasons that early

Muslims in the West didn't push boundaries in this way and that third- and fourth-generation Muslims who have made the UK their home now look to make themselves more comfortable by going to such places. Because food production is changing quickly, Khadija explains that many Muslims are also becoming more questioning of halal; as they try to learn more about their food they are thus forced to go back to the original sources and make new decisions about what is and is not permissible. She concludes that it is always possible to keep learning and moving forward in Islam, and that this is what she tries to instil in her children.

Omar went to school on the outskirts of south Manchester before attending the University of Manchester to study medicine. Of British Pakistani heritage, he is in his late thirties, married with three children, and works as a freelance general practitioner in a local medical centre. He attends his local mosque regularly, and is a trustee there. Omar notes that debate about halal often revolves around meat and poultry and concerns that meat products are prepared appropriately: this means that a prayer must be said at the time of slaughter and that animals must be killed with a swift cut to the neck with a sharp knife so that the blood drains quickly. If stunning leads to death before the proper halal procedure has been completed – and it is his understanding that most stunning does hinder such practice – this renders the meat haram and therefore unsuitable for Muslim consumption. All the necessary conditions have to be fulfilled to make meat halal and Omar argues that humane slaughter is thus central to Islamic practice. This does not mean, however, he claims, that stunning is always unacceptable: if an animal is made comfortable and doesn't die before it is slaughtered, he believes that some form of stunning is acceptable.

Other important areas in halal food production relate to ingredients added to pre-prepared food. If a product has no prohibited ingredients, which is usually the case with vegetarian food, Omar argues that such food is permissible. He recognises that there is ongoing debate about the acceptability of small amounts of questionable ingredients in food products, but states that for him personally this is unacceptable; he gives the example of gelatine and states that there is now enough choice for Muslims to avoid it permanently and 'stay safe'. Omar recognises that enzyme production may pose problems for Muslims, but he admits that he's not familiar with the debates. More generally, when it comes to certification he argues that Muslim consumers need to be clear that organisations involved in the certification of halal meat don't have vested interests, and that they are 100 per cent reliable. In relation to non-food products such as toothpaste, Omar feels that if there is a need for something to be halal that's fine, but he is wary of halal becoming over-commercialised.

Although price can be the overriding concern for many Muslims, he argues that Muslims also need to talk about and recognise the underlying

142

issue of meat quality more often. Omar tends to buy fresh meat from reliable butcher's with appropriate levels of certification, trust and cleanliness. He usually eats chicken, some lamb, beef very occasionally, as well as fish. The family don't tend to buy and eat processed food from supermarkets, but they will occasionally buy branded burgers, for example, if they have trusted halal certification. In general he finds the price of halal food reasonable. Omar wants his children to grow up understanding what halal is and what they can and cannot eat at school. If they are buying sweets for the children he points out that they are told to look for the vegetarian symbol to ensure there are no unacceptable animal ingredients: the same principles apply when the family eat out at somewhere like McDonald's. More generally, when he eats at a restaurant Omar says that trust is important and that he tends to look for restaurants that offer halal meat. While he has to take what the owners tell him about their halal offerings at face value, he admits that this can be difficult sometimes: once he has asked about the food, however, he argues the onus switches to the restaurant if they want to retain his custom.

When he was at school Omar notes that there was no provision of halal food. Today, however, he recognises that this has changed and that his children's school, which has a lot of children from ethnic minorities, has good provision. He also points out, however, that this is changing and that the recent increase in Islamophobic sentiment is turning people against halal food; he supports other religious groups and the Jewish community on such matters. While some Muslims go to great lengths to ensure that the food they consume is halal, Omar argues that they must also pay attention to other ethical issues in their lives, when making financial transactions or driving a car, for example. At the same time, he notes that the younger generation want to know more about what's permissible and what's not and that this renewal and interest in faith is a good thing.

Shabbir arrived in the UK from Pakistan in the mid-1960s and is now in his mid-sixties. Educated to A-level standard in Pakistan, he is married with three UK-born children. Until retirement, he worked as a local councillor in Greater Manchester, but he also worked in engineering, as a bus conductor and in a local cotton mill. He lives north of Manchester and attends two local mosques. Shabbir believes every Muslim has a responsibility to eat halal food and that no one can change the prescriptions laid down in the holy book. He buys halal meat from supermarkets and he always reads the labels provided to see what ingredients are used in production; halal is about purity and he argues that if alcohol is used in food production, for example, a product cannot be halal. As the Qur'an indicates that animals should not be stunned before slaughter, Shabbir sticks rigidly to this position and he states that most other Muslims he knows are of this opinion. In general he trusts the regulation of slaughterhouses and meat production in the UK.

143

If he looks for halal meat from a Muslim-owned shop Shabbir doesn't prioritise one ethnic group over any other, he simply asks questions about the meat, inspects the hygiene and then makes a decision about whether or not he trusts the shopkeeper; his practice is the same if he eats at a previously unknown café or restaurant. Alongside trust, price is a key factor for Shabbir, as he eats meat regularly, sometimes up to three times a day. He is not overly concerned about certification and argues that anyone can put a label on something that says 'this is halal', and that there are now far too many organisations claiming to sell halal food legitimately. For him, the important thing is trust and 'believing that people are telling you the truth'. It is his understanding that halal food can be produced by anyone, just so long as the person involved is hygienic and does not use prohibited substances and ingredients; he also points out that it's widely accepted by Muslims that food marked as vegetarian is halal.

While there are now 'plenty of shops that sell halal food' in and around Manchester, when he arrived in the UK in the 1960s Shabbir explains that there were only of a few places where he could buy suitably slaughtered meat. At this time, many of his friends and family bought kosher meat from a local Jewish shop in north Manchester; he would occasionally go to a farm to buy chickens to ensure they were raised and slaughtered in the correct way. Today his wife and daughter do most of the shopping. Shabbir doesn't think that halal food is necessarily healthier, but he indicates that meat, if produced in the correct way, is: as a diabetic he has to be careful about what he consumes, which means avoiding sugary food and fizzy drinks. When he was in Wythenshawe hospital recently Shabbir was provided with a halal menu every day, yet he also recognises that he sometimes has to consume products, medicines for example, which are not entirely aligned with his beliefs; in such cases he will ask the doctor if alternatives are available. As well as food, Shabbir believes that halal is about many other things in life, including lifestyle and the way Muslims treat other people: he thus likes to give a donation to charity every week whether he can afford it or not.

Javid is from a British Pakistani background. Married with three children, he is in his early forties. An art and design teacher in a secondary school in north Manchester, he is currently developing a school-based health education project using art therapy, whilst simultaneously training as a practice manager in paraplegic surgery at the University of Sheffield. To Javid halal relates to both food and action. In relation to food, this means that animals must be slaughtered in accordance with Islamic law and that other food products mustn't have any unacceptable haram additives in them. When he goes shopping at supermarkets Javid always checks whether foods are suitable for vegetarians, as this is a good indication that they contain no questionable ingredients. He argues that it is more straightforward to consider halal food than halal action and that while factory-farmed chickens are often slaughtered in the halal way 'the halalness about how they were raised and kept is often questionable'.

144

Javid suggests that his wife is very health-conscious. He might only eat meat three times a week and when the family have Asian food it is often vegetarian or fish-based. While he could easily buy halal meat from a local supermarket he prefers to buy it from his local Pakistani butcher, primarily because he has a good relationship with the butcher, who knows how he likes his meat prepared, but also because the butcher has a good relationship with the slaughterhouse, which means that he knows that the meat does not come from animals slaughtered inappropriately. While personal relationships based on trust thus lie at the heart of Javid's everyday food practice, he argues that stunning 'is not really a big deal'. Most animals in the UK are stunned before slaughter and he recognises that there is a position within Islamic law that allows for this practice. He believes that the 'HMC uses emotional language' to segment the market and that they 'have a sales pitch that is in conflict with what happens on the ground'.

Javid argues that the differences between Islamic schools of law about what is permissible and what is haram are not as significant as they are made out to be, yet he recognises that debate on contested issues is healthy. Here he notes a recent 'ruckus' over flu vaccinations for children, which is taken nasally and has some pork elements in it: while some Muslim scholars allow this within Islamic law on ethical grounds, he notes that contested legal discussions on its permissibility continue. Javid and his wife always discuss new products with their children to educate them on what questions they should be asking. Often this is about ethical issues and health, and while halal is often part of this Javid notes that 'it isn't exclusively so'.

In general Javid feels that Muslim needs are well catered for in Manchester. He recognises that views on halal can vary considerably, from the very conservative and orthodox to those who are less so; he also notes that older generations do not necessarily want to eat at a halal-certified restaurant and that they would rather eat food from their local butcher at home with family and friends. When he's travelling or working away from home Javid eats vegetarian food. When it comes to health, he admits that Muslim communities have big problems with diabetes and increased rates of high blood pressure, which has a lot to do with diet. Going back to his original point about halal action he argues that people need to start asking different questions:

> So the question should be how halal is your halal diet, because if it's leading to inevitable illness, and if health is safeguarded within the Qur'an, then the way we eat and the way we live has to be managed better in order for us to say that it is halal.

While it could be argued that halal is becoming over-commercialised, Javid argues that it is also possible to say that such developments are helping people live a life in line with their ethical values and beliefs. As a teacher and artist Javid is interested in exploring issues around mental health, and he argues that discussions of halal, broadly defined around ethics and action, could be of great benefit to the Muslim community more generally.

Ahmed is a professor of economics at a university in the north of England. Now in his late forties he moved to the UK from Egypt 15 years ago to study for a PhD; he now lives in Hulme in central Manchester with his wife and three children. Halal, for Ahmed, is about producing food, particularly meat, in line with Islamic principles and practices. In particular, the name of Allah must be mentioned at the time of slaughter and all blood must be allowed to drain from the body of animals post-slaughter; here Ahmed refers to US research that suggests that this is the healthiest way to produce meat. He argues further that eating pork or drinking wine would only be acceptable if he had no choice; for example, if his life depended on it.

When Ahmed first came England he claims that he met lots of Pakistani and Bangladeshi Muslims who appeared to have a different understanding of halal. If they ate at a restaurant, for example, where they were not sure whether the meat was halal, he suggests that they would simply recite *bismillah* before they ate to alleviate any concerns and worries. Personally he found this difficult to do at the time and he preferred to ask the manager or waitress and then make a decision based on what information they provided, which he argues is acceptable in Islam. This is the same when he goes into a supermarket: if the manager or sales assistant says a product is halal he has to make a personal call about whether or not this is acceptable for him and his family. Ahmed argues that if a product contains even very small a quantity of questionable ingredients it is haram and cannot be halal. If Muslims shop at supermarkets it is therefore essential that they read all the ingredients carefully, as products containing gelatine or alcohol must be avoided completely at all times; he is unaware of enzyme certification.

Ahmed previously lived in southwest England, where lack of halal meat meant that he ate only vegetarian food. Since arriving in Manchester this has changed, and Ahmed can now source halal meat from a wide variety of ethnic sources: while he still eats vegetarian food, and recognises that diet is more important as he gets older, he still eats meat regularly, preferably lamb, sometimes beef and also chicken. He doesn't pay much attention to the politics of certification and suggests that if a logo is visible this is good enough for him. He is, however, against stunning. He believes that the stunning methods used during the industrial production of chicken, for instance, regularly kill birds and that this makes their meat haram and unacceptable according to *sharia* principles; he also raises questions about legislation that allows fast-food chains such as KFC to sell halal meat in some outlets in Manchester and not in others: he finds this odd.

Ahmed prefers to shop at local butcher's and while all ethnic groups within Islam produce meat in similar ways he notes differences in taste and preparation practices. He also explains that his wife has very good halal shopping skills and that she often sends him pictures of products with information about where he can find it. Ahmed prefers fresh halal meat rather than pre-packed and he highlights food similarities between and across all religions, including 'fruit and veg and fish', which people of all religions can eat together legitimately: in this sense he thinks that 'halal' is quite limited. At the same time, he recognises that halal is seen as a way of life by many in that it allows them to do permissible things: Ahmed gives the examples of being unfaithful and gambling as impermissible. He suggests a good way of thinking about halal is to see it as something that allows individuals to lead a balanced life so that they are satisfied on 'judgement day'.

Ahmed recognises that some people he knows have a stricter understanding of halal than he does. He points to some very orthodox acquaintances from Manchester who visit Birmingham, particularly at Eid and on other special occasions, to witness the act of slaughter 'with their own eyes'. Ahmed once bought kosher food in a restaurant because of the similarities with halal, but he argues that this probably wouldn't happen the other way round. Ahmed also admits that during his time in the UK he has (like many other Muslims) become less strict about certain Islamic practices. While he still looks for halal meat whenever he can, he admits that given his job and lifestyle in the UK this can be very difficult in practice. Ahmed once went to the mosque every day, but this is now all but impossible: he blames himself for this. However, while he may say *bismillah* to cover himself if he is unsure about meat in a restaurant, at home he is still very strict.

Saeed moved to the UK from Bangladesh over 40 years ago as a 'young lad'. In his late forties, he is married with three children and lives in south Manchester. He works as an academic specialising in Islamic issues. While Muslims have an idea of what *is* and *is not* halal when it comes to food, Saeed argues that halal has a much broader ethical and environmental dimension than is usually recognised by Muslims, in particular in relation to everyday actions and practices. Here he discusses animal welfare issues, not killing an animal in front of other animals, for example, and using a very sharp knife to minimise pain, as well as the whole ecosystem in which halal meat is produced. Saeed argues that worries over gelatine and inappropriate ingredients are often 'overplayed' and that Muslims have to make their own minds up about whether something is permissible; this, he argues, is about personal choice. He doesn't think Muslims get misled about such issues, more that they have just become obsessed with eating halal meat.

At this juncture he refers to debates that emerged in the late 1990s – the 'certification wars' – on the divergent practices of the two main certification bodies in the UK – HFA and HMC. Saeed argues that this was more about politics than seeing things in a truly halal way, and it is this, he argues, that has helped to bring about the current Muslim obsession with consuming halal food. He suggests that certification isn't really the issue and that personally he simply

147

buys meat from reliable and trustworthy sources. Saeed finds it more difficult when he eats out and states that he is often uncomfortable asking where the meat in restaurants comes from; most of the restaurants he frequents have halal certificates and in general he accepts what is on offer because there is no other option.

At the same time, Saeed recognises that market forces are at play and that while he can afford to make other food choices, and buy organic halal, for example, many Muslims cannot, though he counters this with the assertion that people *can* also chose to stop eating meat. Although he eats red meat occasionally, for health reasons Saeed keeps this to a minimum; the family eat chicken only once a week and red meat once every two or three weeks; they eat fish and vegetarian food as often as possible. While he tries to be ethical about what these things, Saeed indicates that this can be frustrating, 'whether you're a believer in a religion or not', and that the ethics of food consumption constitutes a major dilemma for many people. He doesn't believe that halal food should be produced by non-Muslims, simply because he can't imagine them saying the required prayer at the time of slaughter: he thinks that kosher is probably stricter than halal, but admits that doesn't know enough to make a proper judgement.

In general Saeed thinks that the commercialisation of Islam has gone too far and he gives the example of Malaysian businessmen trying to sell 'halal water' on social media. He suggests that a lot of Muslims 'get compromised' because 'halal sells' and that many thus 'pay lip service to Islamic ethics' without having a rigorous understanding of what Islamic teaching means in practice. As it contravenes some very sacred concepts in religion, Saeed argues that the dominant approach to halal is problematic. It's not entirely clear, he argues, how knowledge of Islam or halal is passed on to the younger generation, with many third- and fourth-generation Muslims having learnt little from attending mosques regularly. In general, when it comes to food, Saeed thinks that Muslims face the same problems as anyone else. Consumers have to be aware of what they're buying and what their consumption practices mean for themselves, both as individual and ethical consumers, and also as Muslims; but he can't see the required cultural changes happening any time soon.

From Cairo in Egypt, *Hussein* is married with two children and in his early thirties. He arrived in the UK in 2007 and started working in his current role as the manager of a restaurant in Manchester in 2011. Halal, for Hussein, relates to the way animals are killed in line with the requirements of *sharia* law and Islam. At the time of slaughter, the head of the animal must be facing Mecca; a very sharp knife must be used for the act of slaughter (so the animal doesn't suffer), and *bismillah* must be recited. He argues that 'it doesn't matter where you are, it doesn't matter where you're from, this is the way that Allah and Qur'an says it has to be done'.

148

When Hussein started working at the restaurant in 2011 it didn't sell halal food. He talked about this with the owners and the potential market they were missing out on and the head chef subsequently agreed to use halal meat; the restaurant now benefits from an increasing number of Muslim customers, particularly Arab students from the university and businessmen. Hussein shows me a certificate from a farm supplier in Greater Manchester and suggests that when people ask if the meat in the restaurant is halal he shows it to them. While he is personally against animals being stunned before slaughter, Hussein explains that customers never ask this question. While he recognises that there are differences in certification practices he doesn't pay much attention to these because it often appears to him that certification is more about making money than doing 'what's right or wrong': when he first moved to Manchester Hussein bought meat from a halal butcher, which was more expensive, he contends, simply because it was certified halal. The restaurant doesn't have to have a certificate for cooking meat and Hussein argues that certification is simply about building trusting in the restaurant. He trusts the restaurant's suppliers much as the restaurant's customers trust him, but he recognises that 'at end of the day you will never know what is gonna happen behind the scenes, you just have to trust the people that you're buying it [halal] from'.

Although he recognises that eating too much meat is bad for his health, Hussein eats meat every day without fail, sometimes three times a day if he's working (which is often), including a big breakfast; he particularly likes rib-eye steak and chicken, but sometimes has fish for lunch. He has never bought or eaten organic food to his knowledge, but says that he once ate kosher food by mistake at a house party, but that he wouldn't engage in such a practice by choice because it's not acceptable.

When he arrived in the UK, Hussein struggled to get halal food in the town where he lived and he explains that he often phoned home for advice. If he was unsure, some people suggested that he could *make* food halal by saying *bismillah* before he ate it. At the time he wasn't sure how true this was and thought the prayer could be recited only at the time of slaughter. Today, however, Hussein eats at a lot of different places around Manchester, and while he always asks if the meat is halal, if it isn't he will say *bismillah* himself. When it comes to strictness about halal observance he says he would probably score eight out of ten.

Rida is a single Muslim woman of Pakistani/Indian heritage in her mid-twenties. She studied law at the University of Leeds and now works in a law firm in Manchester; in recent years she has lived between Manchester and her parents' house in a small town in West Yorkshire. Halal, for Rida, reflects the way meat is prepared in her culture and religion, and she feels most comfortable when she knows that meat been prepared in accordance with Islamic rules. She notes other important things such as not eating pork, but states that halal is mainly about the production and preparation of meat. Rida explains that she often finds it difficult to know who to believe when it comes to trusting in the origins of food; if she goes to a café that states the meat is halal but doesn't display a certificate she will always ask for proof. Rida doesn't consume products containing questionable ingredients such as alcohol, though she recognises that many Muslims she knows will eat such products. Nor is she insistent on halal products being produced by Muslims and she argues that adhering to a recognised standard or certifier is much more important. She is not familiar with the move towards kosher and halal enzyme certification.

Rida argues that today the impact and influence of social media on the opinions of young Muslims going to Greggs and McDonald's, for example, is massive. While there are many on-line posts about the pros and cons of such practice, she argues that at the end of the day individuals have to make their own minds up when they ask whether cheese and onion pastries are vegetarian and therefore suitable for Muslims. Rida finds that Manchester is pretty well catered for when it comes to halal and that the entire Curry Mile is pretty much halal from one end to the other. She doesn't personally buy pre-packed meat or halal-branded items such as burgers and chicken nuggets from supermarkets, preferring instead to go to the local butcher or Asian store on the day fresh meat has arrived: she prefers chicken and will eat red meat if it's in a curry. While these places have certification, she is not sure where from and to some extent she thinks that certification puts up the price of halal meat, particularly in supermarkets. Rida also explains that she has heard conflicting stories about stunning and that she doesn't really have a preference one way or the other. She never asks about stunning when making her enquiries about halal and argues that the overall production process is much more important to her personally: here she notes draining the blood fully and reciting the prayer as key aspects of halal production.

When she goes out with non-Muslim friends to places that don't serve halal food Rida has the fish or vegetarian option; when she caters for non-Muslim friends at home she states she has never had any issues when serving them halal food. When she goes to an Asian restaurant with her family in Bradford she often orders halal steak and chips or halal lasagne. Halal is not necessarily healthier, she argues, as it often contains many of the same ingredients as non-halal mass-produced food: moderation is thus the key to healthy eating. Rida has never tried kosher food and does not know much about it, but she knows from shopping at the Tesco hypermarket in Cheetham Hill that kosher food is situated next to halal food.

Rida understands the move towards and the increasing demand for non-food halal products – personal care items, for example, such as cosmetics and perfumes – but she is not sure how many Muslims pay attention to these products and suggests that she would probably just go for the standard option. What many Muslim consumers are concerned about, she argues, is convenience.

Rida is not judgemental about her Muslim friends who do not eat halal food regularly: she thinks that halal is a lifestyle choice, whether you do it all the time, at holiday time or never.

Imran grew up in Whalley Range, a multicultural area in central Manchester. In his late thirties, he is married with three children and works as a community worker. Although he was bought up in a Muslim household of Pakistani origin, Imran states that he has never been overly strict about what he eats and that he likes 'to have a drink and try all types of food'. Of course, he is also respectful of the stricter dietary requirements of other people. If his mum comes to the house, or Asian friends, he makes sure that all the food is halal and that there is no alcohol around, but this practice varies depending on which friends he is entertaining. Imran says his children can eat what they want and he explains that parents of some his children's friends have expressed concerns about this when they've dropped children off at the house. But Imran says that he always respects their wishes and doesn't give the children anything their parents don't consider halal.

Halal, for Imran, implies than an animal has been slaughtered in accordance with religious teachings. He notes that this practice originated in countries with a hotter climate than the UK, where there was no refrigeration, and that getting rid of the blood completely was more important in this context because the meat would last longer: the health benefits originally entailed have thus turned into cultural and religious beliefs, and benefits, he reasons. Imran argues that knowledge of halal comes down through the generations to illustrate the dangers, as with any religion, of not living in a certain way. When he was a child he explains that he was often told that if he ate something that wasn't halal it was only a problem if he had done it purposely.

When it comes to slaughter, Imran pleads ignorance. He has heard all the major arguments for and against traditional non-stun halal slaughter and he admits that he doesn't really know whether the religious or scientific view is best. The biggest challenge in shopping for halal, he argues, is having good communication with a butcher about how you want 'your meat to feel'. While some halal butchers are still 'very old school' in the way they approach the preparation of meat, he explains that most thrive when consumers know and trust the 'halal quality' of what they sell. Imran has diabetes, which is a massive problem in the Pakistani community, and he watches what he eats carefully. He likes to eat fresh food and vegetables as often as he can, but is aware that he still eats too much meat, which he buys from either an 'English butcher' or a halal butcher if they can provide the service he wants. While most of the places selling halal meat have a certificate on the wall, he indicates that this is not the main issue for him, simply because he is looking for more than this in terms of meat quality, and this, he argues, depends on personal relationships with a butcher. Imran adopts a similar practice when he takes the family out to a restaurant; while they prefer to eat halal meat, he reiterates the point that it's the overall quality of the food that matters at the end of the day. Imran also recognises that different ethnic groups do things differently and that when he buys meat from Somali butchers in Moss Side, for example, they cut and pack meat in slightly different ways from his regular butchers. While there are enough shops selling halal meat in Manchester, Imran thinks there should be more kosher shops in the city, 'because I've just got a perception, it may be wrong … that they give you a better quality of service preparing the meat'.

At the end of the day, he thinks that halal is now just about making money. But this was always the case, he argues, even when the first curry houses opened just outside the city centre to feed factory workers from the subcontinent many years ago. Imran argues that today there needs to be better consensus about halal certification and that debate sometimes gets very political. People want more certainty about halal, particularly the younger generation, who are highly educated, more questioning and to some extent more religious, he argues; whereas older generations just wanted to survive in the UK, young people now want and expect more. They earn more than their parents and are able to enjoy their leisure more, which means that many want to be able to consume halal wherever they go. Halal, as a result, is expanding beyond his own understanding of the term, and is therefore associated with going on holiday, for example. Just as importantly, however, Imran argues that halal is about trust.

Rabia is a single woman of Pakistani heritage in her early twenties. Originally from Leicester, she completed a degree in the history of art at the University of Birmingham before moving to south Manchester, where she works in what she describes as a small, multicultural café. Rabia eats meat on a regular basis and generally this means chicken and lamb. Rabia explains that she associates halal with 'thinking about' – or 'liking to think about' – animals being killed in the right way, and she will not eat meat unless it's halal. This is largely because the production process is important, notably cleanliness, but also because of habit. Elaborating on this, she says that halal means that an animal has been killed in the right way, with a cut to the throat, that the blood has been drained properly and the animal doesn't suffer a long and painful death. She also recognises that there are different understandings and degrees of strictness about this, depending on your peer group and friends.

Rabia suggests that Manchester is pretty well catered for when it comes to halal food and also recognises that there is good availability of halal in public institutions in the UK. She compares this with the difficulty of getting halal meat when she has being travelling, particularly in Germany, where almost everything had pork in it, and she just ate fish. She argues that shopping for halal is the same as shopping for anything else, and that if you've got a favourite local butcher, for example, or a supermarket that sells what you want, you'll shop there. Rabia buys halal meat either from Tesco or the butcher in the Medina Superstore, which are both on Stockport Road in south Manchester.

The butcher in Medina's speaks several languages and has customers from many cultural backgrounds; the shop sells most things and one of the reasons Rabia shops there is price. She often buys a whole chicken and cuts it up to make curries, or does similar things with a piece of lamb. She notes that most places selling or providing halal food these days have some type of halal certificate and that if she shops anywhere else she will look for a certificate, or ask where the meat comes from: her practice thus depends on convenience and sticking to what she knows. Rabia is against stunning, but while she looks for certification when she shops at unusual places, she admits that she doesn't really understand its wider significance or the distinctions made between meat from stunned and non-stunned animals. As she understands it, most, if not all, halal meat comes from non-stunned animals.

Rabia has tried branded halal products from the company Shazans but argues that they are not very good quality. Rabia doesn't think that halal is necessarily healthier than other food, but knowing that it is halal makes her feel better about eating it. For people of her background and heritage, she explains that halal is a big cultural issue and that to some extent it is therefore part of her identity: at this point she states that one of the reasons she likes living away from home is that she can smoke and drink without people back home knowing about it. She also admits that she occasionally displays what she calls the 'oh, well' attitude towards consuming non-halal food. This does not mean, however, she argues, that she will consume non-halal food without giving it a second thought, more that if she calls on friends unexpectedly and they have cooked a risotto, for example, she might, if she's really hungry, be willing to eat it, but only after she's been convinced that there's no pork in it. When friends come to her house she doesn't mind cooking non-halal food, and if it isn't halal she will just use a separate pan. When she eats out with friends and doesn't know the café or restaurant, she will look at the menu and if she doesn't like what's on offer she will just eat fish. Rabia is a bit mystified why products such as Kellogg's Corn Flakes or Kingsmill bread now have halal labels and to some extent she contends that the market is becoming commercialised. On her understanding, halal is simply about meat and she states categorically that this is all it should ever be about: it is this that dominates her everyday practice.

Halal consumers in Denmark

Hassan is in his sixties and he moved to Denmark from Zanzibar in the early 1970s. He is married with three children and works as a constructing architect. With regard to halal he describes himself as 'very observant' and he argues that halal is a central part of the belief of any practising Muslim. Conversely, a person who does not follow the halal/haram binary is not a Muslim. Thus, Hassan and his family are careful about the food they buy and eat. To Hassan, the Qur'an and the *sunnah* are clear guidelines not only to consumption and

153

what to avoid, but also life more generally to avoid 'transgressing bounda-ries': marriage and the legality of one's source of income are examples of this. During our discussions Hassan reads several verses of the Qur'an and passages from the *sunnah* that refer to halal/doubtful/haram. Hassan became more fas-tidious about halal after leaving Zanzibar for Europe. In the early 1970s halal was not a major question, but this changed with Islamic revivalism, and today Hassan and his family consider themselves to be Muslims that are always alert about what they consume.

When going to a halal butchers' shop, for example, he naturally expects the meat to be properly slaughtered according to Islamic ritual principles. If he can't find halal food or if the food at hand is doubtful, he will find something 'neutral' such as fish or vegetables. It's mostly halal meat that is important in Hassan's everyday life, and he reasons that halal meat is also about health and wholesomeness. Draining the blood makes meat healthier and pork avoid-ance is also healthier as pork contains cholesterol and 'bacteria that cannot be eradicated'. In general, Hassan does not trust supermarkets to respect Muslim sentiment and will only buy meat from a supermarket if a halal logo with a recognisable certifier is visible on the packaging – for example the logo issued by the ICCOS on Danpo chicken that he is familiar with: Hassan's wife actually called Danpo to make sure products were halal.

Some shops import non-stunned meat from England and elsewhere and Hassan agrees with the viewpoint that only non-stunned meat can truly be considered halal. Quite simply, stunned meat is not allowed in Islam, as the animal must be conscious when it's slaughtered: a stunned animal will also contain blood, which cannot be consumed by Muslims. Thus, Hassan assumes that meat in supermarkets that does not appear to contain any blood is non-stunned. However, since slaughter without stunning was prohibited in Denmark in 2014 Hassan now makes greater effort to find meat in a butcher's that can guarantee the meat is non-stunned.

To Hassan, food scandals such as those involving the illegal mixing of pork and beef have made him more alert when going about his everyday shop-ping. More generally, the family eats meat, mostly chicken, only twice a week, with fish, which is considered healthier and less expensive, more frequently is on the menu. Hassan and his wife are equally observant and conscious with regard to halal in their everyday lives – they follow religious rules and he states that 'we can't just pick and choose'. He explains that it takes a great deal of 'inquisitiveness' going through E numbers when going about his daily shopping and that more halal logos would be helpful. Actually, he would wel come logos on drinks such as Coca-Cola to be sure it did not contain 'traces of whatever because multinational companies do not give enough info on the packaging'. In contemporary Denmark he argues that it's the obligation of all Muslims to seek knowledge and 'our right to know the contents of what we eat and drink'. Hassan states that he supports other Muslims through his consumption practices. However, some Muslim groups are careless when they sell pork and ham in their pizzerias in Copenhagen and Hassan has stopped buying from these places. Moreover, the same utensils and surfaces are used for preparing all kinds of foods that should not be mixed and on top of that the level of hygiene leaves much to be desired. He argues that these places must decide whether the outlet is halal or not, because there's no middle way. Typically, such outlets are owned or operated by 'careless' Muslims of Turkish origin, whereas Iraqis and Lebanese run more reliable outlets based on Islamic knowledge and sometimes the display of proper halal logos. Several outlets in Copenhagen have started to put up logos in Roman as well as Arabic characters with an identifiable certifier and Hassan is fully supportive of this trend.

The family is also alert when going out to a reception event or a celebration. In these cases Hassan will ask the host about the qualities of the food being served, avoid meat and mainly eat vegetables, cheese or fish. More generally, Hassan explains that his knowledge of halal understanding and practice comes from five sources: The Qur'an; the Prophetic traditions; *ulama* who possess the necessary knowledge; information to be found on the Internet and apps – for example on questionable E numbers and the status of new products; as well as a 'family group' consisting of family members in many countries who share information and 'links' about halal face-to-face and electronically.

When we discuss to what extent halal is boundless, that is, if halal can also be excessive in terms of being used to promote certain products or services that do not warrant certification, Hassan is clear that in principle halal always embodies a useful (and with regard to food, healthier) type of Muslim knowledge that he welcomes: consequently, he would like to know if a leather jacket is made of pig leather or a care product contains unwanted ingredients. At the same time, enzymes and other ingredients should also carry halal certification. Hassan's daughter has started a travel agency that specialises in halal tourism to cater for Muslim travellers interested in Islamic culture and heritage, and to him this initiative shows that halal should not be limited to food, but also extended to services and entrepreneurship. Hassan readily accepts kosher food, as it's stated in the Qur'an that this is acceptable. Jews and Muslims are brothers and both People of the Book. A friend of Hassan's in London works as a kosher supervisor and when in London he finds kosher certification more convincing than much of the vegetarian food sold.

Tahir is in his mid-thirties and single with four children. Of Pakistani heritage and background, he grew up in UK before moving to Denmark with his family; he has a degree in IT. Tahir is engaged in work with the Islamic Faith Community and he manages the organisation's shop, which sells a wide range of Islamic texts, paraphernalia, food products such as olive oil and halal-certified sweets.

Tahir is 'extreme' when it comes to halal: with regard to meat he will ask the seller where the meat is from and if the seller is unconvincing Tahir will not eat it. More broadly, Tahir sees food as a sign of spirituality and of proper religious practice. He clearly prefers non-stunned meat and he found a butcher in Nørrebro that sells this kind of imported meat that is not easy to come by in Denmark. Unfortunately, this butcher had to close and he then found another butcher selling non-stunned lamb from Ireland among other kinds of non-stunned meats. What is more, this butcher guarantees that Muslims are involved in the production of the meat in Ireland: the shop also sells meat from Lithuania and Spain. Tahir hasn't noticed any halal logos on the meat, but there is a logo on the façade of the shop and he basically trusts the butcher. Tahir tries to avoid Danish non-stunned meat because of the risk that the animal is dead before slaughter and because he also feels that non-stunned meat signifies resistance to the fundamentally anti-Muslim political agenda in Denmark. He recalls that his father used to slaughter animals at a farm in order to make sure that ritual slaughter was properly carried out. Tahir explains that he hasn't been a 'practising' Muslim all his life – it was not until his teenage years that halal became really important; one sign of this was when he went with his friends to McDonald's, where he would only eat vegetables or fish. This anecdote fits the bigger picture that surrounds the increasing awareness of 'Islamic lifestyle', Tahir reasons.

Most of the sweets sold in Tahir's shop are from the Haribo brand range (also available as kosher, as we saw in Chapter 1) and are imported into Denmark from Turkey by a German company. These products contain gelatine from halal-slaughtered cows in Turkey and are clearly marked with halal logos. The availability of halal sweets reflects a wider concern among some Muslims regarding non-meat issues such as animal fat and E numbers that is of particular relevance in Denmark, Tahir argues, as very few products carry halal/kosher logos or 'suitable for vegetarians' logos as they do in the UK. Tahir is not only fastidious about his own halal consumption, he also stresses the fact that it is through consumption that Muslim companies and entrepreneurs (the *ummah* – community of Muslims) can be supported.

Tahir's main concern regarding halal is to ensure that meat is non-stunned and he would like greater availability of such meat in Denmark. The relationship of trust between seller and buyer is better in halal butcher's shops than it is in major supermarkets, he argues, which in the eyes of Tahir are not trustworthy and sell only halal meat from stunned sources. Limited availability of non-stunned and pricey meat in Denmark is one reason why Tahir and his family limit their meat consumption to one or two days a week, when lamb is often on the menu. Tahir rarely eats out at restaurants in Denmark – especially after what he calls the 'halal crisis', when an abattoir claimed to be producing non-stunned meat that was actually stunned. Moreover, the law against stunning made him more aware that all or most of the meat produced in Denmark is stunned and he opposes and challenges the position of Islamic scholars who argue that specific types of stunning are acceptable. Tahir believes that halal is healthier, as he argues:

> Clearly there's wisdom behind the Maker's injunction – God only knows what's best for animals and humans and that has been scientifically confirmed. It has also been scientifically proven that pigs contain bacteria and eat their own excrement and therefore pork is clearly prohibited in religious texts.

When we discuss the necessity or relevance of halal toothpaste, Tahir makes the case that these products reflect above all the 'politics' of non-Muslim companies attempting to make their products legitimate for Muslims to consume. Personally, Tahir supports Muslims through his everyday consumption and even if it's possible to buy Colgate halal toothpaste on the Internet or abroad he prefers the Muslim-produced brand Dabur Meswak, which is a herbal toothpaste directly aimed at a Muslim audience. Halal-certified Coca-Cola in Southeast Asia is, Tahir claims, nothing more than corporate over-commercialisation aimed at penetrating the lucrative, global Muslim market. Conversely, he would support the production of halal-certified enzymes because this production in large part goes into processed food products. Tahir argues that kosher and halal are comparable and that the main difference is that Muslims generally accept kosher while Jews do not accept halal.

Hanan is in her thirties and she moved to Denmark from Somalia in the 1990s. She is married with three children and completed her academic education in Denmark and the UK. Hanan currently works for an NGO. She makes it clear that halal has always been a 'major priority' for her: since childhood Hanan has been aware of the dietary laws of Islam and because of improved availability in Denmark she has a 'normal halal lifestyle'. However, compared to the UK, where Hanan studied, the convenience and availability of halal are limited. She goes to the local halal butcher and sometimes asks whether the meat is stunned or not to ensure that the meat is 'as halal as possible', and her preference is clearly for non-stunned meat; but she notes that meat with these qualities is not easy to come by in Denmark. She notes that this issue was particularly topical in 2014, when stunning was made mandatory, but that it is no longer. Non-stunned chicken from the supermarket is therefore a good option and acceptable.

Hanan maintains that knowledge of halal is something 'you learn along the way in Denmark' and that it doesn't really require particular skills except perhaps when looking for questionable or prohibited ingredients such as gelatine and also E numbers. Hanan's knowledge of recent developments in the halal market is not only discussed with friend and relatives, but also updated using electronic resources such as www.justhalal.dk – especially challenging are processed products such as cheese and bread that are clearly more complex than meat. When shopping with her kids she is confident about what to buy and what not to buy, as she explains:

> I do my best. It won't kill you if you don't get it exactly right. You learn from your experiences. Cheese with gelatine is it OK or not? I don't break down if it's not OK; for example I didn't know there was gelatine in chocolate-covered marsh-mallows. Now I know and won't buy them again.

In general she finds that Somalis are fastidious about halal, perhaps because meat is central to Somali cuisine. Hanan's family do not eat meat on a daily basis and they often have vegetable-only dishes, which she has no problem with. Her mother and family thus directly influence her everyday halal prac-tice and she often discusses good shopping deals and quality issues with them. There are some Somali shops in Copenhagen and Hanan occasionally goes to these shops to buy Somali specialities.

Shopping and cooking in the family are shared between Hanan and her husband. While her husband makes enquires about meat before he buys it in halal butcher's shops, she also notes that non-meat issues related to gelatine are puzzling to him: Hanan's husband also discusses the pros and cons of stun-ning versus non-stunning with a local imam. If the family eat out at non-halal restaurants such as McDonald's they eat only vegetables and/or fish; some-times they will also ask the owner or staff at restaurants about the halalness of the menu.

Hanan believes that halal is healthier in that halal slaughter and the draining of blood can be considered as a way of 'purifying' meat. When we discuss the relevance of halal-certified enzymes, Hanan, like most of informants, was not really aware that this is taking place and she feels that it's a complex issue: 'In general, I'm not into halal marks or logos. My main concern is meat, rennet in cheese and gelatine, and everyday convenience in my family plays a large role', she argues. She also argues that there has got to be a balance between the growth of an increasing range of halal-certified products such as care products and common sense. Hanan's understanding of kosher is based on the fact that both Muslims and Jews are People of the Book who to a large extent share dietary requirements.

Basra was born in Somalia and came to Denmark when she was three years old. She's now a student in her twenties, living with her Somali flatmate in Copenhagen. When Basra left home to live on her own she had to figure out how to manage shopping and cooking in a market where food is expensive and halal is not always easy to come by. At the start of each month Basra and her flatmate go to a halal butcher's in Nørrebro to buy meat in bulk: they nor-mally go to the same butcher every month and they frequent this shop because they heard by word of mouth that the quality and price of the meat is very good; they typically buy chicken in a supermarket because they know that almost all of the chicken produced in Denmark is certified by the ICCOS.

Basra notes that meat is essential to Somali cuisine: 'Somalis prefer beef or chicken and we eat a lot of meat – food is not really food if it doesn't contain meat. Serving non-meat dishes to guests would be considered disrespectful.' When it comes to stunning Basra is undecided. On the one hand, she is well aware that religious texts state that meat should be ritually slaughtered without stunning, and she notes that the 2014 public debate made more Muslims aware of the underlying debates. On the other hand, she's not convinced about the arguments that stunning is necessary to ensure animal welfare. She sums her feelings up by stating that: 'Halal can mean a lot of things and I don't think stunning is the major issue.'

Basra notes that recently the focus on halal in Denmark has come to include gelatine and sweets, and not only meat as was previously the case. Halal sweets are now on sale in many places in Copenhagen and she often buys a Turkish brand called Ülker, for example. Basra always looks for E numbers on food labelling: her mother taught her about what these numbers mean. Basra wasn't aware that enzyme production in Denmark is both kosher- and halal-certified so she hasn't given this issue much thought. She speculates that not many Muslims would be concerned about this issue in their everyday lives and personally she's undecided about whether halal enzymes are necessary or not. The same goes for the fact than in some Southeast Asian countries Coca-Cola, for example, is fully halal-certified. Basra states that this is not really necessary and that this type of certification 'doesn't really change anything'. The same goes for halal-certified toothpaste, and she argues that such products are mainly halal-certified to promote them as part of a market strategy and to make them acceptable to more Muslims, but she recognises that as a Muslim it would make it easier to practise her religion if there was better availability of halal in general. In order to support Somalis and find familiar products, Basra goes to a particular street at Nørrebro to buy clothing, creams and shampoos at shops owned or operated by Somalis. Her flatmate, she recalls, was looking for Islamic finance (avoiding *riba* or interest) options when buying a new car, but unfortunately this wasn't available in Denmark.

Reflecting on the sources of knowledge about halal, she mostly learns about this from family, friends when she was at school and the Qur'an. Basra used to have a list of halal products, but access to information using the Internet and apps has made things easier. Moreover, a new Facebook group called 'Halal eating places in Copenhagen' has emerged and this also makes everyday life easier. Previously, it was difficult for Basra to eat out and when doing so she would only have fish or vegetarian dishes. This uncertainty is also reflected in her attitude towards food served in the canteen at her educational institution. Normally, she doesn't eat the food there because she is not convinced it's halal. Basra explains that kosher slaughter is almost identical to halal, but that she would not accept kosher meat.

Fatima is of Palestinian background. In her mid-forties, she grew up in Denmark, trained and worked as a teacher and is married with two children. She maintains that she tries to be as 'observant as possible' with regard to halal, but admits that this is often difficult in contemporary Denmark. If halal observance is compromised in the everyday life of the family, it's because 'we don't have the necessary knowledge'. Fatima and her family do try their best to remain updated on what they can do to meet halal observance in everyday life. For example, when her kids are at a birthday celebration or playgroup, Fatima and her husband tell the kids what to look out for and sometimes they call ahead to talk with parents or organisers about dietary requirements just to make sure everything is fine.

Fatima is fastidious not only about halal meat, but also gelatine and looks at the labels of new products in particular. E numbers such as E471/E472 (types of fat that can be produced from both animal and plant natural fatty acids) and E120 are of concern, but also easy to look for on labels. If it isn't clearly stated on the product that it's of vegetable origin, Fatima won't buy it. Fatima's knowledge of halal mainly comes from her upbringing and this knowledge stresses that dietary observance is an important part of being a Muslim. When we discuss this topic, Fatima has brought a list of acceptable foodstuffs (and care products, as we shall see below) compiled by a Muslim organisation and she also uses the Internet to check on products.

Fatima basically trusts Muslim halal butchers, but if she has doubts about their meat she will ask them about it; Fatima's husband normally buys the family's beef and lamb from their local halal butcher's. As the chicken sold in supermarkets displays halal logos this is where the family buys most of their chicken. The family eats meat a couple of times a week and generally they are happy with the availability of halal in Denmark; Fatima argues that the law against stunning in Denmark is politically motivated. She's aware that a limited number of halal butchers sell or specialise in non-stunned meat, but she doesn't really know whether the meat the family buys is stunned or non-stunned, even if she stresses that in principle animals must be conscious when slaughtered. When eating out the family will only go to outlets that are clearly marked as halal.

Fatima believes that halal is healthier and she refers to research that backs up this idea – for example pork avoidance. When we discuss the necessity to have enzymes or Coca-Cola halal-certified, Fatima's position is clear: 'Yes, I support this – as much as possible. If people are against halal Coke it's their problem – basically it's a good idea.' These notions are also reinforced by Fatima's statement that 'I know for sure that Colgate toothpaste is not halal – there's something in it. I buy Zendium instead.' Fatima supports this claim by referring to the list mentioned above that states that while Colgate toothpaste is not halal, Zendium is a viable alternative. Altogether, Fatima is sympathetic to the idea that more and more products should be halal-certified and offers the example of leather sofas made out of pig leather. Fatima argues that the method of ritual slaughter is very similar in Islam and Judaism, but admits that her knowledge of kosher is limited and thus she's not prepared to eat kosher meat.

Asena is in her forties and is married with two children; she came to Denmark from Turkey when she was five years old. She's worked in different professions and in her spare time she is part of a sewing and cooking network for migrant women. The network is also a forum for discussing halal understanding and practice among Muslims in Denmark. Asena, along with many of the women in the network, is fastidious about halal, especially meat (which is eaten on a daily basis), pork avoidance and gelatine. She also argues that the availability of halal in Denmark has improved and that chicken certified by ICCOS is now widely available in supermarkets: 'When we see the logo on chicken in supermarkets we buy it.'

Conversely, halal beef and lamb are not offered in supermarkets and consequently this is bought at a local halal butcher. Asena acknowledges that going to the halal butcher is simply based on a question of trust: 'We have to trust him.' Upon request she believes that the butcher can provide documentation about the halalness of meat, but normally she doesn't take that opportunity. Butchers are mainly selected from discussions about the quality and price of the meat sold in a specific place among friends and family and the same can be said about halal butchers to be avoided: a friend of Asena's, for example, observed that a 'secular' supplier delivered meat to a particular butcher's and the word quickly spread that this butcher was not halal. The ethnicity of the butcher does not really play a role. Comparing prices in supermarkets and halal butchers, prices in the latter are higher, but the quality is also better, Asena argues; yet she explains that it can also be difficult to find a good halal butcher that maintains high quality. Her parents' attitude towards halal was similar to her own, but as availability has improved she argues that so too has consciousness about what halal is and is not.

Asena states that in principle only non-stunned meat can be considered halal, but she's aware of the law against non-stunned slaughter in Denmark and contends that Muslim consumers must be pragmatic when they go about their everyday shopping for halal meat in Denmark. One of the halal butchers Asena frequents suggested that the meat sold in the shop was imported from non-stunned sources, but Asena explains that questions about the origins of meat are generally not discussed with butchers, as it can potentially undermine the authority and expertise of the butcher and the trust consumers have in them. As Asena states: 'If you're really focused on halal you should not live in Denmark.'

When we discuss sources of knowledge about halal, Asena explains that this is mainly passed on by friends and family, but also through the Internet when exploring whether a specific product is acceptable. Some products or

ready-made meals contain low levels of alcohol – wine vinegar, for example. Asena feels that this is acceptable because the wine 'evaporates' during
cooking, but she often discusses such issues further with friends and family
or checks on the Internet. In general, Asena finds that halal is healthier: 'It's
good for the body to avoid bacteria in pork, many Danes also say that.' Yet
while pork avoidance is central to her everyday practice, non-meat products
such as medication or care products are not subjected to the same scrutiny.
However, Asena speculates that if more non-meat halal products were available in Denmark she would consider buying these to benefit her conscience.

Atilla is a man in his twenties of Turkish background. He was born in
Denmark and is studying at university. He states that halal is very important
in his everyday life: 'What I eat is important for my body and you are what
you eat. For example, when I buy sweets I'm always careful to avoid pork gelatine.' Atilla's family share this attitude and he's thus been brought up with the
notion that halal is important both religiously and physically. Atilla and his
family consume meat on a daily basis. At university he will eat the chicken
that he knows is produced in Denmark and thus halal-certified, but not other
kinds of meat, and sometimes he will ask staff about the halalness of the meat
served. Similarly, he buys chicken with halal logos in supermarkets, but not
meat such as beef or lamb. Instead, he will go to halal butcher's and for cold
meat products he will typically go to Muslim shops in Nørrebro. Atilla believes
that slaughter without stunning is quicker and more humane to animals compared to slaughter with stunning: 'You might as well get it over with without
stunning – I can't see it's necessary to spend money and time on stunning that
only complicates the whole process. For religious reasons I prefer non-stunned
meat and I oppose the law in Denmark that prohibits slaughter without stunning – this law results in conflicts and misunderstandings.'

Atilla is well aware that halal logos on non-meat products are not easy to find
in Denmark, even if new halal-certified products such as energy drinks have
started to appear in local shops predominantly run by Muslims. Generally, he
is not too bothered about E numbers and halal in connection with non-meat
products, but he welcomes better halal availability in Danish supermarkets.
Atilla goes to convenience shops to find what he needs but not to support
Muslims *per se*. However, when going out to eat his general principle is to look
for outlets run by Muslims, although very few of these outlets are certified as
halal. As for alcohol, Atilla occasionally enjoys it and argues that alcohol is an
integral part of culinary culture in Turkey.

Comparing his own generation to that of his parents, Atilla feels that his own
generation is more conscious about halal – not necessarily more religious, but
more conscious about food consumption because more information is available today; for example, friends and relatives of his use the Internet and apps to
check halal and religious issues. These sources of knowledge then supplement
religious texts and scholars. When comparing different groups of Muslims,

Atilla makes the case that Muslims with Pakistani or Arab background seem to be more fastidious.

Atilla believes that halal is healthier physically and spiritually. Arguably, this is the case because non-stunned slaughter is so quick that it does not stress the animals and thus no 'stress chemicals' are transferred to humans through consumption. Moreover, draining the blood and blood cells makes for a 'purer animal', more suitable for human consumption. Even if Atilla believes halal meat consumption is healthier, he also maintains that halal in non-food consumption can be excessive: for example, expensive Muslim-friendly holidays are considered unnecessary and over-commercialised. Conversely, it makes sense that non-meat products such as toothpaste and other care products can be halal: 'If halal toothpaste was available in Denmark it would make me wonder if the non-halal toothpaste next to it is problematic', he points out. Atilla finds halal and kosher to be comparable as both Muslims and Jews are People of Book within Islam and Judaism. Consequently, he would readily consume kosher products if available in his everyday life in Denmark.

Nora is a student of Egyptian background and heritage. She came to Denmark when she was two years old and lives at home with her parents and siblings. Nora often travels back and forth between Egypt and Denmark to visit friends and family. She describes herself as 'very observant' when it comes to halal and this includes sweets and other products as well as meat. Nora is the only member of her family who is a vegetarian. She became vegetarian quite simply because she doesn't like meat, as he explains:

> I never fancied chicken or meat – I didn't care for the taste. The way we treat animals prior to slaughter is not OK – it's unethical and the production of meat is not fair. Becoming a vegetarian made things so much easier.

Nora's family believe that pork is not only prohibited, but also unhealthy in that it contains bacteria. Nora also believes that draining the blood is healthier than not doing so as it lessens the threats posed to human well-being from the consumption of animals products. Altogether, these arguments have been proven scientifically, Nora explains, and she refers to several studies that back up this argument. Nora's family prefer non-stunned meat and they buy this from a butcher's that imports meat from countries where non-stunned meat is allowed. Relatives and friends of Nora are often concerned about local and European meat scandals. Generally she looks for animal gelatine when shopping for food except when it comes to halal sweets that she buys in a shop run by the Islamic Faith Community. Nora would like to see better halal availability in Denmark and more halal logos with reliable certifiers on products. Since she's a vegetarian, eating out does not pose a problem for Nora.

When we discuss the need to have non-halal products such as shampoo halal-certified, Nora argues that in a consumer market such as Denmark where pork and haram products are commonplace it is necessary that a wide range of products explicitly state that they are halal-certified. She also feels that halal enzymes make sense because these are part of a many food products consumed on a daily basis. When we discuss similarities between halal and kosher, Nora argues that there are many similarities: meat, for example, is ritually slaughtered in both traditions, but even so she would not accept kosher products. Nora notes that kosher meat and milk cannot be mixed and that's in general it appears that kosher can be considered more complex than halal.

Ehab is in his sixties. He grew up in Egypt and came to Denmark in the 1980s to study. He married in Denmark and the couple had one child. Before leaving for Denmark Ehab recalls that halal was not a big issue in Egypt until the 1980s. When he first arrived in Denmark he ate pork and sausages because this was widely available/affordable; he also consumed alcohol. However, little by little he was reminded, especially at celebrations and events, that 'You're Muslim – you can't eat pork', and after a while Ehab thus started to become more conscious of food in Denmark. The main issue for Ehab and his friends is pork avoidance and over the last 10–15 years as he has become more observant has also stopped drinking alcohol. Even so, Ehab does not think it appropriate to ask his mother-in-law for halal meat when he visits her in rural Denmark, where halal meat is hard to come by. More generally, he accepts non-halal meat at the homes of friends and family. He argues that in Denmark he has to be pragmatic as a Muslim consumer, although he will choose halal if it's available.

Ehab thinks that it's hard to find a halal butcher who sells halal meat of good quality in Denmark and that when he finds one he buys in bulk and shares the meat with a Muslim neighbour. Quality is important, as is a butcher's expertise, and when a butcher says that meat is halal he trusts them. Ehab's family eat meat every day and they are not overly concerned about whether the meat is stunned or not just as long as the meat is said to be halal. An issue that concerns Ehab is lard in processed foods and so he looks at labels in shops to try and avoid it; food scandals such as BSE also made him aware of avoiding meat from certain countries and producers. When we discuss the relevance or necessity of certifying non-food halal products, Ehab argues that these examples clearly indicate that halal is becoming over-commercialised. He argues that: 'It's a trend right now that stresses a move from Muslim consumption of production to the production of Muslim consumption', that is, the marketing of products and services specifically aimed at Muslims. Even if halal availability has improved over the years, Ehab would still like to see better availability in Denmark. Generally, he's not convinced that halal is healthier even if this is the interpretation of *ulama*.

As long as pork is not served, Ehab feels it is fine to frequent restaurants. He recalls working in a restaurant in which pork and roast beef were put in the same pan – arguably to flavour the roast beef – and to Ehab this make the roast beef haram. Similarly, once he was invited to a barbecue party where utensils used to prepare both lamb and pork were mixed and thus cross-contamination made the meat unacceptable. Ehab is normally in charge of shopping, while his wife cooks. Their son does not have any specific food preferences, so the family eats many different types of food. He recalls that when a Jewish colleague of his visited the house he planned to cook a vegetarian dish, but the colleague indicated that she was used to eating halal meat because she had lived in the Middle East, where both Jews and Muslims were considered People of the Book. Ehab believes Jews would generally accept halal, as there are many similarities between kosher and halal – mentioning the name of God at the time of slaughter, for example.

Danial is a single man in his thirties with a Pakistani background who trained as an academic. He is third-generation Ahmadiyya and his family came to Denmark when he was a child. Danial thinks that generally Ahmadiyya may not be as focused on halal as other Muslim groups: he argues that South Asian Islam is different from Southeast Asian Islam and Muslims from the region are less fastidiousness when it comes to halal. If halal meat is available Danial will buy it, but if not he's flexible and pragmatic as long as pork can be avoided. His family were even more flexible when he was a child because there were fewer halal butchers in Denmark than there are today, but as availability improved, so did the family's views on halal meat.

Danial follows the position of the founder of Ahmadiyya and its present caliph, who stress the linkages between the material and practical, on the one hand, and the spiritual, on the other. 'Basically, I trust a person who states products are halal and it's his problem if they're not.' Consequently if Danial goes to a rural place in Denmark where halal is hard to come by he may eat at McDonald's or elsewhere if the meat can be thought of as halal. In the eyes of Danial many advertisements aimed at Muslims cannot be taken seriously as they only signify the material and not the spiritual. Danial states that it is only following religious rules with the intentions prescribed in religious texts that makes you a good Muslim, and not consuming halal toothpaste. He points out that even the question of gelatine is debated among Muslims, with some *ulama* arguing that gelatine undergoes chemical processes that change its nature and make it acceptable. Danial tries to avoid pork gelatine, however, but he doesn't really feel there's a need for specific halal logos on products and the controversies about E numbers or enzymes to do overly concern him. While alcohol is acceptable as part of industrial processes, when it 'evaporates', he argues that it is clearly prohibited to drink alcohol. Extremely small quantities of prohibited ingredients are not only acceptable, he argues, but also essential to the manufacturing of vital medication. However, whenever possible Danial thinks they should be avoided.

Danial usually buys meat at local halal butchers and chicken in supermarkets. Typically, he eats meat two or three times a week. He follows the position of the Ahmadiyya caliph on stunning, who argues that it's acceptable to stun animals before slaughter if it makes them suffer less. As in the *hadith* traditions, a sharp knife must be used and animals shouldn't be slaughtered in front of each other. To Danial, ritual slaughter is basically about animal welfare, draining the blood and remembrance and gratitude to God on whose authority we take life. Knowledge of halal is first and foremost from religious texts, the Ahmadiyya caliph or the imam of the congregation in Denmark, but everyday practices and habits in families are also important. Danial explains that you can write to the caliph if you have questions and that the caliph is in no way involved in halal regulation or business. Most importantly of all, Danial argues that the food we eat has a direct bearing on physical as well as spiritual well-being and that pork should therefore not be eaten.

Discussion

The empirical data from Manchester shows that the majority of our informants are quite observant about halal and that they generally find the availability of halal satisfactory – even to the extent that several feel that halal is being over-commercialised, on the one hand, and that halal certification by HMC (against stunning) or HFA (largely for stunning) is not as important as it once was. All our UK consumers eat meat and many of them do so on a daily basis, which testifies to the confidence they have in halal meat and meat products. At the same time there are noticeable differences between those who are fastidious about the issue of stunning and those who are more relaxed, and the same goes for questions about certification and health.

In general, UK informants are knowledgeable and conversant about what halal is or ought to be. None explicitly dismiss halal as 'Muslim materialism', even if many of them critically reflect on the ever-expanding market for halal. None were aware of the pervasiveness and scale of halal enzyme production and certification and only a few possessed knowledge about the way in which developments in Southeast Asian countries such as Indonesia and Malaysia over the last couple of decades have transformed global halal. Thus, contrary to Fischer's study on Malay Muslim migrants from Malaysia in the UK (2011), which demonstrated how consumers to a large extent desire ever stricter halal regulation by organisations and the state, our informants feel that as modern religious consumers there is sufficient availability and consumer protection in their everyday lives – for example, these consumers can freely choose stunned or non-stunned meat when frequenting restaurants that are halal-certified. Meat and its qualification thus remain at the centre of halal understanding and practice, even if awareness of non-meat products such as gelatine in sweets or gelatine/alcohol in medication is evident and growing. Although there was recognition that third- and fourth-generation Muslims in the UK have more disposable income than previous generations, and may like to go on halal holidays, for example, other informants such as Saeed expressed concern that the commercialisation of Islam has gone too far.

The Muslim population in Denmark is small compared to that of the UK, but halal availability in urban areas such as Copenhagen has vastly expanded over the last decade or so. Almost all of the chicken produced in Denmark is halal-certified by the ICCOS and thus Muslim consumers can have a wide range of shopping choices. However, compared to UK Muslims, Danish consumers are faced with two challenges: halal beef and lamb is almost exclusively sold in halal butcher's shops and as we saw in Chapter 2 the vast majority of this meat is of Danish origin and thus stunned according to Danish law. Interestingly, out of all our informants only one is a vegetarian and for some meat was central not only to their diet but also to their identity as Muslims. Moving beyond meat, many of the Danish informants are alert about gelatine, E numbers and dairy products such as cheese and often these concerns are articulated in the context of everyday family life and educating children about halal, health and nutrition. A couple of Danish informants are actively involved in Muslim business and they thus idealise halal beyond material products – for example, the informant Hassan explained that his daughter was involved in halal tourism with her own company.

The majority of informants in both the UK and Denmark believe that halal meat produced in the right way is healthier, although in the UK in particular there was also recognition that eating too much meat is unhealthy, which can be seen as an effect of pervasive and powerful discourses about health that characterise welfare state politics. In the UK some informants argued that more attention must be paid to the links between halal in terms of food consumption and actions in everyday life, while others talked about the spiritual benefits of halal consumption. Rabia in Manchester argued that although she doesn't think that halal meat is necessarily healthier, knowing that it is halal makes her feel better about eating it. Eating halal, in this sense, is a type of cultural consumption inseparable from aesthetics and everyday life. Warde's (2016) notion of compound practice captures this complexity nicely in a context where family pressures and concerns about 'health' and 'spirituality', for example, overlap with eating. While some informants in the UK stated that only non-stunned meat is authentic halal, they may also eat non-stunned halal meat or non-halal meat in some circumstances. In both the UK and Denmark, despite different regulatory pressures, many halal consumers trust in the quality of the halal meat sold by Muslims in shops and restaurants. At the same time, pressure from cultural intermediaries makes questions of what and where to eat more open to judgement, thus increasing the need for more elaborate forms of justification when deciding what is and is not acceptable practice (Wouters 2008; Warde 2016).

Comparing informants in the UK and Denmark we can say that they are all aware of being part of a globalising market that increasingly is subjected to expanding and overlapping forms of regulation. However, none of these informants were aware of enzyme production being kosher/halal-certified and this supports the argument that modern forms of transnational governmentality or religious audit culture tend to take on a life of their own: the relationship and cooperation between producers, sellers and certifiers is intensifying to such an extent that most consumers are unaware of these trends and processes.

One noticeable difference between UK and Danish consumers is that Muslim consumers in the UK are generally reassured about the processes of halal qualification (availability, certification and trusted Muslim retailers) and this is quite different in Denmark, where the market is more limited and non-stunned slaughter is banned. Comparable to what we saw among Jewish consumers, Muslim consumers often ritualise not only the buying and consumption of food, but also more contextual practices and items such as utensils. For a number of reasons Muslim ritualisation of halal is not as elaborate as that of Orthodox Jews, yet there is little doubt that the development of the halal market to a large extent emulates what has happened to the kosher market. We speculate that the two markets will be increasingly comparable.

Conclusion

In focusing on the consequences of globalising kosher and halal markets, this book has demonstrated that similarities and differences between kosher and halal consumption, production and regulation in different national contexts are not well understood, and that to better understand global kosher and halal markets they must be explored at different levels of the social scale. This conclusion is organised around the three keywords of the book's title: *religion*, *regulation* and *consumption*. We conclude on these themes by bringing in a few examples from preceding chapters and by reflecting on the 'bigger picture' these conclusions evoke.

It is clear that kosher and halal markets have globalised and been subjected to new forms of regulation within the last two decades or so. However, no matter how regulated these markets have become they are still fundamentally expressions of *religion* as taboos dating back thousands of years. The proliferation and regulation of kosher and halal markets signify, firstly, the way in which religion is given expression in and through production, regulation and consumption – and an important aspect of this is the way in which kosher and halal are moving beyond conventional meat and food production and consumption into biotechnology, for example. Thus, kosher and halal markets signify how material religion has increased in significance within the last two decades or so. Concepts such as transnational governmentality (Ferguson and Gupta 2002), qualification (Callon *et al.* 2002) and compound practice (Warde 2016) are conventionally applied to 'secular' processes, but the empirical data from the UK and Denmark demonstrates that in the modern world religion is not only fully compatible with production, regulation and consumption, but actually thrives or is invigorated in the constituent processes: a couple of examples to illustrate this point.

The UK markets for kosher and halal are vast and expanding because local religious consumers traditionally support the markets for both non-stunned (kosher and halal) and stunned (halal) religiously certified meat (Lever and Miele 2012). As we saw in Chapter 1, kosher and halal fuel a whole range of debates among rabbis/imams and between religious organisations more broadly over what religion is or ought be in the modern world (Bowen 1993). Many of these debates or tensions tend to revolve around the extent to which religious markets are essentially *religious*, and whether it is acceptable to be open about the ways in which certifiers profit and claim (excessive) authority? Following on from this is the question about how local religious authority can be asserted in the context of ever more powerful and profitable forms of transnational governmentality. Thus, all these debates and tensions at different levels reinvigorate old discussions about the role of secularism and religious ritual in modern societies.

Comparing the UK and Denmark, we can say that Judaism/kosher and Islam/halal are less state regulated in the UK and that this allows for slaughter without stunning, for example. This situation has made the UK one of the largest markets for kosher/halal food in the world – a market in which the qualification (Callon *et al.* 2002) of products as kosher and halal is pervasive and expanding in ever more complex ways. On the one hand, the UK kosher market is expanding into the mainstream through hyper/supermarkets as rabbinical authorities attempt to expand their power and control over economic goods qualified as kosher. On the other hand, as these processes expand and questions over what kosher is or ought to be intensify in a globalising context, so greater numbers of Jews are becoming more Orthodox and strict in terms of their *kashrut* and *shechita* requirements.

An example of debate about what Islam/halal is or ought to be is Ahmadiyya in Denmark, which also has a major congregation in London, where the Danish Ahmadiyya imam studied. Ahmadi rely on the teachings of the Qur'an and *hadith* and do not put too much emphasis on buying halal-certified meat and other products. Likewise, the issue of stunning animals before slaughter is not a major concern, since many animals today are slaughtered in a similar way, whether their meat is classed as halal or not. Conversely, the essence of Ahmadiyya theology and practice is the spiritual and moral relationship between God and man. Consequently, in the eyes of Ahmadi, many Muslims are overly focused on the physical and material side of Islam while downplaying spirituality, morality, justice and love. Looking within rather to material signs of piety makes life easier, and instead of competing over material and shallow forms of religiosity, Ahmadi avoid judging the halal/haram consumption patterns of others, for example. Thus, even in the UK, where there is a major market for halal meat, Ahmadiyya is not involved in animal slaughter or halal certification. What is more, Ahmadiyya does not wish to engage in business and what it considers overly commercialised forms religion and unnecessary Muslim dogma; some halal consumers in the UK made similar arguments.

Turning to *regulation*, we have shown how transnational governmentality (Ferguson and Gupta 2002), certification (Bennett and Lagos 2007), standards (Busch 2000) and audit culture (Power 1999), are key aspects of these religious markets. Kosher is often used as an example of not only a niche US market of successful private-sector regulation in an era of growing public concern over the government's ability to ensure food safety, but also more generally increasing regulation of it (Lytton 2013). Within the last two decades or so the Big Five kosher certifiers have achieved global reach: the Orthodox Union, OK Kosher, KOF-K, Star-K and the Chicago Rabbinical Council. However, these major kosher certifiers both cooperate and compete with more local certification bodies in the UK and Denmark. Manchester Beth Din now conducts *shechita* slaughter services in a number of Eastern Europe countries and meat ascribed with kosher qualities in these locations is sold in shops in countries such as Denmark through emergent forms of transnational governmentality that extend the power and authority of these certifiers.

In 2001, a major food scandal in Indonesia triggered a new phase of halal proliferation and regulation on a global scale, covering areas such as enzyme production (Fischer 2016a). Although Novozymes has complied with steadily growing kosher requirements since the 1980s, it was only after this scandal that enquiries about halal certification from Southeast Asia, especially Malaysia, Singapore and Indonesia, culminated in new practices. Yet Halal certifiers such as JAKIM, MUIS and MUI do not have the resources to carry out inspections globally and consequently they have outsourced responsibilities to Muslim organisations such as IFCE and IFANCA. Thus, globally, companies are affected by halal transnational governmentality. Religious enzyme production, supervision and certification at Novozymes in Denmark, for example, fully relies on these increasingly standardised forms, with similar developments being evident at companies such as Biocatalysts in the UK. Kosher/halal qualification in biotech is quintessentially dependent on this kind of transnational governmentality. In many ways, non-animal ingredients are less problematic in the globalised market in an era of food scares and rising religious requirements, and over the last two decades religious principles have played an important role in shaping knowledge, work processes and practices in organisations such as Novozymes and Biocatalysts.

How do our informants understand and practice kosher/halal in terms of everyday *consumption*? We have shown that many Jewish groups are fastidious about their everyday kosher consumption. This point has reinforced regulation of global kosher production and kosher certification and logos are extremely important in the everyday lives of many Jewish groups in Europe. However, many Jewish consumers in Denmark are not so fastidious about kosher and together with local Jewish organisations they feel that the Big Five kosher certifiers have become global, commercial and powerful to such an extent that their certification of thousands of companies and products has taken on a life of its own that is detached from the everyday lives of Jewish consumers. Comparatively, our UK Jewish consumers seem to be more observant about kosher than their Danish counterparts. This is most likely due to the fact that kosher markets are large and expanding in the UK, with many Jewish groups living in increasingly bounded neighbourhoods, where Jewish identity is to a large extent maintained and developed through increasingly strict forms of kosher supervision and consumption. In Denmark, the relatively small Jewish community is more dispersed, and here more of our informants saw kosher as religious dogma.

There are many similarities between our Jewish and Muslim consumers. Both groups for the most part rely on religious texts as guides to their everyday consumption practices. Many of our informants would agree that science is needed in kosher/halal production and many search for knowledge about how to live a pious life. This knowledge comes not only from religious texts, but also from rabbis and *ulama*, family and friends, and from lists on websites and smartphone apps. Most Jews stress the centrality of non-stunned meat to their kosher identity, but comparatively kosher meat is more widely available in the UK than it is in Denmark. After slaughter without stunning was prohibited in Denmark in 2014, non-stunned meat was imported into Denmark, yet interestingly the ban to some extent aligned observant Jews and some Muslims in their focus on non-stunned meat. Since the ban, many Muslims search butcher's shops in Copenhagen for non-stunned halal meat, whereas they previously accepted what was on offer – which was mostly from stunned animals.

Even if meat is still subjected to the most stringent religious requirements, E numbers are also a concern to both groups, who for the most part put a lot of effort into their everyday shopping practices. Some of our observant Jewish informants are focused on non-food products in specific ritual contexts: kosher toothpaste is only of importance during religious festivals, while toothbrushes and dish brushes should have nylon and not animal bristles. Arguably, kosher is more complex than halal for a range of reasons – separating milk and meat, for example – and together with its longer and more pervasive history of regulation there is more of an emphasis on cross-contamination, purification and ritual in everyday life. Thus, in terms of differences we can say that observant Jews in many ways are more fastidious about their religious consumption: they separate milk and meat; have kitchens with different sections for milk and meat; and have different sets of utensils for eating milk and meat dishes. That means that many observant Jews put a lot of effort into maintaining this ritual separation – even in small Copenhagen kitchens. In Denmark more generally the limited availability of kosher products makes these issues more significant in terms of everyday practice. Products like cheese and ice cream are also more problematic to observant Jews. Vegetables can also be of concern in that insects can be hiding inside Brussels sprouts, for example.

Many of our Jewish and Muslim informants are convinced that kosher and halal are not only 'spiritually' but also 'physically' healthier and more wholesome for a range of reasons, including draining the blood (which makes meat healthier) and pork avoidance (as pork contains cholesterol and bacteria). In general they also possess a basic knowledge of the food taboo of the *other*, that is, Jews tend to know that halal is mainly related to ritual slaughter, as well pork and alcohol avoidance, while few Muslims are aware of the kosher prohibition to avoid mixing milk and meat. Almost all of our Muslim informants would in principle accept kosher meat, while observant Jews would never accept halal.

Significantly, contemporary food preference and avoidance also reflects changing social relations between individuals and groups over time, demonstrating how cultural tastes are transformed in line with changes in political power and socioeconomic organisation (Mennell 1985). While our empirical material from the UK and Denmark highlights the ways in which 'food piety' is practised in everyday life, it also illustrates how kosher and halal reflect a type of cultural consumption that is inseparable from aesthetics and everyday life (Warde 2016). Celebrations, religious festivals and 'eating out' are now more complex for kosher and halal consumers for a whole range of reasons, with strategies and forward planning thus becoming more important in a minority religious context. Warde's (2016) notion of 'compound practice' captures this complexity nicely. It illustrates how eating practices are shaped among family members and through concerns about 'health' and 'spirituality', for example, by direction, coordination and regulation by different secular and religious stakeholders, and also by cultural intermediaries and texts that describe and prescribe proper ways of eating. To complicate matters still further, media in liberal state regimes validate pluralism and court dispute simultaneously to reinforce bias towards hegemonic preferences and unpalatable alternatives (Warde 2016). Considered alongside the increasing complexity of food production that has emerged in recent decades, it thus also becomes evident that kosher and halal consumers in contemporary Western societies often have problems knowing what and where to eat, and that they often require more elaborate forms of justification and self-discipline when deciding what is and is not acceptable (Wouters 2008).

Kosher and halal consumption thus remain central to debates about what religion is or ought to be for Jews and Muslims living in countries such as the UK and Denmark. Yet even if the underlying principles behind religious economies and markets retain some form of 'divine order', transnational governmentality is increasingly authoritative as a field of knowledge. While growing numbers of religious certifiers and companies claim authority and generate vast profits through these globalising markets, it is also clear many Muslims and Jews (and also Hindus – Fischer 2016b) are unaware of or uninterested in these processes.

Bibliography

Agriculture and Agri-Food Canada 2012, *The Specialty Food Market in North America*. Ottawa: Agriculture and Agri-Food Canada.

Ahlin, Lars, Jørn Borup, Marianne Qvortrup Fibiger, Lene Kühle, Viggo Mortensen and René Dybdal Pedersen 2012, Religious Diversity and Pluralism: Empirical Data and Theoretical Reflections from the Danish Pluralism Project. *Journal of Contemporary Religion* 27(3): 403–18.

Alderman, G. 1995, The Defence of *Shechita*: Anglo-Jewry and the 'Humane Conditions' Regulations of 1990. *New Community* 21(1): 79–93.

Ansari, H. 2009, *The Infidel Within: Muslims in Britain since 1800*. London: Hurst & Co.

Asad, T. 2003, *Formations of the Secular: Christianity, Islam, Modernity*. Stanford: Stanford University Press.

Bamberger, Ib N. 1983, *The Viking Jews: A History of the Jews of Denmark*. New York: Shengold Publishers.

Barthes, R. 1975, Towards a Psychosociology of Contemporary Food Consumption. In *European Diet from Pre-Industrial to Modern Times*, ed. Elborg Foster and Robert Foster, pp. 166–73. New York: Harper & Row.

Becket, J. and Musselin, C. 2013, *Constructing Quality: The Classification of Goods in Markets*. Oxford: Oxford University Press.

Bell, Catherine 1992, *Ritual Theory, Ritual Practice*. Oxford: Oxford University Press.

Bennett, L. W. and Lagos, T. 2007, Logo Logic: The Ups and Downs of Branded Political Communication. *Annals of the American Academy of Political and Social Science* 611(1): 193–206.

Bergeaud-Blackler, Florence 2004, Social Definitions of Halal Quality: The Case of Maghrebi Muslims in France. In *The Qualities of Food: Alternative Theories and Empirical Approaches*, ed. Mark Harvey, Andrew McMeekin and Alan Warde, pp. 94–107. Manchester: Manchester University Press.

Bergeaud-Blackler, Florence 2005, De la viande halal à l'halal food: comment le halal s'est développé en France? *Revue Européenne des Migrations Internationales* 21(3): 125–47.

Bergeaud-Blackler, Florence 2006, Halal: d'une norme communautaire à une norme institutionnelle. *Journal des Anthropologues* 106–7: 77–103.

Bergeaud-Blackler, Florence 2007, New Challenges for Islamic Ritual Slaughter: A European Perspective. *Journal of Ethnic and Migration Studies* 33(6): 965–80.

Bergeaud-Blackler, Florence 2015, The Halal Certification Market in Europe and the World: A First Panorama. In *Halal Matters: Islam, Politics and Markets in*

Global Perspective, ed. F. Bergeaud-Blackler, J. Fischer and J. Lever, pp. 106–26. Abingdon: Routledge.

Bergeaud-Blackler, Florence and Bernard, Bruno 2010, *Comprendre le halal*. Liège: Edipro.

Bergeaud-Blackler, F., Fisher, J. and Lever, J. (eds) 2015, *Halal Matters: Islam, Politics and Markets in Global Perspective*. Abingdon: Routledge.

Biocatalysts 2015, Biocatalysts Ltd Achieve Kosher Certification. Biocatalysts, Media and Resources, 4 November 2015. www.biocatalysts.com/news/biocatalysts-achieve-kosher-certification, accessed 2 March 2016.

Blech, Z. Y. 2008, *Kosher Food Production*. Ames, IA: Wiley-Blackwell.

Blum, Jacques 1973, *Dansk og/eller Jøde? En Kultursociologisk Undersøgelse af den Jødiske Minoritet i Danmark*. Copenhagen: Gyldendal.

Blüdnikov, Bent 1986, *Immigranter: Østeuropæiske Jøder i København 1900–1917*. Copenhagen: Borgen.

Borup, Jørn and Fibiger, Marianne Q. 2015, *Religion i Danmark*. Aarhus: Aarhus University.

Bourdieu, P. 1984, *Distinction: A Social Critique of the Judgement of Taste*. London: Routledge.

Bowen, J. R. 1993, *Muslims through Discourse: Religion and Ritual in Gayo Society*. Princeton: Princeton University Press.

Bradley, D., Nganga, J., Marechal, A. and Garrone, M. 2015, *Study on Information to Consumers on the Stunning of Animals*. Brussels: European Commission, DG Heath and Food Safety.

Brunsson, N. and Jakobsson, B. 2000, The Contemporary Expansion of Standardization. In *A World of Standards*, ed. Nils Brunsson and Bengt Jakobsson, pp. 1–20. Oxford and New York: Oxford University Press.

Buckser, Andrew 1999, Keeping Kosher: Eating and Social Identity among the Jews of Denmark. *Ethnology* 38(3): 191–209.

Buckser, Andrew 2003, *After the Rescue: Jewish Identity and Community in Denmark*. New York: Palgrave Macmillan.

Buckser, Andrew 2005, Chabad in Copenhagen: Fundamentalism and Modernity in Jewish Denmark. *Ethnology* 44(2): 125–45.

Busch, L. 2000, The Moral Economy of Grades and Standards. *Journal of Rural Studies* 16(3): 273–83.

Busch, L. 2013, *Standards: Recipes for Reality*. Cambridge, MA: MIT Press.

Callon, M., Méadel, C. and Rabeharisoa, V. 2002, The Economy of Qualities. *Economy and Society* 31(2): 194–217.

Campbell, H., Murcott, A. and MacKenzie, A. 2011, Kosher in New York City, Halal in Aquitaine: Challenging the Relationship between Neoliberalism and Food Auditing. *Agriculture and Human Values* 28(1): 67–79.

Charlton, R. and Kaye, R. 1985, The Politics of Religious Slaughter: An Ethno-Religious Case Study. *New Community* 12(3): 490–503.

Collier, Stephen J. and Ong, Aihwa 2005, Global Assemblages, Anthropological Problems. In *Global Assemblages: Technology, Politics, and Ethics as Anthropological Problems*, ed. Aihwa Ong and Stephen J. Collier, pp. 3–21. Oxford: Wiley-Blackwell.

Collins, S. 1957, *Coloured Minorities in Britain: Studies in British Race Relations Based on African, West Indian, and Asiatic Immigrants*. London: Lutterworth Press.

Comaroff, J. and Comaroff, J. 2000, Millennial Capitalism: First Thoughts on a Second Coming. *Public Culture* 12(2): 291–343.

Coveney, J. 2000, *Food, Morals and Meaning: The Pleasure and Anxiety of Eating.* London and New York: Routledge.

Denny, F. M. 2006, *An Introduction to Islam.* Upper Saddle River, NJ: Pearson Prentice Hall.

Diamond, E. 2000, *And I Will Dwell in Their Midst: Orthodox Jews in Suburbia.* Chapel Hill: University of North Carolina Press.

Diamond, E. 2002, The Kosher Lifestyle: Religious Consumerism and Suburban Orthodox Jews. *Journal of Urban History* 28(4): 488–505.

Douglas, M. 1972, Deciphering a Meal. *Daedalus* 101(1): 61–81.

Douglas, M. 1975, *Implicit Meanings.* New York and London: Routledge.

Douglas, M. 1986, *How Institutions Think.* Syracuse, NY: Syracuse University Press.

Douglas, M. 2002, *Purity and Danger: An Analysis of Concepts of Purity and Taboo.* London: Routledge.

Durkheim, E. 1995, *The Elementary Forms of Religious Life.* New York: The Free Press.

Einstein, M. 2008, *Brands of Faith: Marketing Religion in a Commercial Age.* Abingdon: Routledge.

Elias, N. 2012, *On the Process of Civilization.* Collected Works of Norbert Elias 15. Dublin: UCD Press.

Elias, N. and Scotson, J. 2008, *The Established and the Outsiders.* Collected Works of Norbert Elias 4. Dublin: UCD Press.

Engels, F. 2009, *The Condition of the Working Class in England.* London: Penguin Books.

FAO 2006, *Livestock's Long Shadow: Environmental Issues and Options.* Rome: Food and Agriculture Organization of the United Nations. ftp.fao.org/docrep/fao/010/a0701e/a0701e00.pdf, accessed 10 April 2016.

FAWC 2003, *Report on the Welfare of Farmed Animals at Slaughter or Killing. Part 1: Red Meat Animals.* London: Farm Animal Welfare Council. http://webarchive.nation-alarchives.gov.uk/20121007104210/http://www.fawc.org.uk/reports/pb8347.pdf, accessed 12 April 2017.

Fazira, E. 2015, Demand for Halal Food Rising in Tandem with Growth of Southeast Asia. In *Doing Business in the Halal Market: Products, Trends and Growth Opportunities*, ed. Euromonitor International, pp. 10–12. London: Euromonitor International.

Ferguson, J. and Gupta, A. 2002, Spatializing States: Toward an Ethnography of Neoliberal Governmentality. *American Ethnologist* 29(4): 981–1002.

Ferrari, S. and Bottoni, R. 2010, *Legislation Regarding Religious Slaughter in the EU Member, Candidate and Associated Countries.* Dialrel Research Report 14. www.dialrel.eu/images/report-legislation.pdf, accessed 28 May 2016.

Fetzer, J. S. and Soper, J. C. 2005, *Muslims and the State in Britain, France, and Germany.* Cambridge: Cambridge University Press.

Fischer, Johan 2008a, Nationalizing Rituals? The Ritual Economy in Malaysia. *Journal of Ritual Studies* 22(2): 13–22.

Fischer, Johan 2008b, *Proper Islamic Consumption: Shopping among the Malays in Modern Malaysia.* Copenhagen: NIAS Press.

Fischer, Johan 2011, *The Halal Frontier: Muslim Consumers in a Globalised Market.* Contemporary Anthropology of Religion. New York: Palgrave Macmillan.

Fischer, Johan 2012, Branding Halal: A Photographic Essay on Global Muslim Markets. *Anthropology Today* 28(4): 18–21.

Fischer, Johan 2014, Danish Halal and Kosher Ban Leaves Religious Groups with Nowhere to Turn. *The Conversation*, 24 February. https://theconversation.com/danish-halal-and-kosher-ban-leaves-religious-groups-with-nowhere-to-turn-23392, accessed 16 September 2016.

Fischer, Johan 2015a, *Islam, Standards, and Technoscience: In Global Halal Zones*. New York: Routledge.

Fischer, Johan 2015b, Keeping Enzymes Kosher: Sacred and Secular Biotech Production. *EMBO Reports* 16(6): 681–84. DOI: 10.15252/embr.201540529.

Fischer, Johan 2016a, Manufacturing Halal in Malaysia. *Contemporary Islam* 10(1): 35–52.

Fischer, Johan 2016b, Markets, Religion, Regulation: Kosher, Halal, and Hindu Vegetarianism in Global Perspective. *Geoforum* 69: 67–70.

Fortune, A. 2016, Halal Beef Demand Rising as Number of Younger Muslims Grows. *Meat Trades Journal*, 31 May. www.meatinfo.co.uk/news/fullstory.php/aid/19780/Halal_beef_demand_rising_as_number_of_younger_Muslims_grows.html, accessed 24 June 2017.

Freidenreich, D. M. 2014, *Foreigners and Their Food: Constructing Otherness in Jewish, Christian, and Islamic Law*. Berkeley: University of California Press.

FSA 2012, Results of the 2011 FSA Animal Welfare Survey in Great Britain. Report by Andrew Rhodes, Director of Operations. Food Standards Agency Open Board, 22 May 2012 (FSA 12/05/08). London: Food Standards Agency.

FSA 2015, Results of the 2013 Animal Welfare Survey in Great Britain, Food Standards Agency, January 2015.

Gellner, D. N. and Hirsch, E. 2001, Introduction: Ethnography of Organizations and Organizations of Ethnography. In *Inside Organizations: Anthropologists at Work*, ed. David N. Gellner and Eric Hirsch, pp. 1–18. Oxford and New York: Berg Publishers.

Gerlach, M. 1992, *Alliance Capitalism: The Social Organization of Japanese Business*. Berkeley: University of California Press.

Gillette, Maris B. 2000, *Between Mecca and Beijing: Modernization and Consumption among Urban Chinese Muslims*. Stanford: Stanford University Press.

Goswami, N. 2009, The Making of 'Curry Mile'. BBC, 12 May. www.bbc.co.uk/manchester/content/articles/2009/05/12/curry_mile_history_feature.shtml, accessed 27 April 2016.

Graham, D. 2013, 2011 Census Results (England and Wales): Initial Insights into Jewish Neighbourhoods, 19 February, London: Institute for Jewish Policy Research. www.jpr.org.uk/documents/2011%20Census%20results%20-%20Initial%20insights%20into%20Jewish%20neighbourhoods.pdf, accessed 24 July 2017.

Grandin, T. 2004, Preface to the Israeli Article about Kosher Slaughter in South America. www.grandin.com/ritual/kosher.meat.uruguay.html, accessed 23 August 2016.

Granovetter, M. 1985, Economic Action and Social Structure: The Problem of Embeddedness. *American Journal of Sociology* 91(3): 481–510.

Haleem, M. A. S. Abdel (trans.) 2008, *The Qur'an*. Oxford: Oxford University Press.

Halliday, F. 1992, The *Millet* of Manchester: Arab Merchants and Cotton Trade. *British Journal of Middle Eastern Studies* 19(2): 159–76.

Hansen, Thomas Blom 2000, Predicaments of Secularism: Muslim Identities and Politics in Mumbai. *Journal of the Royal Anthropological Institute* 6(2): 255–72.

Hefner, R. W. 1998, *Market Cultures: Society and Morality in the New Asian Capitalisms*. Boulder, CO: Westview Press.

Herzfeld, M. 2001, Performing Comparisons: Ethnography, Globetrotting, and the Spaces of Social Knowledge. *Journal of Anthropological Research* 57(3): 259–76.

HFA 2016, Fact Sheet: HFA Certification of Traditional Halal Slaughter (without stunning). London and Tournai: Halal Food Authority. http://halalfoodauthority.com/fact-sheet, accessed 24 October 2016.

Hirsch, S. R. 1962, *Horeb: A Philosophy of Jewish Laws and Observances*. London: Soncino Press.

HMC 2012, Issues of Mechanical Slaughter and Stunning. Leicester: Halal Monitoring Committee, UK. www.halalhmc.org/IssueOfMSandStunning.htm, accessed 6 May 2012.

Ivry, T. 2010, Kosher Medicine and Medicalized *Halacha*: An Exploration of Triadic Relations among Israeli Rabbis, Doctors, and Infertility Patients. *American Ethnologist* 37(4): 662–80.

Jacobsen, Brian A. 2009, Denmark. In *Yearbook of Muslims in Europe*, ed. Jørgen S. Nielsen, Samim Akgönül, Ahmet Alibašić, Brigitte Maréchal and Christian Moe, vol. 1, pp. 97–109. Leiden and Boston: Brill.

Jacobsen, Brian A. 2012, Islam i Danmark. In *Religion i Danmark: En E-årbog fra Center for Samtidsreligion*, pp. 111–15. Aarhus: Aarhus University.

Jensen, Sidsel V. 2016, Håndtering af Muslimske Praksisser i Danske Folkeskoler: Autoritet, Inklusion og Religion. *Tidsskrift for Islamforskning* 8(2): 17–33.

Jensen, Sidsel V. 2016b, Institutional Governance of Minority Religious Practices: Insights from a Study of Muslim Practices in Danish Schools. *Journal of Ethnic and Migration Studies* 42(3): 418–36.

Jensen, T. G. 2014, Denmark: Islam Classes. In *Islamic Movements of Europe: Public Religion and Islamophobia in the Modern World*, ed. F. Peter and R. Ortega, pp. 281–6. London: I.B. Tauris.

Jensen, Tina and Østergaard, Kate 2007, *Nye Muslimer i Danmark: Møder og Omvendelser*. Højbjerg: Univers.

Jørgensen, Harald 1984, *Indenfor Murene: Jødisk Liv i Danmark 1684–1984*. Copenhagen: C. A. Reitzel.

JPPI 2015, *Annual Assessment: The Situation and Dynamics of the Jewish People 2014–2015*. Jerusalem: The Jewish People Policy Institute.

Kalmus, J. 2012, How Kellogg's Keeps the Corn Flakes Kosher in the World's Biggest Cereal Factory. *Jewish Chronicle Online*, 20 September. www.thejc.com/lifestyle/lifestyle-features/82824/how-kelloggs-keeps-corn-flakes-kosher-world's-biggest-cereal-fact, accessed 1 October 2016.

Karrebæk, Sif M. 2014, Rye Bread and Halal: Enregisterment of Food Practices in the Primary Classroom. *Language and Communication* 34: 17–34.

Kaye, R. 1993, The Politics of Religious Slaughter of Animals: Strategies for Ethno-Religious Political Action. *New Community* 19(2): 35–250.

KLBD 2015, *The Really Jewish Food Guide*. London: Kashrut Division London Beth Din.

Klein, M. 2012, *Kosher Feijoada and Other Paradoxes of Jewish Life in São Paulo*. Gainesville: University Press of Florida.

Knight, J. 1992, *Institutions and Social Conflict*. Cambridge: Cambridge University Press.

Kooy, J. 2015, Survey of World Jewish Demographics. Lausanne Consultation on Jewish Evangelism, International Conference, Jerusalem, 16–21 August.

Kossoff, J. 1998, Sausage Dispute Just Isn't Kosher, Say London Jews. *Independent*, 13 September. www.independent.co.uk/news/sausage-dispute-just-isnt-kosher-say-london-jews-1197893.html, accessed 12 September 2016.

Lamont, M. 1992, *Money, Morals, and Manners: The Culture of the French and the American Upper Middle Class*. Chicago: University of Chicago Press.

Larsson, Göran and Björkman, Nina 2010, South Asian Muslims in the Nordic Countries: An Overview Based on the Existing Literature. *Finnish Journal of Ethnicity and Migration* 5(2): 16–23.

Lee, R. L. M. 1993, The Globalisation of Religious Markets: International Innovations, Malaysian Consumption. *Sojourn* 8(1): 35–61.

Lever, J. 2013, The Postliberal Politics of Halal: New Directions in the Civilizing Process? *Human Figurations* 2(3). http://hdl.handle.net/2027/spo.11217607.0002.306, accessed 11 May 2016.

Lever, J. and Miele, M. 2012, The Growth of Halal Meat Markets in Europe: An Exploration of the Supply Side Theory of Religion. *Journal of Rural Studies* 28(4): 528–37.

Lévi-Strauss, C. 1968, *Structural Anthropology*, vol. 1. Harmondsworth: Allen Lane.

Lewis, P. 1993, *Islamic Britain: Religion, Politics and Identity Among British Muslims*, rev. edn. London: I.B. Tauris.

Lowther, E. 2012, MPs Want Curbs on 'Unacceptable' Religious Slaughter. *BBC News*, 28 May. www.bbc.co.uk/news/uk-politics-18187137, accessed 20 May 2017.

Lytton, T. D. 2013, *Kosher: Private Regulation in the Age of Industrial Food*. Cambridge, MA: Harvard University Press.

Macdonald, A. 2016, Halal Food Authority to Certify Unstun Slaughter. *Meat Trades Journal*, 27 May. www.meatinfo.co.uk/news/fullstory.php/aid/19777/Halal_Food_Authority_to_certify_unstun_slaughter.html, accessed 14 April 2016.

Malnick, E. 2014, Halal Meat Row: Faith Leaders Call for Clear Food Labelling. *Telegraph*, 7 May.

Marcus, G. E. 1995, Ethnography in/of the World System: The Emergence of Multi-Sited Ethnography. *Annual Review of Ethnography* 24: 95–117.

Marranci, G. 2009, *Understanding Muslim Identity: Rethinking Fundamentalism*. Basingstoke: Palgrave Macmillan.

MCB 2015, Criteria or Standards for *Zabiha* or *Dhabh*. London: Muslim Council of Britain. www.mabonline.net/wp-content/uploads/2015/02/Halal-MCB-Zabiha-criteria-.pdf, accessed 25 March 2017.

MCC 2015, Religion Summary: 2011 Census. Manchester: Manchester City Council. www.manchester.gov.uk/downloads/download/5154/public_intelligence_2011_census, accessed 25 March 2017.

Mennell, S. 1985, *All Manners of Food: Eating and Taste in England and France from the Middle Ages to the Present*. Oxford: Basil Blackwell.

Miele, M. 2016, Killing Animals for Food: How Science, Religion and Technologies Affect the Public Debate about Religious Slaughter. *Food Ethics* 1(1): 47–60. DOI: 10.1007/s41055-016-0004-y.

Miele, M. and Rucinska, K. 2015, Producing Halal Meat: The Case of Halal Slaughter Practices in Wales, UK. In *The Political Ecologies of Meat*, ed. J. Emel and H. Neo, pp. 253–77. London: Earthscan.

Miller, T. 2009, *Mapping the Global Muslim Population*. Washington, DC: Pew Research Center.

Mintel 2009, *Kosher Foods: US, January 2009*. London: Mintel Group Ltd.

Mitchell, M. 1998, *Employing Qualitative Methods in the Private Sector*. Qualitative Research Methods 42. Newbury Park, CA: Sage.

Mukherjee, S. R. 2014, Global Halal: Meat, Money, and Religion. *Religions* 5(1): 22–75.

Navaro-Yashin, Yael 2002, *Faces of the State: Secularism and Public Life in Turkey*. Princeton: Princeton University Press.

Nielsen, Anne M. 2014, Accommodating Religious Pluralism in Denmark. *European Journal of Sociology* 55(2): 245–74.

O'Dwyer, G. 2015, Push for Common Halal Guidance in Denmark. *Global Meat News*, 29 May. www.globalmeatnews.com/Industry-Markets/Denmark-pushes-for-halal-meat-guidance, accessed 30 June 2017.

ONS 2015, 2011 Census: Ethnic Group, Local Authorities in the United Kingdom. Excel file. London: Office for National Statistics. www.ons.gov.uk/file?...=/people-populationandcommunity/populationandmigration..., accessed 27 July 2015.

Orthodox Union 2004, *Nestlé USA: Providing Good Food for Kosher Life*. New York: Orthodox Union.

Ponte, S., Gibbon, P. and Vestergaard, J. 2011, Governing through Standards: An Introduction. In *Governing through Standards: Origins, Drivers and Limitations*, ed. Stefano Ponte, Peter Gibbon and Jakob Vestergaard, pp. 1–24. Basingstoke: Palgrave Macmillan.

Power, M. 1999, *The Audit Society: Rituals of Verification*. Oxford: Oxford University Press.

Regenstein, J. M. and Chaudry, M. M. 2003a, The Kosher and Halal Food Laws. *Comprehensive Reviews in Food Science and Food Safety* 2(3): 111–27.

Regenstein, J. M. and Chaudry, M. M. 2003b, Kosher and Halal Laws in the Biotech Era. *Applied Biotechnology, Food Science, and Policy* 1: 95–107.

Regenstein, J. M. and Regenstein, C. 1979, An Introduction to the Kosher Dietary Laws for Food Scientists and Food Processors. *Food Technology* 33(1): 89–99.

Regenstein, J. M. and Regenstein, C. 1988, Kosher Dietary Laws and their Implementation in the Food Industry. *Food Technology* 42(6): 86–94.

Regenstein, J. M. and Regenstein, C. 1990, Kosher Certification of Vinegar: A Model for Industry/Rabbinical Cooperation. *Food Technology* 44(7): 90–3.

Regenstein, J. M. and Regenstein, C. 1991, Current Issues in Kosher Foods. *Trends in Food Science and Technology* 2: 50–4.

Regenstein, J. M. and Regenstein, C. 1999, Kosher Products: A Growing Market for Processors. *NFPA Journal* 1: 11–13.

Riaz, M. N. and Chaudry, M. M. 2004, *Halal Food Production*. Boca Raton, FL: CRC Press.

Roberts, P. W., Simons, T. and Swaminathan , A. 2010, Crossing a Categorical Boundary: The Implications of Switching from Non-Kosher Wine Production in the Israeli Wine Market. In *Categories in Markets: Origins and Evolution*, ed. Greta Hsu, Giacomo Negro and Özgecan Koçak, pp. 153–73. Sociology of Organizations 31. Bingley: Emerald Publishing.

Roth, C. 1978, *History of the Jews in England*, 3rd rev. edn. Oxford: Oxford University Press.

Rudnyckyj, D. 2010, *Spiritual Economies: Islam, Globalisation, and the Afterlife of Development*. Ithaca, NY: Cornell University Press.

Rudnyckyj, D. and Osella, F. 2017. *Religion and the Morality of the Market*. Cambridge: Cambridge University Press.

Schmidt, Garbi 2009, Denmark. In *Islam in the Nordic and Baltic Countries*, ed. Göran Larsson, pp. 40–55. London and New York: Routledge.

Schmidt, Garbi 2011, Understanding and Approaching Muslim Visibilities: Lessons Learned from a Fieldwork-Based Study of Muslims in Copenhagen. *Ethnic and Racial Studies* 34(7): 1216–29.

Schmidt, Garbi 2012, 'Grounded' Politics: Manifesting Muslim Identity as a Political Factor and Localized Identity in Copenhagen. *Ethnicities* 12(5): 603–22.

Seddon, M. 2012, Arab Communities in Manchester, 1839–2012: A Brief History. Paper presented at The Manchester Museum as part of Manchester Cafe Historique's Manchester Men series, 28 January.

Shabbir, H. A. 2015, Non-Muslim Attitude Development towards Halal Consumption: An Overview. Eblex Seminar 2015. http://beefandlamb.ahdb.org.uk/wp/wp-content/uploads/2016/01/Consumer-perceptions-of-Halal-products-Haseeb-Shabbir-240315.pdf, accessed 20 January 2016.

Shapiro, S. 2008, The Food Issue: Kosher Wars. *New York Times*, 9 October. www.nytimes.com/2008/10/12/magazine/12kosher-t.html?pagewanted=all&_r=0, accessed 2 June 2016.

Simoons, F. J. 1994, *Eat Not This Flesh: Food Avoidances from Prehistory to the Present*. Madison and London: University of Wisconsin Press.

Star, Susan Leigh and Lampland, Martha 2009, *Standards and Their Stories: How Quantifying, Classifying, and Formalizing Practices Shape Everyday Life*. Ithaca, NY: Cornell University Press.

Statistics Denmark 2016, Denmark in Figures 2016. www.dst.dk/en/Statistik/Publikationer/VisPub?cid=21500, accessed 25 March 2017.

Thompson, A. and Begum, R. 2005, 'Asian Britishness': A Study of First-Generation Asian Migrants in Greater Manchester. Asylum and Migration Working Paper 4, January. London: Institute for Public Policy Research.

Urciuoli, B. 2008, Skills and Selves in the New Workplace. *American Ethnologist* 35(1): 211–28.

Warde, A. 2016. *The Practice of Eating*. Cambridge and Malden, MA: Polity Press.

Weber, M. 2001, *The Protestant Ethic and the Spirit of Capitalism*. London: Routledge.

Weeks, J. 2012, The Meat of the Issue. *Insights, Magazine of the International Food Policy Research Institute* (IFPRI), 26 October. http://insights.ifpri.info/2012/10/the-meat-of-the-issue-2/#sthash.Tx34CPgq.dpuf, accessed 20 June 2016.

Werbner, P. 1990, *The Migration Process: Capital, Gifts and Offerings among British Pakistanis*. London: Bloomsbury Academic.

Werbner, P. 1999, What Colour 'Success'? Distorting Value in Studies of Ethnic Entrepreneurship. *Sociological Review* 47(3): 548–79.

Wilk, R. 2006, *Home Cooking in the Global Village: Caribbean Food from Buccaneers to Ecotourists*. Oxford and New York: Berg.

Williams, B. 1976, *The Making of Manchester Jewry, 1740–1875*. Manchester: Manchester University Press.

Wise, Y. 2006, The Rise of Independent Orthodoxy in Anglo-Jewry: The History of the Machzikei Hadass Communities, Manchester. Unpublished PhD thesis, University of Manchester.

Withnall, A. 2014, Halal Meat: What Is It and Why Is It So Controversial. *Independent*, 21 October. www.independent.co.uk/life-style/food-and-drink/what-is-halal-meat-the-big-questions-about-religious-slaughter-answered-9331519.html, accessed 20 January 2016.

Wouters, C. 2008, *Informalization: Manners and Emotions since 1890*. London: Sage.

Index

EU authorised representative for GPSR:
Easy Access System Europe, Mustamäe tee 50,
10621 Tallinn, Estonia
gpsr.requests@easproject.com